The Labyrinth of My Life

The Labyrinth of My Life
A NOVEL

Kay Alahakoon

Published by Tablo

Copyright © Kay Alahakoon 2021.
Published in 2021 by Tablo Publishing.

All rights reserved.

This book or any portion thereof may not be reproduced or used in any manner whatsoever without the express written permission of the author except for the use of brief quotations in a book review.

Publisher and wholesale enquiries: orders@tablo.io

20 21 22 23 LSC 10 9 8 7 6 5 4 3 2 1

I dedicate this book to Amma, the woman who made me fall in love with stories and to Asanga and Akka, my two pillars of strength. I love you all very much.

GLOSSARY

This story takes place on the beautiful island of Sri Lanka, also known as Ceylon, in the 1980s and 1990s. As some of the terms used in the story may not be common, the following insights are shared.

Aiya: The Sinhala term for an older brother. Sri Lankans call any older male relative or acquaintance Aiya as a sign of respect.

Aiyo: A term used to express dismay, frustration, shock or grief.

Akka: The Sinhala and Tamil term for an older sister. Sri Lankans call any older female relative or acquaintance Akka as a sign of respect.

Alakamanda/Alakamandawa: This is considered the celestial palace of King Kuvera and King Rawana's heavenly palace. Some think this to be Sigiriya, the ancient rock city.

A-level Exam/AL: Also known as GCE Advanced Level Exam which is similar to British Advance Level and is a qualification and prerequisite for university enrolment. This exam is taken in Grade 12, usually at the age of 18-19.

Almari: The Sinhala term for a cupboard or a closet.

Amma: The Sinhala and Tamil term for mother.

Aney: A term used to express appreciation, compassion and also used as a filler word. It could mean anything based on who is using it and in what context.

Appachchi: The Sinhala term for the father, used primarily in the Kandy region by upcountry clans.

Appa: The Tamil term for father.

Coolie: A term used for low wage or unskilled labourers.

Kandy: This was the last Kingdom before the country fell under British ruling in 1815. It also houses the famous Temple of the Tooth and one of the best universities in Sri Lanka, the University of Peradeniya. Kandy is also considered as one of the Buddhist sacred places of worship. The town was declared a world heritage site by UNESCO O in 1988.

Kandy Esela Perahara/Perahara: Also known as The Festival of the Tooth. This is an annual event held in July and August in Kandy to pay homage to the Relic of Buddha. The procession comprises various traditional dancers, including whip-dances, fire acrobats and parades of elegantly decorated majestic elephants.

Loku Amma: The Sinhala term for mother's elder sister (Aunty).

Malli: The Sinhala term for a younger brother. Sri Lankans call any younger male relative or acquaintance Malli and also used as a polite way to address drivers, waiters, labourers etc.

Nangi: This is the Sinhala term for a younger sister. Sri Lankans call any younger female relative or acquaintance Nangi.

Nuwara Eliya: This town is often referred to as the "City of Light" and "Little England" and is one of the highest cities in the country. It is famous for its colder climate and the ambience of colonial architecture. Today it is known as the tea capital of Sri Lanka.

O-level Exam/OL: Also known as GCE Ordinary Level Exam. This is a qualification and prerequisite for the Advanced Level exam. This exam is taken in Grade 10, usually at the age of 15-16.

Paththirippuwa: The pavilion on the front of the Temple of Tooth (Maligawa) enabled the kings to sit and watch the parades or address their subjects.

Putha: A term used to address a son or a daughter. An affectionate term used by parents and relatives alike.

Sigiriya: This is the famous 8th wonder of the world. It is an ancient rock fortress built on 600ft high rock by King Kashyapa I (473-91BC). Sigiriya is known as The Lion Rock and is famous for its gardens, lost town and World Heritage Sites listed by UNESCO.

Thaththa: The Sinhala term for father.

Theva: This is part of the daily rituals carried out for the Sacred Tooth Relic in the temple of Tooth (Maligawa). Three services are being carried out in the morning, midday, and evening, including traditional sound offerings using various Sri Lankan drums and horanawas (the double-reed instrument).

Trishaw: Also known as a three-wheeler. This is one of the cheapest urban transports used as a vehicle for hire.

Vesak Lantern: This refers to a lantern made of colourful transparent paper that gets hung outside buildings during the month of Vesak (May) to celebrate Buddha's three important life events: his birth, enlightenment, and passing. This is one of the most important Buddhist festivals that illuminate villages and streets with multi-coloured lanterns at night.

Labyrinth: Although maze and labyrinth are used interchangeably, labyrinth doesn't have branches like in a maze and has only a single path to its centre and back.

1 UNEXPECTED

I was late, hours behind my usual schedule. The fog that is part of the cold evenings was already claiming its rightful place, covering the township like a silken cloth. Street lamps have started to spread their weak yellow beams in a poor attempt to illuminate a town, getting darker by every passing minute. Nothing much had changed since I'd last been here; the place appeared the same. I don't know why I was surprised; things are not likely to change in three months. It has taken me that long to return home. Not intentionally, of course. My work makes me travel a lot, making it hard to find a time for frequent visits.

"Move aside," a fellow passenger barked as he brushed past me, snapping me back to the moment, reminding me Malli was waiting for me at the usual meeting point. The central bus station was buzzing with passengers rushing to reach a destination before the thick fog covered the mountainous road. It would be dangerous to drive in the mist, where streets were narrow on the mountain. I picked up my bag and blended in with others scrambling to go to their destinations before nightfall.

I felt peaceful amongst the rush hour commuters; arriving home always made me calm and happy. Especially today, when I was returning for a rest. Earlier, before I left, I'd agreed with myself that I would leave all my worries and concerns behind in Kandy. Even if it was only for a week, the mere anticipation of not having to worry about the next class, the next assignment, the next client, or the next bill put me at ease. A notion I haven't experienced in ages.

I wanted to scream at the top of my lunges to let out my elation but stopped short of doing so at the image of Sula whispering into my ear. *"They will drag you to a lunatic asylum."* I shook my head to shrug off the thought and continued to walk towards the park entrance where Malli was waiting for me. As I was already late, I imagined him phasing up and down the footpath with irritation. He didn't tolerate tardiness.

In my rush to take the next bus out from Kandy to Nuwara Eliya, I forgot to call Amma to inform her I was running late. I was annoyed with Sula for making me miss my usual bus. I regularly rode the mid-day bus, which arrives around four o'clock in the afternoon. Today I was two hours behind. I usually come before dark to make it easy for Malli to pick me up from the central bus station.

Besides that, I enjoy the short walk leading up the entrance to our home, relishing the beautiful array of flowers greeted with prettiness and aroma similar to Haggala Gardens, one of the five botanical gardens in Sri Lanka and the only one in Nuwara Eliya. Amma's love for gardening gifted us with a stunning collection of flora. She made a point of organising the nursery beds with plants radiating different colours and shapes. There was something profound buried in those meticulously laid garden beds that had a magical power to replace the wariness with freshness by the time I reached the front door of our home. Whenever I walked up the driveway, with the fading sun rays fighting for attention with the evening mist, I always thought this must be how the entrance to heaven looks.

When I got to Malli, he was leaning against a street lamp, arms across his chest, in front of Victoria Park's main entrance. The fog was surrounding him like a thick blanket. The yellow light from the street lamp made him look older but flawless for his age. I grinned, noting his perfect body, broad shoulders, lean chest and bulky arms that some of my friends in Kandy tried desperately to build with frequent visits to the gyms. He loomed like a young Greek God in modern attire.

Malli's dark denim jeans fitted him like a second skin. The oversized woollen shirt and the golf cap, which I am sure he borrowed from Thaththa, have given him a rugged but attractive appearance. A sight that would make any teenage girl stop and stare, making their hearts skip a beat. Malli knew he was a handsome teenager and amplified it with his *'I care little about it'* attitude.

I wish I could capture his lazy pose in a photograph. I would name it *'Somebody's Dream'*, which would annoy him big time. The thought of his eyes squinting with irritation made me smile with tenderness.

I wanted to pull him across and give him a bear hug, but I dare not. Although he is still my little brother that I used to cuddle and carry, he is on the edge of becoming an adult. He would not appreciate me hugging him in the middle of the town. Who knew how many of his admirers would see it, which might damage the *'Bad Boy'* image he was proudly parading around.

"How is life, kiddo?" Though he hated being called a kid, I couldn't help it. Malli greeted me with a smile and slapped my palm, following his group's welcoming ritual. At least he still considered me to be part of his gang. It was a privilege that also gave me an edge when dealing with family feuds.

"Not bad at all." He smiled, pulling the bike from where it was parked.

"Sorry I ran late." I removed the backpack from my shoulders and climbed onto the bicycle. "Were you waiting for long?" I asked, searching for any signs of irritation on his handsome face.

"No," Malli replied, shaking his head. "I just got here." He reassured me with a slight smile. "Sula Aiya called. He said you will be late as you missed the midday bus."

I made a mental noted to call and thank Sula when I got home. *'Why should I?'* my inner child questioned. I was still nursing the anger and disappointment I felt earlier in the day after the huge argument I had with Sula. He was why I was running late today. It was proper for him to update Malli with my expected arrival time. "Oh, that's good. I was worried you would be waiting." I said, feeling relieved.

We began our journey home. Malli had me sitting on the bicycle bar holding on to my bag as he peddled. Malli has been picking me up from town ever since he grew tall enough to peddle a bike. Our house was a twenty-minute walking distance from the city centre. It took half that time to reach home on a bicycle.

Although neither one of us would admit it, we both enjoyed the ride. This was our bonding moment, giving us the space to catch up. Sometimes Malli would talk about his friends, and if he were in the right mood, he would tell me about his latest crush.

"How did you go with your competition?" I inquired. Malli is a member of a professional dance group and takes part in competitions. As one of the youngest dancers in the group, I was keen to find out how he scored in the last championship.

"We won third place," Malli said with pride. "I received the newest talent award for my hip hop routine."

"Wow, that's outstanding," I squeezed his hand as I couldn't hug him, thrilled to hear about his achievement. "Well done!" I wished I could see his beaming face. The only thing that gets Malli excited more than computers is his dance competitions. My heart expanded, rejoicing over his success. "So, how are your classes coming along?"

"It's getting tougher," I noted the weight in his voice, the pain of endless hours of studies and preparations required to finish the last challenge in the life of a high school kid in my part of the world. Malli was preparing for the AL exam in grade twelve, a qualification and a prerequisite for university entrance. His dream of becoming a software engineer one day meant he had to work even harder. "Doing past papers helps to pick up gaps in the syllabus we haven't covered." It pleased me he had a plan, and I recollected how the same strategy helped me with all my exams.

"Are you taking a break from dancing to prepare for the exam?" I was hoping he would do the sensible thing and freeze his passion for dancing until the exam was over. Still, I will not be the one to tell him that.

"Yes, I only have two more performances. If I go by the standards of the last three years' papers, this year will be a difficult one. I can't afford to get sidetracked."

The clarity and determination in his tone filled my heart with enormous pride.

"I know you are way too smart to let anything disrupt your goal."

"You give me far more credit than I deserve." There was a chuckle in his voice. "I am not you." Like clockwork, he downplayed himself, expecting a compliment. I am the pushover who always walks right into it.

"No, you are smarter than I am."

As I was sitting in the bicycle's front, I couldn't see his face. Still, I knew he was beaming with pride. I smiled too, appreciating the bond we have and the unique advantage it would give me, at least for a couple of days. We didn't talk again until we passed The Grand Hotel and entered Lady McClum's Drive.

It was already dark, and with that, the temperature dropped. The light breeze that grazed us was bitter and gave me goosebumps. Unfortunately, what I was wearing was not suitable for Nuwara Eliya's evening weather. Although my sneakers and jeans kept my feet and legs warm, the long-sleeved cotton shirt I wore was not thick enough.

"You are cold." When Malli spoke, it was not a question. I held my jaw tight, trying to stop my teeth from chattering and my body from shivering.

"Yes, a bit," I muttered through the shakes.

"I should have brought your cardigan with me." I abhorred his apologetic murmur and pondered why Amma didn't send one - she was aware of my susceptibility to the temperature. Even a day spent outside Nuwara Eliya would make me too sensitive to face the evening's cold.

We were creatures of habit and took pleasure in the regular routine of coming home. Malli picking me up on his bicycle, Amma sending a cardigan to keep me warm, and my parents waiting on the veranda sipping ginger tea for our return - these have always been part of the arrival ritual we all enjoyed. But the pattern had changed today. Something told me that things were not the same.

"Sasoo."

Malli never called me 'Akka' from when he was a toddler like other younger kids did when they addressed their older sisters. He could not pronounce my name, Sakunthala. The closest he got was Sasoo, and that has stuck with me, where everyone in our family and close family friends call me Sasoo.

"What's up?"

"Aunty Nelum and Uncle Sarath are back." Malli referred to our next-door neighbours who were living overseas.

"Oh, that is so nice. How long are they going to be here?" I uttered with a projected enthusiasm to camouflage the uneasiness that overwhelmed me out of nowhere.

"They are here for good. Uncle has retired, so they are not planning to go back unless on holiday. That is what they said."

"I was not aware they were retiring here. It's nice for Amma and Thaththa." I turned my head to glance at Malli, ignoring the deepening restlessness creep in my thoughts. For years, my parents have been best friends with Seneges (the collective noun we gave them). When they migrated to Australia a long time ago, it left a massive hole in my parents' social circle no other friend had filled.

"Guess what?" Malli's voice perked up, as if he was going to share something exuberant.

"What?" I played along, wondering what had him excited.

"Niranga Aiya is also here."

The bicycle tyres screeched when Malli hit the brakes to avoid knocking the dog that ran across the road. My entire body shook as if I was in the middle of an earthquake. That name snapped me back to my childhood. A journey I haven't made in many years.

***

I met Niranga Aiya after Amma got married the second time to Thaththa, and we moved to Nuwara Eliya. It happened a few years after Appachchi, my biological father's death.

Growing up, we didn't have a large family around us for support. Amma's parents had been dead years before we were born. The only family we had was Loku Amma, Amma's older sister. Appachchi's family deserted us after Appachchi passed. It could be because they didn't have any means to support us. So even now, we have no connection.

Amma, Akka and I were dealing with Appachchi's unexpected death in different ways. Amma's laughing eyes were always filled with tears for no apparent reason. Her bright red lips turned to brown. It took me years to understand that was because, with Appachchi's passing, Amma stopped applying lipstick on her lips. Amma no longer wore colourful dresses or sarees. She restricted her attire to white or light colours, which were the colours of mourning.

Akka stayed back after school to return later instead of coming home with me. It left me to my own devices, not having anyone to play with. To this day, I could sense the heaviness that used to hover over us. Appachchi took the brightness and laughter when he left us, leaving us in a dark, unhappy place.

As I was getting used to a life without Appachchi, Amma came home from work with Uncle Rajitha. I recall that evening well. Underneath Amma's glazed eyes, I saw a trace of happiness lingering around, expecting an invitation to stay. When Uncle Rajitha came and sat in the living room, Amma ushered Akka and me to greet him.

"Girls, this is Uncle Rajitha, a friend of mine. Why don't you have a chat with Uncle? I make us some tea."

Although she was smiling, I heard the helplessness in Amma's tone. How weak and defeated she sounded, and her voice begging us to talk to Uncle Rajitha. When I stared at Amma, I saw tears pooling in her eyes.

"Please don't cry, Amma. I will talk to him." I squeezed Amma's hand to reassure her.

I could not bear witnessing Amma's tears. It terrified me to hear her muffled cries when she thought we were at sleep. Her weeping sounds gave me nightmares. Yet, I dared not share that with Amma. She already had enough to worry about. If it was going to stop her from crying, talking to Uncle Rajitha was a small price to pay. I will still do anything to keep Amma's eyes dry. Luckily, Amma is not aware of this; otherwise, I would be handcuffed to her tears.

I sat next to Uncle Rajitha and started chatting. After a quick ' hello ', Akka headed back to her room, pretending she had homework to finish. I knew she was only reading a novel.

After that evening, Uncle Rajitha became a frequent visitor to our house. Amma and Uncle Rajitha worked in the same office. So most weekends, he took us on drives and visits in his white car. I guess that was where I got my love for travel. We met Malli in on one of those outings, who was adorable as now.

Malli's biological mother passed away at birth, making us all want to drown him in love. Malli became my *'Kryptonite'* from the first moment I saw him, making my heart fill with protective instinct. As I got comfortable with the changes, Akka distanced herself from all of us.

Akka had always been studious. She used this as an excuse to avoid family outings on weekends and for evening dinners. When she started constant fights with Amma, I could not understand why. I got angry with Akka for making Amma cry. That resentment made us drift apart, leaving traces of permanent damage in our relationship.

I turned into Akka after Amma got married to Uncle Rajitha. The day Amma asked us to call him 'Appachchi,' Akka and I both cried for hours.

"I don't want to call him Appachchi. He will never be my Appachchi," Akka screamed with anger and stormed out. But I wanted to please Amma, so I promised her I would call Uncle Rajitha 'Thaththa' as Malli did.

Changes that shaped us into who we are today didn't stop there. When one of Thaththa's distant relatives had proposed selling the Nuwara Eliya house and land at a lower price, it was too good to pass up. Amma and Thaththa got a transfer to Nuwara Eliya's office, and we got uprooted from Kandy. Akka refused to move. Loku Amma stepped in and offered to take her in. Amma and Akka's relationship was so brittle that Amma agreed to let Akka continue her studies in Kandy, living with Loku Amma. The same day Akka moved into Loku Amma's house, I said goodbye to my beloved school friends in Kandy. That was the day I began my war with Amma.

Even before we came to Nuwara Eliya, I hated everything about the move, from its cold weather to the colour of my new school uniform. Nothing pleased me: I missed our old house, my friends, and I also missed Akka. Although we didn't get along as we used to after Appachchi's passing, I felt the void in Akka's absence left and didn't know how to fill it.

Forming new habits wasn't my thing. Though we didn't talk as much as we used to, sharing a room with Akka, and having her as my companion to school together comforted me when we were in Kandy. New rituals made me uneasy. I didn't enjoy sleeping on my own. Or walking alone to school when the roads were still tainted with the dissolving fog. They were too depressing. Moving from a girls-only school to a class mixed with noisy uncultured boys ready to tease at any opportunity angered me. I hated everyone who made any attempt to become my allies.

I spent the day being livid and annoyed. The coldness of Nuwara Eliya amplified my anger. I can't recall if I ever smiled or laughed. From morning to night, I stomped around in a daze. I was making more enemies than friends, as I was unresponsive even to the kind gestures of my teachers.

Those days, I took solace visiting the small stream I stumbled across on the little hill behind our house. When I came home after school, I would head straight to the stream. I spent my afternoon there jumping from one stone to another, having conversations with my imaginary friends, until it was time to head back home.

I met Niranga Aiya on one of those miserable days. It was a day where the sky was dark with pregnant clouds. I didn't stop to listen to Lechchami, our domestic helper, when she asked me not to go to pinewood as she forecasted rain. I ran through tall pine trees, not paying much attention to their needles piercing my arms. Maybe it was the need to defy Lechchami that made me climb further up the stream. Whatever the reason, I was buried in the pinewood when the rain fell. It got dark in seconds. I became scared.

The towering pine trees swayed with strong winds and screeched with weird noises I had not heard before. The scenery and the sound reminded me of the Baba Yaga, the flying witch I discovered in Russian folktales. Baba Yaga was famous for eating children wandering off in the woods. I scanned the mourning trees and the dark sky, expecting Baba Yaga to appear at any moment on her giant mortar and pestle and swallow me in one big mouthful for her dinner.

Little did I realise the most challenging part of hiking was the descent. Climbing was difficult but safe; the descent was easy but unsafe. Not being aware of that basic rule, I run down the hill, fleeing from the imaginary Baba Yaga to be in the safety of home. I paid little attention to where I tread. Distracted and panic-stricken, I stepped on a stone that was already loose, and I slid to the bottom of the slope. I remember calling for Amma.

I landed on an enormous pile of mud with a splash. The rain was bucketing down with wind and thunder, and visibility was poor. Closing my eyes, I wailed for Amma, too scared to open them, imagining Baba Yaga in the face of me. I didn't have any hope that anyone in the vicinity would hear my screams. Still, I continued to yell, making no attempt to get up.

"Here, give me your hands." The first time I heard his voice, I thought it was Baba Yaga, the flying witch looming in front of me. When I picked up the voice for the second time, I opened one eye and saw a boy's silhouette with his arms stretched towards me. It was the boy next door, who I had observed playing on his own. I had ignored his past attempts to smile and talk.

That evening, he got me out of the mud pile I fell into. In retrospect, not only did he rescue me that day, but he also pulled me out of the self-pity I was drowning in. That incident is tattooed on my reflections. If I could carry memories into my next life, that would be something I would take with me. It doesn't matter how hard I have tried to keep those recollections hidden; a mere whiff of bubble gum would be enough to recall how Niranga Aiya smelled on that rainy day and how safe he made me feel.

Niranga Aiya wiped the mud off my face, and half carried and dragged me to his house. His presence subdued the fear. I recall being housebound after that fall with a twisted ankle. By the time I recovered and was ready to go back to school, Niranga Aiya and I were best buddies. Our parents have likewise become good friends.

Niranga Aiya became an extended part of our family. He not only played with me, but he was also kind to Malli. His friendship made me a different person. I enjoyed my life in Nuwara Eliya, waiting to go to school with him and returning home to the wonderland he created for me when we became friends. Any time spent with him became my favourite time of the day.

Niranga Aiya became my star. And I started orbiting around him like a planet.

2 DISGRUNTLED

"Anytime today would be good."

Malli's sarcastic voice pierced through my daze, pulling me back to the present. We were at the bottom of the stone steps leading up to our house. I have missed the last ten minutes of our commute, lost in the past.

A million thoughts were running through my mind, with little time to process them.

"Oops... sorry, I was elsewhere," Malli smirked when I turned to him. He held the bicycle steady for me to get off, saying nothing further.

I glanced at Niranga Aiya's house up on the slope a few yards away from ours. It was glowing like a vesak lantern, yellow lights cutting through the mist spreading across the hill. The lights illuminating through all windows, reminding me of the charming house I used to admire as a young girl. The memories started rushing in, forming a massive lump in my throat. I tried to suppress the unexpected burning sensation that was brewing inside.

' How is he?' I wanted to ask, wanting to find out the details. Yet, I was too afraid to voice it. Overwhelmed by emotions, I wished I could turn around and head back to Kandy.

Instead, when Malli took the stone staircase leading up to the veranda carrying the bicycle, I tagged behind in silence. Unlike other days, Amma and Thaththa were not waiting for us sipping ginger tea on the front veranda. A deserted and abandoned notion washed over me, spreading emptiness, making my heart heavy. While Malli set off to store the bicycle in the shed, I headed inside the house to search for my parents.

"How are you, my child?"

The moment I stepped through the front door, Thaththa walked out to greet me, pulling me in for a bear hug as if he had been waiting for my arrival. He smelled full of his favourite soap and hair oil, warm and homely, reminding me why I love coming home. I snuggled in his warmth, inhaling deeply, filling my lungs with his familiar aroma I adored so much.

"What is this?" Thaththa stretched his arms, pushing me back to study my face. "You think I am your blanket? Go and put on a cardigan before you catch a cold."

Thaththa sounded jovial, more energetic than he had been. Since he retired, he had aged. His hair had turned grey, and I have also noted a slowness in his movements, similar to a tortoise. However, today, he appeared more vigorous. He sounded happy, as if the old Thaththa, who used to crack jokes and play pranks, was peeking out from a small gap to remind me, *'Hey, I am still here.'*

"Why can't I stay longer?" I pleaded. "Amma didn't send my cardigan today." It hadn't been a minute since my return, and I was already complaining. Noting this, he grinned. Thaththa rubbed my arms to warm me up and pushed me towards my room.

"Go put on a cardi."

As the night progressed, the temperature started falling. Not having any heaters, we always layered up to keep warm. Once I moved to Kandy, I observed my body was more sensitive to outside temperature than it used to be. Malli and Akka always teased me, saying I was reacting as someone from down south of the country, throwing a jumper even on the days the sun was out.

I went into my room and grabbed my favourite Ralph Lauren jumper. It was old and tattered. Though I pretended I cherished it because it was comfortable to wear, I will never admit the real reason I have not discarded it. I can't remember how I ended up with it. It was over thirteen or fourteen years old. Cleary it had seen its better days as the colours have long faded. The jumper had grown with me; threads have reached their maximum stretch. Despite its appearance and wariness, it still keeps me warm.

On second thought, I put it back on the clothes hanger. I was not in the mood to wear it today, so I picked up another timeworn jumper and headed towards the kitchen. I was grinning, ready for Amma's scolding at seeing me in the old rag.

The powerful aromas that greeted me made me hungry. Amma and Akka were busy cooking in the kitchen. There were many pots and pans on the kitchen table I had not spotted in ages. "Whatever you are cooking, it smells divine." I hugged Amma, and I picked a fish cutlet from the serving dish on the table.

"Aney, you didn't have to go into so much trouble to welcome me home. A warm cup of ginger tea would have been enough!" I joked.

"You are late today!" Amma stopped staring at the hearth and threw me an annoyed stare. "We expected you home two hours ago." She didn't sound pleased, which was normal for her. She always got irritated when I didn't turn up on time.

"Aiyo, sorry, Amma, I had to tidy up a few loose ends. But I am here for a week." I tried to score a few points with Amma by reminding her I was home for more than a few days. Still, she didn't flinch and continued to stir the pot she had on the stove; her focus tied up somewhere else.

"Is Saman Aiya back already? Is he bringing any of his friends for dinner today?" I moved across to Akka to hug her. "I thought he was still in Singapore."

Saman Aiya is Akka's husband who travels back and forth to Singapore for his business. They are expecting their first child, and Akka lives with us to make it easy for Amma and Thaththa to keep an eye on her while Saman Aiya is away.

"Hey there, little fella, how is it going in that dungeon?" I rubbed Akka's belly and talked to the baby growing inside.

"Aney, no, he is still in Singapore." Akka sounded sad. But in an instant, her voice bubbled up, and her eyes glittered. "Seneges are coming for dinner."

"What?" I glared at Akka in shock.

Akka rolled her eyes, implying, *'How dumb are you?'* We have been fondly referring to our neighbours by their surname whenever we refer to more than one of them. "Aunty Nelum, Uncle Sarath and Niranga are going to join us for dinner." Akka beamed with no attempt to suppress her delight.

"Oh!" I did not expect to face the Senege family on the day I returned. I was distracted with memories to realise I would meet them before I headed back to Kandy.

'What did you imagine? Were you hoping to stay under the radar, avoiding crossing paths with them altogether?' A tiny voice mouthed.

As neither Amma nor Akka showed no intention of making me a cup of tea as they usually did, I stepped closer to the fireplace to keep warm. Since I became independent and I moved to Kandy, I only get spoiled when I come home. Clearly, that was not on the agenda today, so I started making my own tea.

Except for the noise of crackling firewood in the hearth and the sound of the knife hitting the chopping board, the kitchen was silent. I had so much to ask about Niranga Aiya, but I didn't want to bring up the subject. I sensed unsettled, as if I was stranded in a place with no bearing.

"Nangi, go and change. Seneges will be here any minute. They have been dying to catch up with you." The joy in Akka's voice was making me agitated. I pretended my focus was on the task at hand, ignoring her. "Niranga has changed so much. If you run into him on the road, you wouldn't recognise him. He is striking like a Bollywood movie star now." Akka continued with her rambling without expecting a response from me. Something still plastered the beaming smile I saw earlier on her lips. Her happiness was apparent as her eagerness to share her view of Niranga Aiya.

I was not into watching Bollywood movies. The only stars I could recognise were from movies I watched with Akka when I was home, a devoted Bollywood fan. I was trying to recall if I knew any famous actors in Bollywood who were bulky and not made of the same cookie-cutter lean framework as most of the prominent artists were. Niranga Aiya was towards the plump side, a chubby boy with puffy cheeks.

Then I realised. I can't rely on Akka's choices in men. She finds both Saman Aiya and 'Govind' handsome and has a habit of exaggerating. I could relate to her sentiment of Saman Aiya as she is in love with him, but for the life of me, I couldn't understand how she found 'Govind' to be attractive out of all the Bollywood movie stars.

"Then it is a good thing Saman Aiya isn't here, isn't it?" I am not too sure why I said that. It slipped my tongue before I could do anything about it. It flustered Akka as she dropped the knife she was using to cut onions. I picked it up and handed it back to her, noticing her blushing cheeks. Akka continued to chop onions with trembling hands, trying to cover her agitation.

"Sakunthala, go freshen up! You are dressed like a street beggar and stink like a coolie."

Amma never approved of what I wore. So it did not surprise me when she asked me to change; I expected her disapproval even before entering the kitchen. Conforming to her usual behaviour, Amma always scolds me when I wear my faded jeans and haggard jumpers with a tone filled with love and affection. Her eyes glitter with the excitement of having me home, and I ignore the smile she tries to hide behind her pretence of anger. We both have acknowledged that neither will alter our behaviour, but we do the same dance as part of our bonding ritual.

Though her reaction was not unexpected, the tone in her voice was. Unless she was angry, she didn't call 'Sakunthala'. Instead, Amma addresses me as *'my little Sasoo.'* When Malli became the *'little one'* for all of us, Amma didn't stop calling me her little one. She added Sasoo to the end. That is the only time I really didn't mind being called Sasoo.

Today her voice wasn't soaked in affection that clutched my heart in a tender hug. It burst the balloon full of warm fuzzy feelings I carried with me to the kitchen. She was fumbling with the curry she was cooking and was avoiding my eyes. I felt neglected and discarded.

"For the love of mother Kali, I just got home!" Amma's already annoyed face scrunched when she heard me swear. I was the only member in our family to openly curse, as Akka and Malli only do it behind our parents' backs. I picked the phrase from Lechchami, one of the domestic helpers we had who used to call upon the badass Goddess as her witness when she had a point to stress. It was a cool tag to repeat as a kid, especially when many adults seemed to fear the ferocious Goddess Kali. Somehow it got stuck with me, probably because Amma thought it was beneath my social status to use such a pedestrian term. Now it has become part and partial of my vocabulary that comes out when I am irritated. "Let me at least have some tea to warm myself." Amma didn't respond and let me continue with my task. I gathered the tea mugs and walked out of the kitchen.

I joined Thaththa and Malli, who were in the living room, glued to the television. Both of them grabbed a tea mug, each without waiting for an invitation. In our house, we go through warm ginger tea the same way joggers go through bottles of water.

"It is all about Seneges today!" I plunked down next to Malli and aired my frustration on no one.

"What's wrong, my child?" Thaththa picked up the pain in my voice. He turned around, giving his full attention with an air of concern.

"Why? Did you get demoted from the Queen Sasoo to a third-class citizen?" Malli grinned with the pleasure of knowing I had fallen from *'honorary'* status that generally lasted for a couple of days after returning home.

"Amma didn't even notice I am home," I said with more anger than disappointment. "She didn't even make me a cup of tea. It's all about Seneges!" I was annoyed with Seneges for stealing my spotlight. I returned home after three months, not to be pushed to an edge by my neighbours.

"Funny how life changes people!" Thaththa gave me a snobbish glare, something he rarely does. "I remember a time when you wanted to become a Senege!"

***

Since we became friends, I was not used to being separated from Niranga Aiya unless when we retired for the night and went to school.

Niranga Aiya went to the only private school in town while I attended one of the public schools. Our families got so used to us behaving like twins they let us be in each other's shadows. We did everything together; homework, playing, having our meals, watching TV, and we also fell asleep in each other's beds.

When we attended parties (Senege's parties, as we did not have any other friends of their calibre), I could conjure up times staying together and falling asleep in each other's arms. Malli sleeping on my lap, I am on Niranga Aiya's, with his hands around me, keeping me warm, preventing me from falling off the sofa. I can recall hundreds of times when Amma and Aunty Nelum laughed about how Niranga Aiya and I used to hold on to each other tight in our sleep and become dejected by the slightest attempt at separation.

The first time when they set off on a foreign trip, I couldn't understand why I could not accompany them the way I did when they travelled around in Sri Lanka. Been spoiled by Aunty and Uncle with luxury toys, clothes, and treats all year round. My little brain knew it had nothing to do with the expenses. Still, they did not inform me about the stringent visa application processes involving overseas travel.

"Why can't I come with you?" I asked Niranga Aiya with my eyes filled with tears and a sob stuck in my throat. I couldn't imagine being away from him for a month.

"Because you are not a Senege," Niranga Aiya gave me a *'what a stupid question'* stare with an air of superiority.

"Why? Only Seneges can go abroad?" I stood in my Wonder Woman pose, hands on my waist, challenging him, not ready to back down despite the amusing expressions our parents exchanged over their teacups.

"No, silly," Niranga Aiya rolled his eyes and smirked. "Anyone with a passport can travel. You can't come with us because you are not a Senege."

"That is easy. I can become a Senege to go with you." I proposed, always the problem solver. My parents sat there, allowing me to make an utter fool of myself by not educating me why I couldn't fly with the Seneges. For the four adults who were indulging in afternoon tea and sweets, our exchange was entertainment.

"Then I have to marry you to make you a Senege." Niranga Aiya straightened his back, eyeballing me, implying he was not keen on the idea.

"Oh, ok." I plunked myself on the floor next to Aunty Nelum with disappointment, accepting my defeat.

"Why, Sasoo, don't you wish to wed my Niranga?" Aunty Nelum tossed her teacup onto the coffee table and pulled my chin up, peering into my face. She wiped away the tears that were sliding down my cheeks and stroked my hair with empathy. I shook my head, showing, *'I don't want to.'*

"Why not?" Aunty perked up with curiosity, still holding a compassionate stare on her face.

"He is just a knight. I am going to marry the Prince Charming!"

★★★

"Do they have to come tonight?" I complained to disguise the embarrassment that surfaced remembering the incident. Not wanting to let go of my grievances, I sat there feeling miserable. This home is my sanctuary. I come here to rest and recharge. To be loved, and to be spoiled and to be admired. Instead, today I am being treated as a stranger in my house.

"You were supposed to come home yesterday. That's why dinner was set for today to give you some time to settle. It is not their fault that you changed your plans at the last minute and got home late as well." This time around, Thaththa sounded stern, trying to put me in my place. His manner showed he expected more from me and he was disappointed. I said nothing and drank my tea in silence.

We watched television with no further interaction, each to their own thoughts. I let my mind drift to my 'happy place', a moment in the future that I have created for myself to immense in luxuries I can't afford today. It was more to keep my mind from becoming curious about Seneges.

I didn't want to lace stories about meeting them. So I let my mind travel to a place where I felt light, free, and liberated.

3 RESTLESS

I changed into a fresh pair of faded jeans and a thick woollen jumper, knowing I would fail in Amma's eyes again with my wardrobe choice. Not in a mood to care, I combed my short hair and applied some moisturiser to keep away dry patches appearing on my face.

As today was not an ordinary evening, I was self-conscious about my looks. I glared at my reflection in the mirror, wondering how the Seneges would perceive me. Unlike Akka, who is more like Amma, curvy, fair, and gorgeous, I took after Appachchi. I have dark but clear and smooth skin. My skinny silhouette screamed years of neglect being exposed to the harsh tropical sun. If there was anything I could call an asset, it was my elongated neck that held my small head and childlike face.

I stood near my bedroom door, listening to the voices that floated through. My room has direct access to the living room, where the guests were conversing with my family with the television operating in the background. I tried to subdue my inner chatter, as my mind was deafening. I live with a child and an adult in my head, helping me process my thoughts and feelings; having constant battles about what is right and wrong. Most of the time, the three of us abide in perfect harmony. However, on days like this, my mind becomes restless with anxious outbursts of my inner child throwing tantrums while the adult fades into the shadows to observe.

Seneges have arrived. I tried to catch Niranga Aiya's voice before I went out to join them. It bothered me not knowing if he had come, as I only heard traces of Aunty Nelum and Uncle Sarath's voices. I was jittery, unable to imagine what to expect; I hadn't seen Niranga Aiya for over ten years.

After a few minutes of standing at the entrance with apprehension, I realised I had to muster the courage and join the visitors. Whether I wanted it, I couldn't stay hidden in my room the entire night. I had to face them.

'Come on, girl, you got this. It's only for a few hours.' The wise one cajoled, knowing it was better to go before Amma called out and avoid another

disappointing glare from Thaththa. I rubbed my sweaty palms on my pants, took a deep breath, and stepped out to join the others in the living area.

I noticed the change in the air quality as soon as I walked into the living area. It smelled like a fragrant cocktail. Not overpoweringly, but I inhaled the mixture of fruity, sandalwood, pinewood and mint scent that was light and refreshing, as if we were in a flower garden on a sunny day. The room seemed different with just the mere presence of the Seneges filling the room, making it appear smaller.

"Sasoo, my sweet daughter," Aunty Nelum, who saw me first, screeched with delight. "What a pleasure to see you after so many years." I strode across the room and hugged her.

"Don't you feed this young woman, Thanuja? She is all skin-and-bones." Uncle Sarath glared, pulling me away from Aunty for a hug.

"Hello possum, you look younger than when we saw you at Amali's wedding." He stepped back, beaming over, and pulled me in for another cuddle. "It must be your short haircut." He ruffled my hair with an adoring face.

They reminded me of the first time I met them—that day when I fell into the mud pile and twisted my ankle. When Niranga Aiya half carried, half dragged me to his house. It was Aunty Nelum who bathed me with warm water and dressed me in one of Niranga Aiya's long sleeve shirts that was way too big for me. I was dressed funny in that shirt with sleeves folded a few times, so my wrists were visible, and the hemline reached down almost to my ankles.

It was Uncle Sarath, who just got back from work, checked my ankle, and wrapped a bandage around it to keep the swelling from getting any worse. Then he carried me across the shrubs that separated our yards, with Aunty and Niranga Aiya towing behind after the rain faded away. That's how Aunty and Uncle met my parents and formed their strong friendship.

When growing up, they were my second parents. Since they migrated, the only time I saw them was at Akka's wedding. Even at that time, I avoided them like the plague and somehow stayed away from home when they visited Sri Lanka. They tried to meet me in Kandy in the early years, but they gave up after noticing my lack of interest.

I wonder if Amma has sensed my active avoidance of the Seneges. She did not mention their visit last occasion I was home or when I called home for my regular check-ins. I didn't want to bring this up in case it ignites a string of unnecessary conversation.

Aunty kept on stroking my cheeks with such love in her eyes while Uncle had his arm around my waist, making me feel guilty about not being in touch. Sandwiched between them, I didn't have time to spot Niranga Aiya until he walked across to us from where he was sitting.

"Hey stranger, how have you been?" His voice sounded different; his Australian accent had no trace of the musical vibe I carried in my memories. Although he had a pleasant smile on his lips, I noticed it didn't reach his eyes. It seems as if he was trying very hard to be civilised and warm. I don't know what I was expecting. But it was not this formidable-looking man.

For once, Akka did not exaggerate his attractiveness. I was gawking at a powerful-looking person. This was not the Niranga Aiya I knew. He was not the chubby boy I used to outrun when we played cops and robbers. Aunty Nelum used to say he never could shed the baby fat he gained in his younger days. Somewhere over the last ten years, he had lost all of it and had become lean. He was taller than I recall. I wouldn't call him handsome because he was much more than that.

Niranga Aiya was wearing a slim fit shirt over faded Levis that made his legs appear longer. His short hair just touched his shirt collar, a style that matched with his skinny cheekbones that didn't look like the *'papadams'* I used to pinch.

He knew his presence unsettled me. Of course, I could recognise that demeanour, as I have witnessed it a thousand times, both on Malli's and Sula's faces - those who are aware of how desirable they are that wear it with arrogance. But, as I was still trying to digest how striking he had become, I couldn't muster a single word before he politely kissed one of my cheeks.

"Oh! Two! I keep forgetting its two cheeks here," He said with awkward politeness when he missed my other cheek. Those who often travel get confused with how many cheeks one needs to kiss when greeting in different countries. Americans and British do it twice while French go for three, and Australians only kiss one cheek for some reason. Remembering Sri Lankans follow the British custom, Niranga Aiya quickly corrected himself.

I noted the smoothness of his skin on mine and the warmth of his fingers on my shoulder when he hugged me. *'Show off'*, my inner child smirked. As my heartbeat raised and I worried if he could hear it pounding. My throat got dry, my palms began sweating, and my knees turned into jelly. I wondered if I grabbed a chair and sat, would others notice my edginess.

"Come, sit and tell us all about you."

I was grateful when Aunty Nelum pulled me across to sit opposite her and Uncle. Amma, Thaththa and Akka let us chat and continued with watching one of their favourite television dramas. Aunty Nelum and Uncle Sarath were so eager to learn about me. I tried to calm myself and have my heart rate return to normal while responding to their questions.

There was three of me in the room. The adult, calm and composed; the child, overexcited and giddy, while me in the middle talking about life while trying to settle my racing pulses and stop my thoughts from wandering to Niranga Aiya. Over the last ten years, I can't recall how many times my mind had conjured up stories, imagining how I would process meeting Niranga Aiya again. Yet, in none of those scenarios, I was this agitated.

'Sweet mother Kali, this is not fair. How can you put him in front of me with no warning?' I was talking to myself, trying to get a hold of my emotions. My senses were overloaded. My mind was in a blender, swirling around, building up one big pulp of gooiness. His Australian Sri Lankan mixed accent was so smooth and charming. And he smelled divine with an invisible fragrance cloud of mint and pinewood around him. My body was still in awe of his touch. I made a mental note to check if his touch had left any permanent marks, as I still could feel the tingly sensation. If I were not already sitting down, my legs would have collapsed by now.

'Get a grip on yourself girl.' The adult hissed with annoyance. Once my breathing turned to normal, my thoughts also settled down a bit. Maybe because we started to talk about my work.

When I mentioned I returned home after travelling in the Wilpattu National Park with a group of tourists, Aunty and Uncle's eyes widened, and brows went up with curiosity. It didn't surprise me Amma had chosen not to tell Seneges I also work as a tour guide in one of her many correspondences with Aunty Nelum. Amma and Akka never got around to accepting me as a tour guide, and they both preferred not to talk about it.

"How did you become a guide?" It surprised me when Niranga Aiya leaned forward and peered into my face. In my nervousness, I forgot he was also listening to my conversation with Aunty and Uncle.

"It was pure accident." I closed my eyes, stretching my neck, reminiscing the incredible moment that paved the way to the most rewarding career in my life. When I turned to him to share my story, he jolted back as if he got shocked by something.

How I became a tour guide always makes me smile. It was not because it made me discover one of my passions at an early age in life, but because it made Sula embarrassed.

***

I was at the Maligawa, the famous Temple of the Sacred Tooth Relic of Buddha, in the royal palace complex in Kandy with my best friend, Reshani. We were on the ground floor, near the entrance, listening to the evening theva. The theva is the daily service being carried out for decades to worship the tooth relic of the Buddha. A young man came with a group of Japanese visitors, attempting to explain the history and meaning of the traditional sound offerings, but he was doing a terrible job at it. It was clear that the Japanese language was not his cup of tea.

"That guy is butchering Japanese!" I leaned across to Reshani, pointing to the guide with my eyes. "Those poor tourists are going to think theva was King's lullaby."

"Here is your chance to practise Japanese," Reshani nudged me with an encouraging smile. "Show him how it is done, girl!" She shoved me towards the visitors. It was the first time I met Sula.

I was studying Japanese in school and was quite good at it. History and Japanese both being my strengths, Reshani didn't have to encourage me further. I walked across to them and took over the conversation.

Little did I know the group was Sula's father's business colleagues. They had given a glowing recommendation about my good Samaritan act when Sula's father came to meet them after the tour. As Sula was studying Japanese at school, his father had requested him to assist him with his clients. But, in his usual fashion, Sula had overplayed his ability, not admitted he was a lousy student of the Japanese language.

Sula's father is a well-known business owner in Kandy. He always has many trade partners visiting him from Japan and requesting translation work. Later he introduced me to an owner of a tourism business in Kandy, who allowed me to practise my skills as a translator, which was the first stepping stone into my current career. When I was in university, I started taking groups around Kandy and became a full-time tour guide after graduating.

As I became one of the few females in the industry, I offered specialised services to female tourists who prefer Japanese, German, or English-speaking tour guides.

***

"You should take Niranga around and show him how the township has changed since his last visit."

Aunty's suggestion made me eye Niranga Aiya. I wasn't sure if that was something he would be interested in. He was not new to the town as he grew up in a city full of colonial-style buildings that have changed little in the last ten years. For me, its beauty lies in the approach to the township and on the way out of the citadel.

It was comforting when Niranga Aiya said nothing. "Unlike Kandy and Colombo, Nuwara Eliya town has changed little," I reported, supporting his silence.

"So now you don't lecture at the university anymore?" Bound by her traditional ideas, Amma must have told Aunty my primary job was being a lecturer at the university.

"Aney, no,…… I still teach Aunty."

"I can't understand why she doesn't tell anyone she is a lecturer at the university." Amma chipped in with some annoyance, sharing her disappointment with my choice of career. It was clear though Amma was sitting with others pretending to watch television, her ears were glued to our conversation.

"Aiyo, our Niranga is the same. Instead of telling people, he is a mathematician, he tells everyone he is a game designer. God only knows what that means. I think these kids are trying to shock us."

Pride in Aunty Nelum's voice made me take a sideways glance at Niranga Aiya. When our eyes connected, we both shared a smile, identifying our need to defy the norms. For a moment, I felt spellbound. I was in the presence of my childhood best friend, who used to know everything about me and could read me like a book.

"What do you teach?" Niranga Aiya brought me back to the present with his question.

"I cover European History and Basic Archaeology."

"That is a lot to cover." Aunty straightened up in her chair, casting a curious look my way.

"Yes, a bit Aunty. But my tours help me set up practical assignments and get students to excavation sites. So, it helps," I said. "European History is hard, especially when I have visited none of the places."

"Ah, get Niranga to take you along on his trip. What do you say, putha?" When Uncle Sarath interjected in the usual jovial manner, Niranga Aiya shifted in his chair, avoiding my eyes.

"Um...... yah.... why not." He said with unease. I was curious about his travel plans to Europe, but I kept quiet, seeing Niranga Aiya fidgeting in his chair.

"Doing two jobs can't be easy. Do you have time for all?" Then, as if he could sense I was aware of his agitation, Niranga Aiya asked with interest.

"My lectures are only on Mondays to Thursdays. I cover the weekend tours and leave the long stints to Sula. Assignment grading is the hardest as I have to balance with touring and exam schedule." Niranga Aiya stared at me with some curiosity, trying to gauge how I managed it all. I craved to tell him, *barely*. For me, it was not a *want*; it was a *need* for survival. I hardly share that with anyone. It surprised me I wished to disclose it with Niranga Aiya.

"Sasoo, Sula Aiya is on the phone." When Malli called out from the other room, I was glad as I needed to flee away from the uncomfortable notion building inside me. An invisible thread pulled me, bit by bit, towards Niranga Aiya, and I didn't like it. Ignoring the concerned frowns Aunty and Uncle shared, I excused myself and left the room.

4 UNEASY

"Hey Sula, so sorry I didn't call you," I muttered into the receiver, ignoring the guilty sensation as I didn't bother calling him when I arrived home.

"I don't know why I still get anxious after all these years," Sula muffled, more to him than for me. "I know the moment the bus crosses Mahaweli River, you forget my existence!" His voice was heavy with hurt as he referred to a change in my attitude with the shift of geographical borders, the mighty Mahaweli River that separates Kandy town. Not that I forget his presence. Once I am home, I dive into being in the moment and absorbing as much of family time.

"Saku, all I wanted was a quick call to say you arrived home safely." Now he was using his sad voice, trying to take me on a guilt trip.

"Don't be so melodramatic, Sula! If I didn't come home, Malli would have called you." I snapped, not having the patience to entertain his whimsical dialogue.

"My, my, what's with the short fuse?" Sula picked up my irritation, realising his strategy would not work today.

"I am tired and hungry," I let out a long sign. "A good night's sleep will fix me." I wasn't ready to share my unsettled mental status with anyone, not until I had processed it myself. Sula was not aware of Niranga Aiya's existence. Niranga Aiya was a person I have kept hidden from everyone around me in Kandy. When I moved there, I kept my past separate from the present. So, no one in my current life, not even Reshani, my best friend, knows about the chubby boy with laughing eyes who dominated my adolescent years.

"Okay, rest well. I was just checking on you...... I will catch up with you in a week?" There was the usual question. Sula always wondered if I would stay longer when I came home, but he dared not ask. Sometimes I stayed back when there was no university work, and Sula knew that.

"Are you going to fix it?" Sula knew what I was referring to - that was what our fight was about before I took the bus back home. When there was no response for few seconds, I imagined him slouching in his office chair, twiddling the pen with unease.

"I promised, didn't I? ...... I will not let you down, Saku," He sounded defeated and tired.

"You better not! Or...... I will walk away." It wasn't a threat. Sula knew I was at the end of my tether, having no strength left to fight anymore.

"I know......" There was a sob in Sula's voice that he was trying to contain within. I signed and let go of my anger for the moment, knowing his eyes would be filled with tears.

By the time I finished the call, everyone was making their way to the dining room. I scanned the room for Niranga Aiya when I saw him helping Akka get up from the chair. There was such warmth and care in the way he was leaning over her.

Out of nowhere, I became angry and irritated, wanting to storm out of the room. I thought Akka was behaving as a damsel in distress. Though it is tough being pregnant, on other days, she manages on her own. I couldn't recall anyone giving her a hand when she had to be on her feet.

'Oh, who are you kidding, girl?' I ignored the inner child's taunt, eyeing Niranga Aiya, pulling a chair and helping Akka sit down for dinner. Akka was still the centre of his attention. Nothing much has changed in the last ten years.

"Was that your Gorky?" Niranga Aiya interrupted my thoughts sitting opposite me.

"Gorky?" I blinked, not following him.

"Didn't you say you were going to find a boyfriend like Maxim Gorky?" He leaned forward and snorted, picking up my cluelessness.

'What's with him now? He was all lovey-dovey to Akka earlier to look so pissy now....'

"I grew up," I muttered with annoyance. Not keen on continuing the conversation, I ignored Niranga Aiya's disheartened glare and focused on the food.

Both our parents were sitting at one end of the table having their own conversation, leaving us to have our own. I recalled many such nights we had over the years. The difference was our side of the table would be more disruptive back then. This room used to buzz with our elevated voices; Malli and I arguing with Akka, or Niranga Aiya and I debating about something that happened during the day. The night would not have ended without having one adult demanding us to keep quiet and settle down a few times.

Today, all of us were much more civilised. Malli and Niranga Aiya were in an in-depth conversation about computers and the next big *'thing'* that will disrupt the world of information and technology. Despite the vast age gap between those two, Niranga Aiya always had a way of connecting with Malli, even when Malli was a little kid, annoyingly following us everywhere we went. It was comforting to observe that trait hadn't changed with time.

Akka looked tired and ate little. Being in her last trimester of pregnancy must be so hard on her, and I guess to top it off, to have to sit next to Niranga Aiya must be even harder.

★★★

I recollect the day we had that conversation about Gorky. It was a gorgeous day in April. The sky was blue, and the entire city was buzzing with colours and the unique sounds of migratory birds. On my way back from school, I received my first love letter.

As a teenager, I had little interest in love or sex. I found boys to be boring and lame, except Niranga Aiya. Perhaps that was my defence mechanism, as I wasn't getting any attention from the opposite sex.

I have always been an ordinary girl, not one to get a second look from a passer-by, which I accepted with grace. Maybe growing up with Akka, gorgeous like a movie star, and Malli, adorable and attractive, made me settle into being the mediocre middle child way early in my life.

I can't recall how many times I read the letter. I was excited that someone had taken the time to write to me. Finally, a boy believed I was worthy of his time and attention, although he was a stranger. When Niranga Aiya found me, I was sitting outside my favourite place in our yard, facing Mount Pedro and reading the letter once again.

"Why are you grinning on your own?" He startled me, peering into my face. I was so lost in my thoughts that I didn't hear him coming. When he stood closer to study my face, I sensed the warmth spreading through my cheeks. I bit my lips, glancing away to avoid Niranga Aiya's piercing eyes that were trying to pry into my inner thoughts.

"What is going on? You look flustered."

Niranga Aiya was my best friend, and I did not want to keep it a secret from him. More than anything, I was dying to share my first love letter with someone. I didn't have the patience to wait until the next day to share it with one of my school friends.

"My first love letter!" I remember sounding proud, more than shy. Niranga Aiya was stunned, as if he couldn't believe what I had just said.

"Who gave it to you?" It was clear he didn't expect me to receive a love letter. I wanted to tell him, *'Me too. Who would have thought I would get a love letter?'* but I didn't.

"Janaka Aiya from your school. He was waiting near the church and gave it to me today."

"Why did you take it?"

"Why shouldn't I?" I asked with irritation. "He has written it for me; I wanted to read it."

"Give it to me!" He said as he grabbed the letter. I let him read it, focusing my eyes on the mountain.

Our house sat on a small hill, blessed with a spectacular view. That day white clouds had spread across the tip of the mountain, making shadows that lay across its slope, forming part of it to appear blue-grey while the rest of the hill loomed in bright green. April's breeze was refreshing. I was sitting on the bench beside the only pear tree on our property that bore no fruit. Amma said after the cyclone in the late seventies, the town had produced no pears at all.

"Cookie, are you going to say yes to this guy?" Niranga Aiya took a long time to read the letter, and when he spoke, there was some anxiousness in his voice.

"No." I can't recollect what made me glance at Niranga Aiya. It was as if he had his breath on hold until I responded. He exhaled slowly and looked pleased, with a hint of a smile playing on his lips.

"How come?" For the first time that afternoon, he smiled, expanding his cheeks into giant *'papadums.'*

"I am not crazy to say yes to a guy that I know nothing about!"

"I don't think you need to know everything about a person to fall in love. Why, don't you believe in love at first sight?"

It sounded like a trick question, as I didn't expect him to interrogate my reasoning. Instead, I thought he would be pleased I was not interested in his schoolmate. "I haven't thought about it before," I told him the truth.

"So, what kind of boy are you looking for?"

"I am going to find someone wise like Maxim Gorky!" I boldly declared with all the confidence a fourteen-year-old could muster. On reflection, I was deluded. I didn't have any insight into boys or love to make such a proclamation.

"Gorky? What is so special about him?" Not understanding my idolisation of one of my favourite writers, Niranga Aiya arched his eyebrows with curiosity.

"I want to love someone soft as a kid, yet possess the strength of a thug and can be a wise sage… Someone who would have experienced the world, its beauty, the good, the bad, and the ugly. Someone who would have the strength to let me make my own mistakes, hold my hand when I am weak and let it go when I need space to grow."

I can recall the delusional excitement tickled my heart. Not living in the real world, I was harbouring a fantasy I had latched onto from a book I had read. The memory made me want to vomit with disgust. Have I been that naïve? I wanted to travel in time and tell my younger self to get real, stop dreaming and be realistic.

"That is a tall order for any guy to fulfil." He warned me with some sarcasm.

"Listen, you are too young to fall for anybody." He took my hands and peered into my eyes.

We sat there for hours. Niranga Aiya did the talking while I enjoyed being there. He was guarded. I could tell he never shared what was on his mind. He skirted around the topic, the way we walked around Lake Gregory on sunny days, without taking the plunge for fear of the icy cold water.

Soon the light started fading, and the sun crawled behind the mountain. As the atmosphere got colder, I felt the warmth in his hand and offbeat pulses. I recalled how he avoided looking at me, pausing and collecting his thoughts as if he was trying to find the right words.

"You think Gorky is great because you love his characters in the books you have read. In real life….. he may not be as pure and admirable as you think him to be."

"That may be the case, but it doesn't hurt to hope for someone like him." I dismissed his concern with a shrug.

"I thought you had a crush on Apu." Niranga Aiya referred to one of the main characters created by the Indian author Bibhutibhushan Bandyopadhyay in his book Pather Panchali that we both enjoyed reading.

"Nah, I always thought Apu had a weak personality. He is someone who is self-obsessed and so much in love with himself." I had a crush on Apu's character when I started Bibhutibhushan Bandyopadhyay's trilogy, which soon faded away when I finished reading the last one from the collection.

When I was a teen, we had little access to information, not as today's teens do. We were the generation that grew up playing outdoors, climbing trees and building playhouses. In those days, watching a movie was considered a treat. I was a kid that got lost in books. My fantasies revolved around the characters I found in them. Earlier on, Niranga Aiya and I were Peter Pan and his shadow. Later, I thought we were more like Apu and Durga, the two main characters from Bibhutibhushan Bandyopadhyay's trilogy, going about enjoying childhood innocence. However, our roles were reversed in real life, where Niranga Aiya was the one protecting me.

I was not the only one in love with an author or a character in a book. I remember Aunty Nelum saying that when she was pregnant with Niranga Aiya, she got the idea for his name reading the Bibhutibhushan Bandyopadhyay trilogy. She has been determined to name her daughter 'Durga,' the main character from the novel; if she ever had one and always joked, she would ask Niranga Aiya to call his daughter 'Durga' one day when he has kids.

As a teen, I can't recall having any preconceived ideas about boys. I couldn't pinpoint a particular character I admired. Although I read many romantic novels and fancied the tall, dark and rich guy as most other girls did at that age, I sensed it would be different in real life - not every girl was lucky enough to get her Prince Charming. I was receptive to a happy ending for sleeping beauty with a hard-working dwarf.

Maybe that's why I was obsessed with those who were like Maxim Gorky, whose characters they inked with faults and baggage but had larger-than-life ideas. It helped me to accept people were not just black or white but lived in many shades of grey.

"Keep your heart to yourself for a few more years, Cookie. You are too young to get it crushed." I wish I had listened to his advice, but it was too late. My heart was already lost.

***

When Malli kicked my foot under the table, others had moved on to dessert, and I hadn't even finished half of what I had on my plate. I was not hungry anymore. Scanning the room, I caught Niranga Aiya watching me. It felt like he was searching for something he wanted to hang onto. His gaze was intense, as if he could pick up the awkward unease swirling around my mind. I turned my eyes away, fearing he could sense I was still trying to glue pieces of my shattered past.

I had a sudden urge to leave the room and curl up in my bed, forget about everything, and let the coldness carry me into a deep sleep. Feeling exhausted, I suppressed a yawn, checking the wall clock for the time.

"You have changed little." Niranga Aiya chuckled, following my gaze. "Still a sleepyhead. Can't keep your eyes open after ten at night." This time when he smiled, it reached his eyes, making them glitter like stars. I stopped breathing for a second. He reminded me so much of the teenager I grew up with.

'Holy mother of Kali, why does he have to be so gorgeous?' I muttered to myself. I didn't know how to ignore him when he still remembers our childhood details so vividly. He had all my senses over working from smell, sight, hearing to touch. The only thing missing was the taste, and I didn't want to imagine what it would be to taste him. I felt a warmth spreading through my body, making me blush. *'How am I going to salvage myself when he got all my senses in disarray?'* I was not sure who could give me the answer when I felt so distressed by the mere presence of this arduous man.

I glanced away to avoid his intense glare. The last thing I wanted was for him to hear my internal thoughts or know how uncomfortable I was with the feelings turning in my head.

"Aunty and Uncle, thank you so much for such a wonderful dinner. I am going to call it a night." To my enormous relief, Niranga Aiya pushed his chair and got up to leave.

"Are you sure, putha? I am sure Sasoo would love to catch up with you. You two haven't seen each other for more than a decade." I was horrified when Aunty Nelum questioned. I didn't want her to know I had no intention of catching up with her son when I was not in my best state, sleep-deprived and emotionally bruised.

"Saku must be tired after her long day today. Look at the poor girl, she is about to fall asleep, and I will have to carry her." Although he was teasing, there was kindness in his voice. It was the first time I heard him address me by my name in years, making me yearn for the way he used to call me *'Cookie.'*

When he eyed me charmingly, he reminded me of the boy who used to put me to bed when we were kids. I had always been the first to give in to sleep when we were trying to stay up as kids. Even Malli could stay up longer than I.

"I can always catch up with Saku on another day," There was a spark in Niranga Aiya's eyes, as if he could sense my intention was the opposite. "She will be here for a couple of days for us to catch up properly," he said with full authority, making me nod in silence.

"That is true. You kids go on and retire. We have so much catching up to do." Uncle Sarath wasn't ready to call it a night. That didn't surprise me. It had always been like that when those four adults got together. Most of the time, Aunty Nelum had to drag Uncle Sarath kicking and screaming black and blue when he had a bit too much to drink.

It was refreshing to witness the strength of their friendship over a decade that ignored caste, class, and geographical boundaries. A heavy sadness filled my heart for Niranga Aiya and me I. We made their friendship possible, but somehow, we didn't survive the test of time.

We all left the dining room and regrouped in the living room. I said good night to Aunty and Uncle. I ended up being the last to say good night to Niranga Aiya. When I was about to head to my room, he stretched his arm and enfolded me in an unexpected hug.

He held me much tighter and closer than he did when he greeted me a few hours ago. I stiffened, standing there holding my breath with unease, not knowing what to do with my hands. I brushed off the strange squint in his eyes, making no attempt to interpret his actions.

"Good night, Cookie," My heart squeezed when he uttered my childhood pet name. "Dream well." Niranga Aiya whispered following our childhood parting ritual. He left, leaving a bit of his pinewood and mint mixed scent behind as a daring reminder that no matter how much I try, his charismatic and masculine presence would not be easy to erase.

5 APPREHENSIVE

Some voices outside adjoining my room on the veranda work me up. The voices belonged to Akka and Niranga Aiya, reminding me that what happened last night was no longer a dream. Niranga Aiya was here, back home. I couldn't understand why they were up that early. The clock on the bedside table showed it wasn't even eight in the morning. Without trying to comprehend what Akka was doing without going to work, I snuggled back into my quilt and drifted back to sleep. It was way too early for me to ponder about either of them.

When I woke up, it was after eleven, and the house was so quiet. Akka had gone to work and Malli to school. Thaththa and Amma were nowhere to be seen. As they both are retirees, it was unusual. Usually, I would find Thaththa reading the daily newspaper and Amma cooking or mending an old blouse or a skirt sitting on the veranda.

After wandering from room to room like a lost puppy, I made it outside, trying to locate either of them. Expecting Amma and Thaththa to be in the plant nursery, which has become Amma's new means of income, and found Amma in the corner of the yard, tending to her plants.

"Good morning, my little one," Amma lifted her gaze from the plants she was potting, giving me a blazing smile. "Did you get anything to eat?" After hearing Amma's greeting, I let go of the breath I was holding, seeing Amma was in a better mood than last night. I was curious about what made her agitated and stressed yesterday to be so annoyed with me. It can't be only because of my late arrival. I made a mental note to ask Akka about it later.

"Not yet." I shook my head. "I came searching for you and Thaththa. House was silent. I didn't want to stay in."

Amma was repotting some oriental lilies. I joined her and grabbed an empty pot to help her out. Mount Pedro stood tall and gallant, covered in snow like clouds, far across from where we were. Morning sun rays were peeking through the thick clouds trying to kiss its peak.

I felt the coldness in the morning's fresh air sneaking through my woollen cardigan. Pulling it closer to my chest, I turned my face, stretching my neck towards the sun to let my cheeks greet its soft presence, enjoying the gentle warmness spreading across my face. It felt like a caress of a lover warming your body ever so gently. I wondered if this was what the mountain top was feeling when morning rays were sneaking through the fortress of clouds.

"Thaththa has gone to the golf club with Sarath. Now that Sarath is here, it has become Thaththa's new routine."

Amma sounded happy and calm seeing Thaththa out. Since he retired a couple of years earlier, he was pretty much homebound. It makes me sad when I think about my parents, who got forced into retirement way too young and are deteriorating. It was hard for Thaththa to find a purpose in life and get used to not working daily. The early diagnosis of Parkinson didn't help his case, either. It challenged him when he had to shift from being the provider to being cared for.

"Can he play?" I have noted how Thaththa struggles with the tremors that come and go with the early onset of Parkinson. So I was sceptical if he could play a game of golf uninterrupted and keep his stamina up without getting tired.

"He is going there for the company, not the game. It has been good for him to be out and do something other than reading the daily newspapers."

We both continued to work in silence. I helped Amma to repot her plants from smaller ones to medium size pots. After her retirement, Amma turned her hobby into a small business. It didn't generate much income, but it kept her occupied and gave her something other than cooking and cleaning to focus on during the day.

I watched Amma going about with repotting, noticing that she, too, showed signs of ageing. There were more grey hairs around her temples and sagging of skin around her neck and arms. She was rubbing her back in between repotting when she thought I was not watching. It appeared she was nursing back pain.

"Amma, have you been lifting heavy pots?" I waited for Amma to rub her back again to confront her. "Let's get someone to help you with the heavy lifting." I was worried about Amma. I knew she wouldn't ask Thaththa to help her because his grip was not firm enough. Malli was also not around during the day with school work and after-hour classes.

"I can manage." Amma instantly dropped her hand from her back and picked up another orchid plant. "There is not much heavy lifting, anyway." She dismissed my suggestion in her usual manner.

"Oh, yeah? How do you get your plants onto a trishaw when you take them to the flower stall?"

"I have seen you rubbing your back every five minutes!" I continued, as Amma said nothing to dismiss me. I wish she would open up and share things with me instead of keeping her worries within.

"We don't need the extra expenses, love. I can manage."

"Nonsense. Let's get someone to help. It wouldn't cost much." The saddest part of retirement was that having to be frugal with your money. I watched the worry lines on Amma's forehead, wanting to smooth them out with some reassurance.

"You are doing enough already. I don't want you to worry about other stuff." Amma sounded defeated and uncomfortable.

I know that Amma and Thaththa are not comfortable receiving the money I send them. The only reason they haven't turned it down was that their pension couldn't cover increasing medical and living expenses.

Until recently, I never understood the sacrifices my parents had made for us. I went through school and my first year of university, demanding whatever I wanted from my parents, not understanding how hard they had to work to allow those luxuries I took for granted.

We are from a lower-middle-class family, where both our parents were ordinary government workers. Akka, Malli and I went to national public schools. However, the three of us grew up enjoying the comfort of upper-middle-class children.

Perhaps it was because of the influence of the Seneges, who were all born into the upper class, or perhaps Amma and Thaththa were trying to compensate for the things we lost in our lives - Appachchi's demise and losing Malli's birth mother. None of us saw the price tag attached to the lifestyle we assumed and lived. I came to realise this when I eavesdropped on a conversation.

Amma and Thaththa were talking about our bleak financial situation when they thought we were all sleeping. They were unaware that if I listened in, I could hear the conversations in the living room. Oblivious to my presence, they were going on about selling a part of the land to finance Akka's wedding.

That conversation happened a few months before the wedding. Thaththa was planning on giving Akka a reasonable dowry. I never found out how they financed the wedding and the dowry, as they kept those details from us. But I remember Akka had a lavish wedding in Kandy, as Saman Aiya demanded it. Most of the guests were from his side, as we didn't have many relatives or friends. Aunty Nelum and Uncle Sarath came from Sydney for the reception, but not Niranga Aiya. Maybe it was too raw for him to witness Akka getting married.

Eavesdropping on that conversation made me grow up, take responsibility, become independent. I took on translation assignments and guiding tours during university breaks. I was careful how I spent and turned down the allowance my parents gave me.

"You need to save for your own." There was a trace of a stern warning in Amma's voice.

"You can't spend all your earnings on us. Soon you have to get married and start your own family." She was trying to stress her point further.

"Why are you in a rush to marry me off?" I stopped pulling the oriental lily plant I was working on. "Are you planning on running a baby nursery, is that it?" I tried to make her smile. "You will regret pushing me into a marriage."

As she didn't grasp my joke, I dug a little deeper, seeking a smile as she would normally dismiss me with a cynical slur, but today, she didn't. I wished I could tell her she wasn't alone, that I understood her worry and the fear she was grappling with, wanting to give the same comfort to Malli as she gave to Akka and me. The heaviness of the guilt weighed her down. I wanted to put my arms around her hunched shoulders and hug her tight, stroke away her worry lines and wipe away the tears lingering at the bottom of her eyes. I didn't do any of that.

'Covered.' I ignored the tiny voice that screamed inside me.

"Amma, I am going to marry rich. Can you please stop worrying about me?" To give some comfort to Amma, I spoke the only language she knew, pretending I had aligned my dreams with hers.

"I am going to Jeevani's house this week. Devan can find someone to help you, don't worry, it wouldn't cost much." To avoid seeing the tears welling up in Amma's eyes, I shifted my eyes away. She shouldn't be embarrassed than she already was. We both lifted our heads at the same time, hearing a ruffling sound. And saw Aunty Nelum watching us with discomfort, as if she had listened to a good part of our conversation.

"Good morning. I didn't realise you would be helping Thanuja, Sasoo." Though she was trying to sound cheerful, she was flustered, shifting her legs as if she was trying to shake off invisible ants climbing up her legs.

"What are you doing here, Aunty?" As I asked, Amma fired a warning stare.

"Well, I was bored at home," Aunty Nelum grinned as it was a good enough reason for her appearance. "Niranga was supposed to take me out shopping, but either he has forgotten about his promise, or he is having a busy day at work. So, I came to help Thanuja."

"What? Helping Amma in the nursery? Dressed like that?" I asked in doubt.

I didn't believe Aunty would change that much. She was not a person to get her hands dirty working with the potting mixture. She is the type that wouldn't mind sewing or doing a bit of occasional cooking when her domestic helper was not around. I failed to picture her in a garden other than to cut flowers for her vases. Ten years of Australian life wouldn't have changed her that much, especially with how she was dressed - in three-quarter length shorts, a matching polo shirt with a cardigan wrapped around her shoulders. Aunty Nelum was dressed to go on a picnic than working in a backyard. She had a big brim hat and sunglasses, which turned her into a page out of a Vogue magazine than a woman coming to help her friend.

"Aiyo, don't be silly," Aunty shook her head with horror. "I mean helping Thanuja to take a break." She waved her hand, dismissing me.

"You know, the only work I am good at is exercising my credit card with a good dose of shopping!" Aunty Nelum said, making both of us laugh.

"Thanks again, Nelum. It is so nice of Niranga to drop off Amali in the morning. The poor child doesn't even get proper sleep on his holiday." The weakness in Amma's voice made her sound like an apple polisher, and I shifted my feet in discomfort.

"Aney, Niranga loves doing that. He is an early bird. It helps him get through his emails and calls with his friends in Sydney as they are about four hours ahead of us."

So, that was the reason I caught Akka and Niranga Aiya's voices outside my window in the morning. Niranga Aiya had taken the chauffeuring role and had driven Akka to work. Akka would find it to be so comforting. It is difficult for anyone to take the rush hour bus ride, let alone a pregnant woman. Though

I should be grateful for his goodness, I was annoyed. *'There must be a motive behind his kindness,'* a tiny voice inside me murmured. However, underneath that suspicious sense, I knew Niranga Aiya was born benevolent, one who cared about the well-being of others. Still, I couldn't understand why he would spend his holiday driving around someone else's wife.

Was he the kind of person who would help a friend while on his holiday? Doesn't he have any friends to hang out with? Wouldn't he have sophisticated places to be rather than be around his parents and neighbours when he is on holiday? Indeed, there has to be a reason for his gallantry kindness. Is he planning to win Akka's heart and steal her away from Saman Aiya?

My thoughts were in a hyperactive panic, crisscrossing all over, making me agitated and uncomfortable. I conveniently ignored the knowledge of his kind-heartedness, as I wanted to believe there was something dubious about it.

"Still, it is very nice of him. Amali is not having an easy time with the pregnancy. If only Saman had left his car keys with us…… at least Manoj can drop her at work."

I wished Amma would stop talking and get back to repotting as I wanted to scream, *'You don't have to be grateful; he is not doing it as a favour… He is after Akka.'* I had a very suspicious mind, and it was working overtime.

"Niranga got his grandfather's qualities. He would help anyone. You wouldn't believe how many kids we had staying on and off at our place when he was in university. Now that he lives alone, I don't know who stays in his apartment, but I can assure you there would be a few strays sharing his place." Aunty Nelum started rambling to suppress the helplessness we both heard in Amma's voice.

"Aney, yes, Niranga is born like that. If he didn't help my little Sasoo, none of us would have met!" I was glad to hear a bit of happiness finally in Amma's voice.

"Yes, I still remember that day. How scared and worried you were, Sasoo……. I couldn't stop you from crying for a long time. You know, you were so cute in Niranga's shirt. I wish I had taken a photo….. oh, you were so adorable." To make my embarrassment worse, Aunty Nelum came across and pinched my cheek. That small action dragged me from being a woman in her twenties to a ten-year-old in an instant. I couldn't resist the memories that started flooding in. Traces of that windy night and how the events unfolded formed a lump in my throat.

"What are you so happy about, Amma?"

We didn't hear Niranga Aiya coming. His voice sounded warm and open. From where I was sitting, he looked even better in natural light. As the morning sun was behind him, I couldn't see his facial expressions clearly. He was taller and leaner than he appeared yesterday. The polo shirt he had on was hugging his torso in the right places, showing off his muscular arms and flat belly. His face was darker, which can be because he had not shaved in the morning and was wearing dark sunglasses.

"We were talking about how we all met when you carried Sasoo home after her fall." Aunty Nelum turned to Niranga Aiya with a beaming smile. "Remember how scared she was with mud all over her and with a broken ankle?"

"You mean twisted ankle," Niranga Aiya said with an air of authority, correcting his mother's oversight.

"What?" Aunty Nelum turned to Niranga Aiya, not picking up the arrogance superiority in her son's voice.

"Saku didn't break her ankle Amma, she twisted it when she fell." Though he was addressing his mother, his eyes were on me. I wished I could read those hidden behind the sunglasses, wanting to find out what caused that lazy smile on his lips.

"Ah, yes, that is right. Sasoo twisted her ankle." Aunty Nelum nodded her head, agreeing with Niranga Aiya with a whimsical smile on her face.

"Oh, do you remember how cute she looked in your shirt? It was up to her ankles, and that was the only thing I could find to change her into." It embarrassed me further when Aunty started talking about me wearing Niranga Aiya's shirt, as it sounded inappropriate.

Niranga Aiya shifted his gaze from his mother to me, running his eyes over my head to toes. I hoped, unlike me, he was not trying to imagine how one of his shirts would fit me now if I had to wear one. I watched the lazy smile already on his lips, reaching his eyes.

"Who could forget that day?" I was not sure if it was a statement or a question. Instead of joining their conversation, I got up and brushed the dirt off my palms. It was time for me to head back home.

"Amma, I am heading back inside. Catch up with you all later, Aunty and Aiya." I walked away, ignoring the disbelief that crossed all three faces, not giving any explanation. I wanted to flee from their company fast, as Niranga Aiya's presence made me uncomfortable and edgy.

"Saku, wait up." I stopped when I heard Niranga Aiya's voice and his quick steps behind me. I turned around and waited for him to catch up, not having any other option.

"Have you been to the stream?" When he came and stood facing me, I took a step back to build some distance between us. I couldn't handle inhaling the smell of his cologne or standing so close to him. He studied me oddly, but said nothing. He waited for my response as I shifted my eyes to gaze at the pine forest that was looming in front of us.

"No, I haven't been there in years."

"What? It used to be your favourite place on earth!" Once again, his ability to recall details about our past disturbed me. He was tugging some invisible cords I didn't realise existed, making my heart feel warmer, melting the protective shield of the ice layer I had around it.

'Used to be,' I said nothing as I had no plans to explain how my favourite place in Nuwara Eliya turned into the most detested place in my mind. An uncomfortable silence stretched between us, and I stood there like a statue, not understanding how to break the silence.

"Well, I would like to visit the place," Niranga Aiya gazed at the pine forest before turning his eyes on me. "I like to do it while you are here. Shall we go for a stroll?" he sounded enthusiastic about visiting the place, not sensing my discomfort.

"Do you mean now?" I inquired, concerned as I was trying to overcome the anxiousness that was brewing inside.

"No, not now. How about tomorrow morning? If you are free?" When he smiled, I felt the same squashy sensation I experienced last night. It was unfair for him to look that attractive, just standing there and smiling as if everything was normal.

"How about another day? I've already got something planned." I dismissed his suggestion, as I didn't want to tell him I was not planning to visit the place ever again or go there with him in this lifetime.

"Oh, sure, maybe another day. Why don't you tell me when you are not so busy?" I sensed my response had made him uncomfortable. Niranga Aiya's voice changed, and he sounded angry or hurt.

"Sure, I will," I uttered, none committing, and without waiting for a response, I headed back home. I wanted to turn around and take another peek at his handsome silhouette, but I didn't. His presence disturbed me in a way I didn't fathom understanding. Imagining he was staring at my back made my body shiver with anxiety. I hope the next few days will soon pass without having to worry about visiting the stream or bumping into him.

6 BENEVOLENCE

When Jeevani called to tell me, she was only working half a day, I visited her instead of waiting around for the weekend. I have always enjoyed visiting Jeevani. Their house was a small dwelling with a tin roof and thin brick walls. Jeevani was a natural homemaker, and despite their financial position, she always kept the place clean. The house smelled a mixture of jasmine flowers that decorated her hair and fried vada. I knew she made the vada especially for me as Jeevani knew how much I loved her spicy dhal based appetiser.

"So, are you still with Sula?" Jeevani started her usual interrogation while putting away the grocery bag I bought for her on my way here.

Jeevani and Devan did not enjoy the best luck in the world, as they faced one challenge after another. Their first hurdle was getting married. Jeevani was the only girl in their middle-class Sinhalese family. And Devan was the eldest in a Tamil family from a local tea plantation. Either party, because of social status and different cultural backgrounds, did not bless their union. So, they did what any couple in love would do and eloped. As Jeevani's own family disowned her, they moved in with Devan's family - so it was a struggle from day one.

She didn't make it to university, but was lucky to get a job as a bookkeeper at a local factory. Daven was qualified to enter university, but could not afford to attend. Their fate had them working in the same factory, and when they met, they both claimed it was love at first sight.

No one, including me, blessed their union. I had nothing against Devan. He was a nice guy, and now we are friends. Still, I was looking out for Jeevani. I knew it would be an uphill battle for her to be with someone like Devan, who could not provide the same level of comfort she was used to. As a realist, I struggle to understand her rationale. I was a reluctant witness to their marriage. Although I disagreed with their actions, I was not ready to turn my back on our friendship.

I remember Jeevani telling me, 'There is more to life than having financial security, Saku. You can't choose who you fall in love with, and if your love is strong, you make it happen.' She was not one to give up. She took everything in her stride and got used to her new surroundings. When Devan's mother passed away, she inherited the responsibility of looking after his father and the two young siblings who were schooling, on top of minding her own two toddlers. Jeevani was a natural caregiver and took this responsibility seriously, with no complaints.

"Why wouldn't I?" I was not pleased with having to provide the same answer every time I visited Jeevani.

"How many jobs not get paid in the last two months?"

"Who is counting?" I smiled and shrugged off her comment.

"When are you going to get off that sinking ship?" Jeevani was referring to our tour agency's bleak financial status. Sula hasn't managed the finances well. I was helpless, as it was not my area of expertise. Though Thaththa was an expert, asking for his advice was a bad idea. That would become the last ammunition Amma needed to declare war against Sula.

I didn't want Amma to find out I lost the rainy-day fund I worked so hard to save. Nor did I want her to know about my sleepless nights worrying when the house of cards would tumble. Amma already disliked Sula for no reason, and I didn't want to give her one. If she asked me to choose, no matter what, she would win.

I am not as sturdy and independent as the world saw me. My weakness is my family. I would lie down in my life for their happiness.

"How would you have felt if I deserted you when you eloped with Devan?"

"It is not the same thing, Saku, you know it. Sula is dragging you down with him. You shouldn't go through it, especially when you know there are other options for you."

Ever since Devan came across details of the agency's financial status when he was in Kandy, Jeevani has been worried.

"I can't, Jeevani," I told her the truth. "It will destroy Sula. I need to fix it." Jeevani's face softened with some empathy.

I haven't figured out a way to mend it. The tour agency is the only means of income for Sula. Unlike me, he didn't finish university. He was too good for an outdated syllabus and couldn't wait to use his newfound business skills. So, he opened the tour agency with the money he borrowed from his father, making me his working partner. Since then, most of my savings have been going into it to keep up with the expenses.

Until now, we have done well. Between a few other part-timers and us, we built a powerful presence in the market. As I was too busy juggling my studies and touring, I left the business's management duties to Sula. Though my intuition screamed something was not adding up when I didn't get paid on time for my work, I ignored it.

I realised the gravity of the situation when the leasing company ceased our only asset, the Hiace van used to transport guests. There were too many things going on in my life to take time to question him when Sula became inhibited than usual. I expected him to share his troubles. No matter how well one believes you know someone, I know hidden layers are invisible in plain sight. In all the years I have known Sula, I never saw his ego to be in control, perceived as a leader or shrewd proprietor. Still, I didn't have any right to be angry with him.

We all are the same; we share bits and pieces. We go on believing we are open to our dearest and the nearest. Yet, in reality, we compartmentalise. We open a window and let someone peek through; for another, we open a door. Few are welcome to stay for longhaul, while others just pass by. Most of the time, we keep many of the rooms closed and well-guarded.

I always believed one couldn't understand the actual personality without collating many faces of the same person. Like working on a jigsaw puzzle, to understand a person, one must start with a corner, get the framework completed, and try your best to fill in the middle. If you are lucky enough, you will complete it in one lifetime. I am living proof of this - I am not the same person when I am with Sula or Reshani or with Jeevani, a different person when I am at home or in front of a lecture room. Not that I become another person, but situations and people bring out distinct qualities and aspects of my life to the surface.

I have allowed no one to peek into my soul, opening every door and window, going through the rooms, checking every nook and cranny. How can I allow anyone else to walk through my corridors when I haven't done the walk myself?

There are so many who could help Sula. For anyone to help him, he needs to admit he needs help. If he can't be honest with himself, I am unsure how he could open to others. I would share none of these thoughts with Jeevani. The little she knew had got her worried and have made her dislike Sula. I would not add fuel to the fire.

"All businesses have highs and lows. You wouldn't leave Devan because he doesn't have enough money to support you, would you? So don't be a hypocrite and start lecturing me, woman!"

I laughed while I was pacing around her tiny kitchen. Jeevani had already moved on to making tea. She stopped adding sugar into the tea mug to study my face. I watched her contemplate a response in her head and was relieved when she disregarded it, returning to her task.

"Hey, is that Appa outside in a wheelchair?" I stopped to stare, noting Jeevani's father-in-law in a wheelchair playing with Jeevani's two boys. Jeevani and Devan's latest challenge was a significant blow to the entire family. Devan's father was hit by a drunken bus driver, making him paralysed from the waist down. After the accident, their household income decreased from three to two; they had to take up the extra cost of caring for their father's medical expenses. Devan's younger sister, Rani, stopped her studies. She became her father's full-time caretaker, while the other, Meera, became a domestic helper.

"Oh, yes, we got a wheelchair donated by Meera's new master," Jeevani, following my gaze, peered through the window, beaming with happiness. "Did I tell you, Meera is now working for this family in the hills? It must be close to your place. I still haven't been there." This was a piece of good news. Finally, some positive changes were taking place in Jeevani's life.

"When the family came to pick up Meera, they saw Appa and, seeing how he was struggling even with the smallest task; they got him a wheelchair. You can't imagine what a change it has been for all of us." I heard the gratitude and relief in Jeevani's voice.

"Rani doesn't have to carry him all the time. Appa also prefers the outdoors. He is now helping with the kids and minds the vegetable patch."

"I am so glad, Jeevani, especially after the lousy collection we had to buy the wheelchair."

A couple of Jeevani and Devan's friends, started a fund collection to buy a wheelchair for Appa. After months of effort, the pool didn't cover a quarter of the amount required for a cheap wheelchair. What had taken place was a miracle.

"The son gave Devan a job in their factory, and he has told Devan he will give one of his old computers so Devan can improve his skills. A nice guy."

"Oh, there is a son in the picture?" I found this piece of news intriguing. "Is he married?"

"I am not sure." Jeevani paused for a moment and shook her head. Then, as if she had insight into my following questions, Jeevani answered before I asked. "He must be in his late twenties... a handsome guy."

"I wonder if Meera has smitten him, and he is helping Devan to win her heart." Jeevani placed the teacup in front of me with a bang and sat down facing me, giving me a quizzical stare.

"Oh, so you have some romance in your bones?" Her voice was heavy with sarcasm. "That is the only romantic thing you have said in all the years I have known you."

Last night I watched a Bollywood movie with Akka where a tycoon's son fell for their maid's daughter. I didn't want to tell Jeevani; the movie plot got my imagination running wild.

"Oh, come on, I am romantic as long as it is practical." I grabbed the teacup, taking a large sip to warm me up as the evening cold was creeping inside my jumper.

"You know it is an oxymoron, don't you?" Jeevani's voice was laced with sarcasm.

"Why? Do you think there is no middle ground? It shouldn't always be one or the other!"

"Because you are too rigid and don't like any complications." Jeevani's eyes were daring.

"Isn't life hard enough as it is?" I was thinking of all of us who were struggling to make some sense of life. "Why do we have to make it harder? I can be romantic if it is practical and makes sense."

"Why become vanilla when you can be fruit and nut or chocolate chip?" Jeevani's voice sounded sad, and I knew it was because she believed I was settling for less.

I was content with my vanilla life. I had my priorities, so I didn't get offended when Jeevani teased me. There were already enough worries in my life to let her comments weigh me down.

"Enough about me, tell me about Devan's new job." I change the topic, taking a bite of my third vada.

"Aney, we have to thank you for that." Jeevani leaned forward and squeezed my hand with gratefulness.

"Remember how you helped us when Devan wanted to study computers? Not only did you lend us money for the course, but you also let him stay with you during the classes. Without you, this wouldn't have happened."

That was more than a year ago. Devan wanted to study computers, but the course fees were unaffordable. I remember how distressed Jeevani sounded when she called me to ask if there was any way to help. All the years I have known her, Jeevani had been so careful not to share her difficulties with me, no matter how hard life became. She had her pride and dignity that kept her head high, so I knew it was a tough conversation for her to have when she called.

I didn't have enough money to make the upfront payment for the course. However, as Sula and I have done enough favours for people over the years, we talked to the company's Managing Director running the training course to work out an instalment-based payment plan for Devan. I lent them the money he needed to register for the course. During the four months of the study, Devan came to Kandy on Fridays, stayed in my annexe, and left on Sundays after classes.

"So, he got the job he wanted?" It was pleasing to hear Devan's hard work was getting paid off.

"Yes, and it was you who told Devan that computers are the future. Everything seems to fall into places Saku. The pay is good, and soon we can return what we borrowed. This is the break we were waiting for, and it is all because of you." Jeevani squeezed my hands again to show her appreciation.

"You should listen to me more than mocking my vanilla life!" I joked, being uncomfortable with Jeevani's gratefulness.

"Hey, you know I admire you as hell, don't you?" Jeevani leaned forward and staring into my eyes. "I wish I have your clear thinking and determination." I heard the cry in her voice before I saw the tears in her eyes.

"What is wrong?" Jeevani was not a person who got emotional. In the years I have known her, I can count the number of times she cried. Yet, despite all the hardships she weathered at such a young age, Jeevani has always been resilient.

"Jeevani, is everything ok, hon?" I leaned in, squeezing her hands as she was scaring me with worry.

"No..."

"I mean... Um...... Yes." She stammered, not knowing her feelings. Jeevani slumped down in her chair as if she had been defeated.

"Just tell me. We can figure out how you are feeling later." I tried to reassure her, although I didn't know what else could have shaken her up like this.

"I am pregnant." after a few minutes of silence, Jeevani whispered, turning her face away from me.

"Are you fucking kidding me, Jeevani?" That was not a piece of news I expected, making me spatter with no filters. I felt as if I got dragged down to a dark bottomless pit, making me feel claustrophobic.

"It was not planned... it just happened." Jeevani shook her head; her voice laced with embarrassment.

"What? You haven't heard of birth control?" I was so irritated and annoyed with her for her recklessness. How can she bring another child to this world when she barely fed the two kids she already has?

"Is there anything you can do about it?"

Jeevani gaped in horror, not believing what I had just asked. To her credit, she quickly recovered, accepting that was how my rational mind worked. I rather have an abortion than bring a child to a world where suffering would be the only inheritance.

"It is a sin!" Jeevani cast her eyes down and started drawing circles with her index finger on the table.

"Fuck the sin. Do you want it?"

"I can't do anything about it now. It is too late, and I can't risk my kids not having a mother." She sounded beaten, slouching further into her chair.

"That's it. Let's get ready to have this baby." I tried to smile, masquerading my fear for her, Devan, the two toddlers, and the unborn child. It was going to be hard, seeing how much they were already struggling.

"I disappointed you, didn't I?" When Jeevani lifted her eyes, her voice was heavy with sadness.

"It doesn't matter what I think, Jeevani. What matters is how you feel." I didn't want to lie to her. Still, I didn't want to hurt her any further than she already was.

"It does to me. You are my best friend." Jeevani was pushing me to the edge, demanding a reaction from me.

"Of course, I am fucking disappointed. I can't understand why you are prone to create one suffering after another. Things were just turning around for you, and instead of letting things get better, you have added another complication." I looked into her eyes as I shared the truth.

"Hey, that is how I think, Miss Practical. You are not me, and your brain is wired differently. So we will not see eye to eye on this." As Jeevani's eyes glazed with tears, I turned away, not being able to bear her pain.

"I was kicking myself when I found out," Jeevani attempted to smile and, failing at it, wiped the tears before they ran down her cheeks. "You wouldn't believe it. I went and bought two raw papayas to terminate the pregnancy and doing my penance afterwards. But life will never be easy for people like us, Saku. I couldn't risk my life and put my kids' lives in danger."

With my hands under the table, I could maintain my composure. I squeezed my fingers with agitation as I disagreed with Jeevani, seeing how she created her misery.

'Don't blame life when you are the one who has been irresponsible.' I bit my lips to keep my thoughts to myself as there was no point in aggravating her helplessness.

"Oh, who knows? Meera's new boss could be your saviour, and you may all get invited to the castle." I wanted to take her pain away and make life smooth and perfect for her and the baby. I tried to lighten the situation by disguising my anxiety.

"Yes, that could be the saving grace. Anyway, the lesson for you, young lady, is not to have an unplanned child because you would be a lousy mother." Jeevani mocked with a feeble attempt to smile.

"What I can do to help you? Now is the time to look after yourself instead of fussing over others."

"You are doing more than enough for us, Saku. I am glad you still consider me as one of your friends."

Glancing outside the window, I noticed it was getting dark as the mist was descending. I got up from where we were seated to wash the cup and the empty vada plate.

"Leave them there. I can wash them later." Jeevani came behind me, pushing me away from the water bucket she had ready.

"Hey, I need some help from Devan. Can you ask him to find a boy to help around in Amma's nursery? She shouldn't be doing any heavy lifting. I can't pay much, so someone who can do half a day of work is okay. We can give him food and lodging."

"I will ask Devan. When he finds one, can I get him to bring him to your place?"

"Yes, please, tell him I can't pay much."

"Yes, I understand." Jeevani nodded with a tight smile, already aware of my financial difficulties.

"I should get going before it gets dark. It is getting colder."

"Yes, you should," looking outside the window, Jeevani agreed. "I will walk with you to the bus stop. There should be a few coming back from Bambarakelle town."

"You could have taken a trishaw if you didn't spend your money to buy that bag of groceries for us." Jeevani glanced at me with sadness. We were about to step out of the house when we heard Devan's voice outside the door.

"Jeevani, make some tea. Sir is here." I turned to Jeevani, wondering who their guest was.

"Oh, that would be the young master from Meera's house. He must have brought the computer with him." I watched Jeevani's face filled with appreciation and was glad to note the sadness that loomed earlier had vanished.

"You stay behind and serve him." I mocked, scanning the room for my bag. My overactive mind doubted if this guy was interested in Meera. Could this be a real-life Bollywood script? "That is first class service, coming to you and all. You better get on his good graces." I nudged Jeevani, squinching my face.

We laughed and hugged each other when Devan and the mystery man walked through the door carrying a couple of boxes. My heart dropped with heaviness, sighting Niranga Aiya there with a box in his hand, realising he was the young master Jeevani was raving about earlier.

"Saku, what are you doing here?" Niranga Aiya stared at me, equally surprised. I could sense that he, too, was trying to understand the coincidence of our meeting in this tiny little house.

"Oh, hello, this is my friend Jeevani. We took the same math tuition class. I am not sure if you would remember." I managed a quick response, masking my shock.

"Not really," Niranga Aiya shook his head without even glancing at Jeevani. Since entering the house, he did not take his eyes away and was watching my every move.

"Hey Devan, how are you?" To break his stare, I turn to Devan.

"Congratulations, you must be elated." I reached out and hugged Devan and whispered, "Don't be so nervous," as he appeared uncomfortable than usual.

"Thanks, Saku."

"Are you leaving?" Niranga Aiya asked, dropping the box on the small table in front of him. "Stay, you can go back with me. I am picking up Amali on the way." He said, noting I was getting ready to leave.

"Oh, thanks,..... Um........ I need to hit the town before the shops close." I chucked the handbag over my shoulder and pretended to lock the side pocket, not wanting to meet his eyes.

"Sir, please take a seat." Jeevani's politeness towards Niranga Aiya made me unease. I shift toward the front door, wanting to disappear from the room.

"Devan, add some firewood to the hearth; I will drop Saku at the bus station." Implying she would be back in time to prepare tea for their guest, Jeevani put her arm around me and dragged me through the front door.

"Stay; you don't need to come." I tried to leave Jeevani behind, ignoring the *'Don't you dare.'* stare Jeevani cast my way.

"Nonsense." Jeevani shook her head, dismissing me. "I will be back before the water has boiled. Let's go." The moment we were outside, safe from anyone's hearing distance, Jeevani turned to me.

"How do you know him?"

"We grew up together. Niranga Aiya was my next-door neighbour until they migrated to Australia."

"So, why do you want to avoid him? Did he bully you?"

"My gosh, no, nothing like that." I shrugged off her question and continued to walk towards the bus stop.

"Oh, yeah? Is that why you are avoiding him?" Jeevani wasn't ready to let it slide. She grabbed my hand, stopping my stride.

"I am not avoiding him." I peer into her eyes longer than necessary, trying to convince her.

"Really?" Jeevani sneered. "Then why did you give that bullshit excuse? For your information, the shops are already closed! This is Nuwara Eliya, and no one works at this hour."

"Woman, is it a crime to go home early to be with my family than hang around until he finishes setting up that damn machine? I just want to get home." I turned to Jeevani with irritation.

"Aney, don't lie to me, missy!" Jeevani was too quick to dismiss me. "You complain all the time how crowded the buses are, how dark it gets after four, how cold it is………… and you turn down a lift?" Jeevani was relentless and watching me with determination.

"Hey, if you don't stop your interrogation and head back, Devan is going to share all your secrets with Niranga Aiya. Believe me, that would include how you became pregnant. Did you see how nervous he looked? You know your man can't stop talking when he is nervous………… You better hurry and get that tea. You don't want Devan's rambling to piss off Niranga Aiya, do you?" As I rambled, Jeevani's face darkened with anxiety. We both could easily recall times when Devan's nervous rumbling got them into trouble.

Jeevani stopped her probing and hugged me. I held on to her longer, filling my lung with the jasmine fragrance that oozed out of her hair. Wrapped in Jeevani's warm embrace, I felt small and weak. Perhaps it must be the icy wind that made me I wanted to cry. I closed my eyes, letting the tears dissolve into the eye cavity.

"There, the bus is coming. Let's talk next time when I am back."

"No, I will come and see you before you go. You are not getting off the hook, missy." When Jeevani cheerfully threatened, I knew she would somehow visit me before I headed back to Kandy.

7 DECEPTION

"How is Jeevani?" Akka asked when we were having dinner that night. Clearly, Niranga Aiya had told her about our meeting, as Akka wasn't aware I had visited Jeevani.

"She is okay."

As I was not in a mood for conversation, I hoped Niranga Aiya hadn't shared news about Jeevani's pregnancy with Akka. I rather not reveal the details to my family yet. I didn't want Amma to get worked up and go on a rampage about what a foolish girl Jeevani had been getting married to Devan. After seven years, Amma had not stopped reminding me that Jeevani could have made better life choices. After years of fruitless debates with Amma, I have learned to let go. Today, I didn't have the energy to engage in futile talk.

"Niranga said you didn't want to wait to ride home with him." Akka's comment made both Amma and Thaththa stop eating and glance at me with surprise. I was annoyed. Akka made it sound as if I had done something unacceptable.

We do only a few things together as a family: having afternoon tea and dinner were those moments I cherished the most. Dinner was a tradition I loved taking part in when I was home. I was not pleased about Akka bringing Niranga Aiya into our conversation when it was supposed to be a time for our family.

"Yes, I had to go to Cargills." I am glad no one asked me what I bought from the town's fancy supermarket, as they usually inquisitively asked.

"Well, you could have asked Niranga to stop there on your way back."

I continued to eat without responding to Akka, as it wasn't a topic I wanted to entertain. Niranga Aiya was consuming enough of my time already.

"Niranga was very impressed that you are helping them."

I observe the temper building inside me. If Akka thinks, I gave two hoots about what Niranga Aiya thought, her pregnancy hormones were doing a number in her brain, making it slow picking up cues. I didn't have the energy to say he got it wrong. One helps strangers, and Jeevani was family to me.

"Amma, is Meera a pretty girl?" I asked.

"She is a boney girl with long hair. I didn't know she was Devan's sister until Amali told me today."

"Why are you curious about her looks?"

"Oh, no reason. " I shrugged my shoulders, wanting to do something mean to spite Akka.

"Are you implying Niranga is interested in Meera?" Akka's comment did not bother others as they continued with their dinner, letting us dominate the conversation. I managed a fake surprise to show I hadn't considered it.

"You would know better as he chauffeurs you around these days."

"Holy mother of Kali, are you jealous?" Akka's unexpected question made everyone stop eating and glare at me. It clearly surprised Amma and Thaththa, as neither scolded Akka for swearing at the dinner table.

"Saman Aiya would be if he knew how well you are being pampered these days!" I deflected Akka's question, reminding her how possessive her husband is.

As I watched, Akka's face turned pale, and her eyes glazed. Malli was glancing at Akka and me, trying to understand what I was implying. There had always been underlining friction between Akka and me. Ever since she returned to Nuwara Eliya, we have been trying to patch it up. But it always raises its ugly head and lashes out on rare occasions like this. Though we have been at each other's throats before for many reasons, I have never insinuated a liaison between Niranga Aiya and Akka in front of Thaththa or Malli.

"Do you think you are the only benevolent person around here?" Kudos to Akka when she quickly bounced back. I shrugged my shoulders to say I really didn't care and continued to stare at her.

"Anyone going to eat that last piece? I am going to have it." Always the peacemaker, Malli broke our glare, reaching out for the last piece of bread on the table. Both Akka and I took that as a cue and continued with our dinner in silence.

***

I was still pondering Akka's question while sitting on the veranda when she joined me with two cups of tea.

"What is the matter with you, missy, missing your Loverboy?"

"Oh, piss off." I grabbed the tea mug from Akka, pretending to be annoyed. But I was so relieved she made the first move toward peacemaking.

"Hush… The baby will hear you." Akka was always worried when Malli or I swore, assuming her baby would pick up our bad habits.

"Oh, my baby is going to be just fine, aren't you, sweetheart?" I rubbed Akka's belly, talking to the baby. I felt a little kick, and Akka and I both looked at each other with delight.

"Oh my, did you feel that? Baby agrees!" I screamed with pleasure.

"Saman and I are going to have a tough time raising this one with you around!" Akka complained and slumped opposite me. I point to her to lay her legs on my lap to give her a foot rub. Her legs were getting heavier and puffier as she progressed through the pregnancy.

"Oh, that feels so good," Akka purred like a kitten leaning back in the chair, "You are an angel."

"I know." I grinned. Akka made a face and continued sipping her tea, enjoying the foot massage. "When is Saman Aiya back?"

"He will be back in three weeks." I sense the longing and sadness in her voice. I pondered how Saman Aiya would react to Akka and Niranga Aiya's friendship. Would Saman Aiya be open to having his wife close to a younger, wealthier, and attractive guy like Niranga Aiya? As if she read my thoughts, Akka warned me, "Hey, do not tease me about Niranga when Saman is back."

"Does he have anything to worry about?" I inquired innocently. Akka pulled her legs, trying to sit up to straighten herself in the chair, attempting to show her annoyance, but found it challenging because of her condition. I suppressed the laughter inside me and raised my eyebrows to hint, *'I am waiting for your answer.'*

"Nangi, what sickening thoughts are going through your head? There is nothing between Niranga and me. There is nothing between us other than a friendship."

That came out forcefully. I watched Akka, wondering, *'Who are you trying to convince? Me or yourself?'*

"So, what's his deal? Chauffeuring you around to work and back?" I asked, not shying away from my curiosity.

"He only wants to help. I would do the same thing for my friends if I had a car and time on my hands." We both knew that was a lie. Akka wasn't one to go out of her way to help anyone unless there was a nifty payback for her.

"Surely, he can find better things to do on his holiday rather than becoming your chauffeur?" I was not convinced.

"I guess it is better than jogging in the morning." Akka grinned, calling up one of her early memories. "I bumped into him in the morning on my way to work one day. I am sure he felt sorry for me struggling with the bus ride and all."

"He is jogging in the morning?" I was very intrigued to find out who this new person was. Niranga Aiya wasn't the most physically active boy I grew up with. He was a bookworm, and most days, I outrun him when we were kids. So Niranga Aiya jogging early in the morning when the air was still heavy and damp was something I did not expect.

"Yes, he follows a rigorous exercise regime. How do you think he keeps up with his physique?" I sensed a slight resentment passing through my mind, noting how impressed Akka was with Niranga Aiya.

"Did he replaced jogging with driving? I can't see if that would help with his strict exercise regime!" Akka didn't appreciate my mockery and scrunched her face.

"He just shuffled around his schedule. Niranga is here to revamp Uncle's business, so Uncle has something to do instead of playing golf every day. Now that Sarath Uncle has retired, Niranga is worried he will deteriorate fast if he doesn't have something to do. Niranga is actually dropping me off on the way to the factory and picking me up on his way back."

I completely understood his concern about Uncle's wellbeing after retirement, having experienced this with Thaththa over the years. Maybe Thaththa can help with their bookkeeping as he was an accountant before. I made a mental note to do some checking before I approached anyone with the idea.

"Akka, is everything okay with Amma?" I asked, remembering the lousy mood Amma was in on the day I returned home.

"Why do you ask?" I heard the concern in Akka's voice as if she had missed something she should have noted.

"Amma was in a pissy mood the evening I came home. Did I miss something? Why was she so angry? Is everything ok with her?"

"Oh, that's because your Loverboy called!" Akka laughed. Amma never liked Sula and never wanted me to come home late. But I sensed Amma's behaviour was not related to either of them.

"Why get so pissy just because Sula called? He always calls when I come home."

"Amma is worked up these days. Aunty and Uncle have been asking why you are not married or engaged. Amma is pissed because she doesn't know much about Sulakkana or your plans."

"Why on earth are Seneges concerned about me? They should focus on their boy." I got annoyed. They should get their house in order before trying to tidy up others. Deep down, I was aware Aunty and Uncle always considered me as one of their own and an integral part of their household. It was natural for them to care about my future.

"Oh, don't worry, Niranga is not getting off the hook. Aunty is on a mission to find a girl for him. If she could, she will have him engaged before he heads back to Sydney." Akka said with a bit of amusement. Surprisingly, I didn't sense any jealousy or regret I expected from her.

"Why is it so funny?" I couldn't contain my nosiness, wanting to learn about Niranga Aiya.

"It's funny listening to Niranga complain about his parents dragging him on making house visits to meet girls." I watch the smile playing on Akka's lips with heaviness in my heart, envying the friendship she has with Niranga Aiya, which should be mine. I met him first, and he was my knight in shining armour. We were inseparable best friends. But today, we have become strangers.

"When did he ever do something, he didn't want to?" The Niranga Aiya I knew was stubborn and unpersuasive.

"Niranga fears Aunty Nelum." Akka smiled with amusement.

"So he is a mama's boy." I was annoyed thinking he had changed.' *Hypocrite,*' The adult in me murmured sarcastically. There I was, criticising Niranga Aiya when I would do the same if Amma made a stand. To protect me from Amma's demanding nature, I learned to act rebellious from my early days. If Amma pushes me into a corner, I will not hesitate. Maybe Niranga Aiya is more like me than I imagined him to be, willing to give in to his mother's love.

"Oh, that will never happen. It is all pretence on Niranga's part. He isn't fooling anyone. Aunty and Uncle are aware Niranga is going along to entertain them. They both hope he will fall for someone along the way." Akka spoke with confidence, implied that she had more information about Niranga Aiya than she was letting on.

"Apparently, Sarath Uncle had met Aunty through a proposal, and it had been love at first sight for him. So, Sarath Uncle believes it could be the same for Niranga. Aunty hopes Niranga will get tired and say yes to a nice girl. Niranga thinks Aunty and Uncle will eventually give up and leave him to his own devices. So they all are going on a merry-go-round." Akka giggled as if she was watching a comedy.

'If only we were talking, I could have given him a few tips,' Not aware of my internal dialogue, Akka continued with her rambling.

"Niranga has agreed with Aunty, promising to give it a shot while in Sri Lanka. It will be tough to find someone in this part of the world that can keep him in line. We all know how difficult it is to get Niranga to listen to anyone."

I remembered the times when I could manipulate Niranga Aiya to get my way. I grew up with a warm and fuzzy sensation, believing he had a soft spot in his heart for me and that I was special. But did he let me believe that way while he got away with what he always wanted? I was in a daze, reminiscing about our childhood days, when Akka brought me back to the moment.

"That is why Amma is angry with you. Even Niranga is ready to get married when you are not."

"But he isn't. He is pretending."

"Amma doesn't know that! She questions if Niranga can, why can't Sulakkana? Aunty and Uncle suspect you are dating a player who isn't ready for commitment."

I felt guilty getting Sula into trouble when it was not even his fault. I recalled one conversation we had a couple of months ago when we gathered in Reshani's house for our usual Thursday night dinner.

"All you have to do is say yes, Saku. I will marry you in a heartbeat?" Sula turned to me with an earnest look in his eyes, and I knew I only had to nod, and he would move heaven and earth to make it happen.

"Of course, you would. That would solve all your troubles!" Before I could say anything, Reshani mocked from the adjoining room, making me laugh.

"Aiyo, yes. Resh is right. If we get married, you benefit more. What is in it for me?" I played along, challenging Sula.

"You get free lodging and your mother off your back." Sula gave me a sheepish grin.

"Not much of an incentive to tie myself to you for a lifetime." If Sula got hurt by my sarcasm, he kept it to himself.

The memories made me smile. I was curious; would Amma be a little kinder to Sula if she knew I was the one who was not ready to get married.

"Let's go to bed. I am sleepy." I slowly placed Akka's legs away from my lap, faking a yawn.

8 DISCOMFORT

"Sasoo, can you help me with rehearsing my dance steps?" Malli strode into the room, disturbing the serenity Amma and I had. When I am home, Amma expects me to be an ornament in her living room while she goes on with her chores. I give into her pleasure, engaging in meaningless impromptu conversations while trying to read a book or work on my course work. Today I was working on preparing notes for next week's university lectures.

"You mean now?" I turned to Malli with irritation, hoping to complete the section I was working on.

"Not now, silly," Malli smirked ear to ear, displaying his lily-white teeth. "This Saturday at the Academy." He was after a favour. I could tell by the way he was grinning.

We both love dancing. Growing up next door to the Seneges meant, by default, they invited us to every party they had in their house. Aunty and Uncle loved organising large gatherings for their family and friends. One wedding anniversary, a lavish Christmas lunch, then three birthday celebrations meant we had five events to practise our dance moves. Seneges parties were something everyone looked forward to all year round. They always held their gatherings on a different scale. And to this date, I have only come by a few that could be considered better than the Senege's events.

From the very first evening, I saw Aunty and Uncle dancing; their elegance and energy spellbound me. They would transform their large living room into a dance floor and grace it with their movements. Their dancing screamed of passion and sensuality. It mesmerised my young mind. I thoroughly enjoyed squeezing between the adults, who were swaying to the music with wide grins on their faces.

Not able to take any more of my clumsy attempts to move my arms and legs, Uncle Sarath put his best effort into turning me into a cultured dancer. He made me stand on his feet to teach me the steps for ballroom and foxtrot routines. Though Uncle and Aunty loved dancing, Niranga Aiya was not much of a dancer. Yet he, too, ended up following me together with Malli to the dance floor just to be near me.

Niranga Aiya and I used to take turns carrying Malli and dancing with him when we were kids. I would lift him onto my hip with one arm around him, with the other arm stretched, pretending he was my partner. Niranga Aiya would usually have him on his shoulders, swaying to the music.

Uncle Sarath paved the way for Malli to learn to dance by enrolling him at the local dance academy at a very young age. This turned Malli into one of the youngest contenders in the competitions. Since then, Malli's talents grew, and he started taking part in professional dance events. When I am home, I assist him in perfecting his steps. Though I enjoyed it, I had neither the talent nor the patience to become a professional.

"Not this weekend, Malli," I said, returning to work on my notes. "I can help you in the evenings." When I paused my writing to look at Malli, he was no longer grinning. A disappointment had spread across his face.

"Aney, Sasoo, please, only for this weekend." Malli placed his arms around me, hugging me with a pleading voice. I pushed him away, wrinkling my nose to express my disgust. "Take a shower. You stink like a dead rat!!" Back from school, still in his uniform, Malli was full of body odour too strong to bear.

"So, will you come with me?" Malli pulled his arms away and inquired in a pleading tone.

"What is wrong with Menaka?" Menaka was Malli's usual dance partner, the girl he has on and off again love interest. I wondered if she had enough of Malli's passive interest and had called it quits.

"Um...... The thing is........." Malli drew random patterns on the coffee table with his index finger, avoiding my eyes. "We are doing doubles and are short of a female partner........." Malli softly murmured, his eyes focused on the coffee table.

"Who is the other guy?" I stopped my writing, giving Malli my full attention. Malli was hiding something as he was shifting back and forth nervously.

"Kasun." After a bit of silence, Malli reluctantly uttered.

"Not a chance!"

Kasun, the group leader in charge of the routines and schedules, is an older boy in Malli's dancing group. He always talked to me about my favourite authors and my dream car, the Volkswagen Beetle. Only recently, I got to know he has been nursing a crush on me for a while. I was naïve and unaware that Malli and his friends had been taking advantage, manipulating his feelings every time I showed up at the academy.

"Whatever favour you are after, you have to do it without getting me involved!" When Akka spilt the beans with me on their schemes, I was amused by the youngsters' ingenuity. I was not angry with them for using me as bait, but it hurt me they didn't trust me enough to share their secrets.

"It is only for two hours, Sasoo. Please..................." Malli lowered his voice and made a pouting face, knowing he looked adorable.

"I said no!" I raised my voice with irritation. "Now, leave me alone. I need to finish this assignment."

"I wouldn't let you go until you say yes." Malli slid next to me, pulling me over to him in a headlock, something he and I started doing when he discovered wrestling. Malli would have me wrestle with him if I had to get away from one of his demands. Usually, I would play along and let him try his skills. Although both of us were too old to have childish sibling arguments, that's how we behaved most of the time. Amma always scolds me for behaving like a teenager and not acting my age. Though I didn't mind an occasional tussle, I was not in the mood today, sluggish and tired, so I tried to pull away from his tight grip.

"If you don't let me go, I am going to hurt you so bad you wouldn't be able to dance this weekend!" Failing to get away from Malli's clutch, I threaten. Though I tried, I couldn't shake off Malli's hold. The weight of his upper body was pinning my head down with pressure and strength, making me dizzy. Topping it, the odour from his sweaty armpits was suffocating me.

"Not until you say yes! Come on; you love the attention." Malli tightened his grip, pulling himself closer to me. "Imagine what a great boyfriend he would be? Kasun wouldn't be like Sullakana Aiya," Malli hissed in my year. "Kasun adores you." He was purposely looking for a fight.

"Amma," I screamed, seeking her help. "Please ask Malli to leave me alone."

"Manoj," Amma took her eyes away from the blouse she was mending. "Leave Sasoo alone. You are hurting the poor girl." Though Amma raised her voice, she was not convincing enough. Having witnessed hundreds of our disagreements, it was clear she wasn't keen on meddling. Amma's lack of interest only encouraged Malli, as he didn't alter his grip on me.

"Come on, Sasoo, Kasun has bought the newest Wilbur Smith book for you," Malli pushed my head a little further to the floor, making me gasp for air. "There is nothing he wouldn't do for you. Wouldn't he be a perfect boyfriend?" He was trying to wheedle me, in his usual fashion.

"Malli, you are hurting me, let go, or you will break my neck." I lower my voice, lacing it with a soft cry to change his mind.

"Manoj! what are you doing? Let her go!"

Malli and I both froze when we heard Niranga Aiya's deep command. Malli's grip loosened a bit, but he still didn't let me go free.

"What is this, mate? You need to find someone your size to wrestle with, not a matchstick!" With a deep and authoritative tone, I haven't heard before. Niranga Aiya swiftly removed Malli's grip and plunged on the sofa between us, shuffling Malli aside.

"Are you alright?" Niranga Aiya peered into my face. I could tell he was angry, as his lips were in a tight pucker when he rubbed my neck. I inhaled his masculine fragrance, which was like heaven after Malli sitting next to me before. A warm rush ran through my body when his fingers made slow but firm strokes on my neck.

I was breathless. I couldn't distinguish if it was because I struggled to get away from the deadlock earlier or because of Niranga Aiya's proximity. An unexpected tingling sensation spread across my body.

"Oh, you are underestimating Sasoo. She is lazy today. She got the moves of the Lady Killer!" I heard Malli pipe in with a voice loaded with pride. He always admired that I could easily emulate the famous wrestling champion's signature moves.

"Are you all right?" Ignoring Malli completely, Niranga Aiya asked, still caressing my neck smoothly. I wanted to say, "Yes, I am okay, thanks." But the words didn't come out as if they were stuck in my throat. I nodded my head, looking at Malli. He avoided my eyes and glanced away with embarrassment.

"What is going on? I keep telling you not to go with Malli's schemes, Sasoo. Why are you encouraging Kasun?" Akka's voice sounded infuriated, and then I realised why Niranga Aiya was in our living room. He had fetched Akka from work.

"How is it my problem if Kasun has a crush on me?" I found my voice to challenge Akka with annoyance I felt.

"You are bloody encouraging him when you go dancing with him."

"Why do you have your knickers in a knot? Dancing with him doesn't mean I am going to sleep with him," I lashed out, not bothering to correct Akka. I sensed the pause in Niranga Aiya's hand on my neck as our exchange mortified him.

"Sakunthala! Watch what you are saying. You are talking like street trash!" When Amma raised her voice and spattered with contempt, I understood her anger was knitted with embarrassment. I shouldn't have spoken to Akka in such an uncultured manner, especially in front of Niranga Aiya. He is a stranger, and he would not remember the intricacies of sibling relationships.

"Aney, Amali Akka, I was joking." Malli got distressed, noting the friction between Akka and me. "She doesn't dance with Kasun. When she comes, Sasoo dances with me. Sasoo doesn't take any gifts from Kasun, either. I made it up." Malli's voice was oozing with regret, trying to remove the stigma Akka plastered on me. I felt grateful, and my anger towards him turned to vapour. I gave him a slight smile, appreciating his efforts.

"You should be ashamed of yourself, dragging Sasoo around to get favours from Kasun. Don't say I didn't warn you when you get into trouble with Thaththa."

My breathing was still elevated. I realised as long as Niranga Aiya continued to rub my neck, it would not be normal. On the surface, I was annoyed - how dare he invade my personal space without my permission. I was neither his younger sister nor his friend. I didn't want him sitting close to me, let alone touching me. But inside, I felt warm and precious by his way of caring. Still, I could not handle Niranga Aiya's closeness. He was disturbing my equilibrium with his presence - his smell was intoxicating, and his touch was melting me in places I was not comfortable with.

"I am going to make some tea." I got up abruptly, not able to take it anymore. The heat building inside me made me uncomfortable, as if I was inside an oven, all warm and short of breath. Without waiting for any response, I headed to the kitchen. The coldness in the kitchen was welcoming and soothing. I added some firewood to the hearth and refilled the kettle with water, kept it to boil, and went outside.

It was getting dark, and the fog was descending. The air was frosty and wet, and I shivered as it nipped my nostril and the coldness wrapped around me like a thick skin, calming me. Standing in the dusk, I breathed in deeply, trying to flush out the pinewood mint aftershave from my lungs.

After a few minutes of standing outside, the uneasy sensation I had carried into the kitchen earlier left. I moved inside to make tea. I squashed a fresh piece of ginger root to extract its essence, then slipped it into the teapot before pouring boiling water. My mind started doodling, reliving the sensation I encountered when Niranga Aiya rubbed my neck. As I was distracted, a ruffling sound and footsteps near the door caused me to nearly drop the kettle and spilling hot water all over my left hand. The pain that rushed through me was unbearable, making me moan in agony. Tears pooled in my eyes, blurring my vision.

"Oh, my god. Cookie, are you okay?" Niranga Aiya rushed in and dragged me to the sink, turned the tap on, holding my hand under the running cold water. My entire body shivered when the cold water hit my hand, and I pulled it away in pain.

"Hold still," Niranga Aiya barked. "Let the cold water run a bit longer, or you will end up with a blister." He softened his voice as if he was explaining it to a child. Though I couldn't see his face, I sensed his eyes would hold a tenderness no different from his voice.

Niranga Aiya pushed my hand back to the sink and held it under the tap with force, which sandwiched me between Niranga Aiya and the sink. He had his arms around me, holding my burnt hand under the running water. As it pressed my back to his chest, I could feel the warmth of his breath in my ear. If I leaned back, I could comfortably rest my head on his shoulder. And for a second, I wanted to close my eyes and rest in the comfort of that warmth.

I have wasted my time earlier shivering outside to remove his scent from my body, and it is back there again. Now his musk was hitting my nose like a sack of rice. I fled his presence earlier to escape from the unbearable closeness I felt. And now I was standing here, closer to him than ever before. My emotions were running pretty high. On one end, I was dealing with the pain of a scorched hand, and on the other, I was trying not to melt away by the exhilarating burning sensation I was experiencing.

"Let's leave this for a bit." After a few minutes of keeping my hand under running water, he spoke closer to my ear, his warm breath kissing my cheek. I didn't move, fearing my legs would give in to the weakness that took over me. Niranga Aiya slowly laid a cold, wet piece of cloth on my hand. It appeared to be a man's handkerchief, and he gently tucked its corners to cover my wound.

I struggled with the pain in my burnt hand and the annoyance building up with Niranga Aiya for invading my personal space again. Despite this, I was grappling with the nervous excitement I felt. I bit my trembling lips, hoping to hide my nervousness, which was a dangerous move as it drew his attention to my lips. Niranga Aiya's face had turned soft, making his eyes sparkle resembling the morning sun. He slowly leaned towards me with a glitter in his eyes. When I turned my face away with unease, he stretched his arm, cupping my chin with his fingers before turning it to face him.

"Are you all right?" he asked.

Tears of pain were scrolling down my cheeks, and Niranga Aiya softly wiped them away with his thumbs. "Oh, gosh, Cookie, you are such a crybaby." His touch was soothing and gentle. It reminded me of the boy who pulled me out of the mud pile so many years ago. My heart got heavy with the yearning to get back to those perfectly happy days. I shook my head with irritation to get rid of the longing in my thoughts.

"Why don't you try it? See how well you can bear the pain?" Once I found my voice, I murmured with bitterness. It was easy for Niranga Aiya to judge when he was not the one who got burned.

"Fair enough. Hey, I am so sorry for making you spill hot water on your hand." He was remorseful. I was clumsy, and it was not his fault. But I didn't say it. The mean girl inside me wanted him to suffer a little longer.

"Why are you here in the kitchen?" I sounded unfriendly, as I didn't want him in the kitchen near me, disturbing my peace and tranquillity.

"Oh, yes, fathers are back from golf. We need two more teas."

"Malli couldn't come?" I bet he sat there, refusing to come over, letting Niranga Aiya be the messenger. *'He can bloody well find his dancing partner,'* my anger returned.

"Oh, no. Aunty asked me to come. She was worried you two would start another wrestling match." Niranga Aiya grinned innocently.

"Oh, okay, thanks. I will make some more." I toiled with the wet cloth in my hand and waited for him to leave the kitchen before I started making the tea. "Go and join the others. I will bring the tea later." After an uncomfortable silence, I glanced at Niranga Aiya. He stood there, not making a move, as if he was waiting for me to make him leave.

"You just sit there and let me make the tea." It was not a request. I always recognise when Niranga Aiya was angry. Not bothering to argue, I ebbed across to the chair in the corner and watched him go about with the task at hand methodically.

Niranga Aiya was comfortable in our tiny kitchen, as if he had done this kind of task a hundred times before. The charcoals of the firewood, the light smokiness in the kitchen, or the occasional sparks flaring out of the hearth did not bother him. I perched in the chair while he moved around the kitchen effortlessly, locating utensils and filling in mugs with tea.

"So, you still love dancing?" When he asked, I smiled without responding to his question. "Manoj mentioned you help him practise his routines?" Niranga Aiya wasn't ready to take my silence and was probing for a response.

"When I have time...."

"So, how serious is this, Kasun?" It surprised me he raised that question. I didn't expect him to cross personal boundaries without an invitation, especially with his Australian education. Instead of spatting, *'None of your bloody business.'* I lined up the teacups on the table. "How long have you been following wrestling?" Ignoring my lack of interest in conversing, Niranga Aiya changed the topic.

"I don't." I dismissed it, not wanting to entertain any further questions.

"That is not what Manoj said." He raised his eyebrows, holding his stare.

"I wouldn't believe everything Malli tells you!" I watched Niranga Aiya's eyes slide to the floor. Then, to avoid him raising another question, I crept away to get some biscuits ready. Before we headed back with the tea, Niranga Aiya gently took my hand and removed the handkerchief to inspect the wound. The skin had turned red, but luckily there were no blisters.

"Is it still hurting?" His voice was filled with remorse. The way he was holding my hand and his dilated pupils made me tingle all over, making me pant. My heart was racing, and I was sweating.

"A bit," I admitted. "It will be okay."

"Come on, let's go before the tea gets cold." I led the way with a plate full of biscuits to flee from the unfamiliar emotions brewing inside.

9 TORMENT

"What took you two so long? I thought Niranga went to help, not to hold the process," Akka sounded irritable and tired of waiting.

"Oh, we had an accident." Niranga Aiya blurted, drawing everyone's attention.

"What happened?" Akka was the first to ask what was on everybody's mind. They all straighten in their chairs like meerkats on parade.

"I startled Saku when I went to the kitchen, making her spill hot water all over her hand." Niranga Aiya sounded regretful, and I felt sorry for him. I almost missed the warm way he addressed me earlier when we were in the kitchen. Except for Niranga Aiya, no one else calls me 'Cookie', the childhood nickname he gave me.

"Oh, my poor child, are you okay, little one?" Thaththa grabbed my hand with worry to inspect. He rubbed my left thumb in his haste, which was still raw, causing me to cringe. The reaction got him flustered, and the tremors started showing. I ignored the concern I saw on Niranga Aiya's face and pulled my hand from Thaththa's grip.

"Don't worry, I am okay, Thaththa. It was only a small spill," I assured him, pointing to the angry red patch appearing on my left thumb.

"Oh, she is now, but she was crying like a baby when it happened," Niranga Aiya said, ruffling my hair as he used to do when we were kids. I elbowed him off, not appreciating his joke or regarding me as his kid sister.

"Well, you better make it up to her Niranga." Uncle Sarath warned him. I suppressed the laughter building in me. It reminded me of many times Niranga Aiya got into trouble when we were kids and Uncle punished him.

"Of course, anything you want, Saku, name it." Niranga Aiya sounded too eager, not like a guy who was seeking to make amends when he slid next to me on the sofa.

"Give me some time; I will think of something." I grinned, pretending I was enjoying the talk. *'Perhaps I should ask him to stay away from me until I head back to Kandy,'* the inner child murmured.

"Oh, no… It would be best if you didn't hand over her a choice. You are in trouble." Malli slurred, shaking his head in disapproval.

"Yes, giving her the option is a bad idea." Akka echoed Malli, causing both Niranga Aiya and Uncle Sarath to raise their eyebrows with interest.

"Why is that?"

"Don't even go there, Uncle. Sasoo makes very tall demands." Malli's voice was full of irritation.

"Yes, she will make you do crazy shi.."

"… tuff." I was more amused at how quickly Akka and Malli aligned themselves than hearing Akka, who claims she never swears, nearly dropped a curse word in front of everyone.

"Okay, on second thoughts, how about I take you out to lunch before you head back to Kandy?" Niranga Aiya pushed my shoulder with his signature smile, transferring his face into a striking man. I want to kick both Akka and Malli with frustration. Now I had to find a polite way to decline the offer.

"I thought you were the one who had to pay for what you have done?"

"What do you mean?" Niranga Aiya turned to me with eyebrows raised.

"How would it be a treat for me when I have to see you gulp food down as if there's no tomorrow?" When I asked, others howl with amusement. Niranga Aiya's obsession with food was no secret to anyone.

I watched him, pretending to be irritated while suppressing a burst of laughter. "It isn't my fault if you have a weight complex." To my annoyance, everyone nodded their heads, agreeing with Niranga Aiya's comment. As he could sense the fury boiling in me, Thaththa called out from where he sat.

"Come, my poor child, I will give you a head rub." Typically, I have to coax Thaththa to give me a head massage, so I didn't wait for a second invite. I dashed across and sat next to Thaththa on the floor. It also gave me the perfect excuse to move away from Niranga Aiya, who was sitting way too close to me, making my skin burn every time his thigh or arm touched mine. It freed me from wanting to give in to the desire and slide a little closer to his warmth.

When Thaththa started patting my head. I closed my eyes, following the way his fingers shook when they touched my skull. His fingers began with rapid shakes and then settled into light, random strokes. Once stable, they were no longer pounding my head.

When I come back home, I spend most of my time with Thaththa. We filled our days going to town to run errands or lounging around discussing politics, history, or books we have read. We never ran out of topics as he had to wait for my arrival to have a decent conversation since the other three had little interest in his areas of fancy.

But this time, Thaththa was behaving like a young boy courting his first girlfriend, fascinated by Uncle Sarath's return. Uncle takes up most of Thaththa's time, so he hasn't been home much. They have both been playing catch up on years they have missed.

I knew he felt guilty for not spending enough time with me in the last few days unless when we had dinner. Perhaps he must miss our time just as much as I.

"You are spoiling her, Rajitha; she is not a little girl anymore". Usually, Amma would scold Thaththa every time I sat beside him for a massage.

"She is always going to be my little girl." Thaththa would shrug off Amma's comment with a laugh.

"She isn't. All you are doing is making things harder for her husband. Who is going to have time to massage her head when she gets married?" Amma would shake her head with disappointment.

"I will come home to Thaththa. Isn't that right, Thaththa?"

"Absolutely!" Thaththa and I always played alone, ignoring how Amma suppresses her smile. It must be because we had visitors. Amma said nothing today.

Everyone settled into drinking tea and continued with their conversations, reminding me of similar evenings we had when we were young. In those days, it was natural for Uncle Sarath to drop by for a cup of tea on his way home, as Thaththa used to catch a ride with him after work. Some day's Aunty Nelum would join us. And on an occasional evening, Seneges would end up at our house for an early dinner. Niranga Aiya, Malli, and I used to sit on the floor working on a puzzle or watch 'Sesame Street' or 'Casper the Friendly Ghost' on TV.

My mind floated back to the warm, queasy sensation I experienced earlier, sandwiched between Niranga Aiya and the sink. Lost in my thoughts, I did not notice Thaththa had asked me a question. He gently pulled a handful of my hair to draw my attention.

"What is it, Thaththa?"

"I told Sarath I can't join him for deep water fishing as you would disown me. He is asking why?" Thaththa grinned, implying I should be the one to explain.

"Yes, tell me, Sasoo, what is wrong with deep water fishing?" Uncle Sarath turned to me, squinting his eyes. "I thought you would be happy, as it benefits tourism."

"What is so fascinating about fishing, Uncle?"

"Why haven't you gone fishing? The pleasure is in the activity. It is such a great way to relax and be stress free. Fishing is a process of pinning insects on your hooks, putting them in water, waiting for hours, and finally, hooking a fish if you are lucky. It is such triumph." I could see fishing was one of Uncle's great satisfactions. I tried not to display the loathing I felt listening to his jovial voice talking about catching innocent fish.

"Okay, let me ask you a question." I pulled my legs, hugging them before turning to Uncle, pretending not to care about Niranga Aiya's keen eyes following my moves. "How will it be for you if a superior being came around and started hunting you for fun?"

"Imagine you are a fish, swimming around in your home, finding food and going on with your life. Then, one day, you bite into a worm, thinking it is food, just to get yanked with force, ripping off your lips. They pulled you out from the water, making you suffocate," I watched bewilderment spreading across Uncle's face. I couldn't understand why I had to explain this simple concept to anyone. No one spoke for a while. Uncle turned away with unease. Niranga Aiya was shifting around and combing his hair with his fingers, something he used to do when agitated. I could tell Amma was uncomfortable and was trying to make me stop talking with her gestures. But now that I had started, I couldn't stop.

"When you go fishing, for you, it is relaxation. What you are doing is causing terror on another living creature. Fish have nerves and experience pain and suffering. That is why Thaththa promised he wouldn't go fishing."

"Oh, we just catch and release" after a brief silence, Uncle stammered. I knew it was a lie when Niranga Aiya scrunched his brows with embarrassment.

"It doesn't change the torture you cause, Uncle. Pain is pain. Sometimes it could be more merciful to kill the fish than releasing one with a deep wound. If you are after a nice relaxing holiday and still want to enjoy the deep sea, why don't you go whale watching? It is unwinding and far more rewarding because you are not hurting anyone." When I stopped talking, Uncle Sarath appeared upset, and Amma looked mortified.

★★★

By the time the Seneges left, my head was pounding with a tension headache. Though I wanted to leave the room to lock myself in my bedroom's serenity, I didn't dare do it. I couldn't fabricate an excuse that wouldn't attract too much attention. So I sat through the discomfort, masking my uneasiness and discontent with politeness. Once Seneges left, Amma came to inspect my burnt hand. The part that got burned had an ugly purple colour bruise and was throbbing with pain.

"Keep an eye on the wound. Don't break the skin. Otherwise, there will be an ugly scar." As usual, Amma was concerned about having blemishes on my body. I could remember the countless times when I was running around in the pinewood, climbing cypress trees, how she scolded me with a fear of me falling and bruising myself. Despite her best effort, my body is full of scratch marks from old wounds. Every imperfection had its own funny backdrop story. I was not a child scared of scars, and they still didn't bother me much.

"Nothing your Aloe-Vera cream can't fix, Amma." I smiled and kissed her on her cheek, appreciating the love she showed weirdly.

"Why did you turn down Niranga? You should take him around and show him Worlds End." Earlier, when Niranga Aiya asked if we could visit World's End, the famous cliff in Horton Plains National Park, which was not that far from Nuwara Eliya, I politely declined. I said I had made plans for the rest of the days I was here, although I could have easily accommodated a visit to the place. I found Amma's comment to be odd. Usually, Amma preferred me to be home, not hang out with others. It was also unusual, as Amma never allowed me to go on trips with males without at least one other female companion. She was unaware of the touring side of my work, where I never get to choose my companions.

"What is this double standard? You don't tell anyone I am a tour guide, but you want me to escort Niranga Aiya to visit Horton Plains?" I asked. "Holy mother of Kali, what would people say? They will believe I have a new boyfriend now." I joked, paraphrasing Amma's standard remarks, mimicking her voice.

"Niranga would be a better boyfriend than that lame boy you hang out with!" Amma's unrelated remark and backhand dig at Sula threw me off guard. I found it to be uncalled for and mean.

"I have better things to do with my time than be Niranga Aiya's tour guide." I got up to leave, but I stopped, hearing my name.

"Sakunthala, can you leave your moral high ground talks to your friends?" We were back to my full name, which meant Amma was annoyed with me again. "Didn't you get it? They both love fishing! You should not have talked about taking lives and all....." I couldn't understand what had triggered Amma's anger. It couldn't just be my talk about fishing. Amma has always been a supporter of non-killing.

"How about next time I stay in my room to make sure I don't annoy your guests?" I was tired and irritated and was getting hurt by Amma's verbal attacks.

"Sounds good to me!" Amma dismissed my angry outburst as if she didn't notice or care about it. "Especially if you can't wear some decent clothes!" Amma said, running her eyes from my head toes with disgust. She was in a foul mood for sure as she circled back to my wardrobe choices. "Even Meera dresses better than you do!" She commented, glaring at me. I watched Amma walk away with dismay. She never liked my faded jeans and baggy t-shirts or sweaters. But she had never sounded this nasty. The way she spoke to me was the way she would address a domestic helper.

"What was that about?" I asked Akka.

"Oh, that is because you disappointed her........ You didn't behave like a proper young lady in front of Seneges."

"Why does she want me to be someone else? I am not a stranger to Seneges." The comment baffled me, wondering what was going on in Amma's head these days.

"Forget about Amma's moods. Tell me, why don't you like Niranga anymore?" Akka asked, not interested in answering me.

"What do you mean?"

"You two used to be best friends!" Akka paused, resting her eyes on mine, trying to read my expression before continuing. "You treat him with such hostility these days, I can't understand what he has done to you."

"I don't understand you Akka."

"Come on, you usually would have jumped to visit World's End. It is not like you to pass such a great opportunity to show off what a great tour guide you are! Why are you avoiding Niranga?"

"I am not." I shook my head with irritation.

"Is that why you hardly speak to him these days?"

"I have little in common with Niranga Aiya now. I don't know what we can talk about? I hardly know him."

"Maybe you should put in some effort to rekindle. Niranga is a bit hurt with your unfriendliness." Her voice sounded disenchanted. It appears everyone in my family were dishearten with me for something or another.

"Someone is overly invested in how Niranga Aiya feels." I mocked Akka.

"You don't need to worry about me." Akka sounded displeased as she had enough of my remarks. "Niranga and I are friends." Though Akka's eyes were on me, her dilated pupils looked the way when someone was calling up memories. Akka was reminiscing about something from the past. "Stop implying things that are not there because you are trying to find fault to stay pissed at Niranga."

"Why would you say that?" I blinked; a bit surprised.

"Because dear sis, you are still mad at him!" Akka gave me a knowing look.

"What for?" I uncoiled myself, fearing the worst.

"You are pissed with him for ridiculing your first boyfriend, Channaka. You can pretend all you want. But you can't fool me." Akka was full of confidence. I relaxed, noting Akka didn't have a clue of what was going on in my mind. I breathed in, letting go of the worry I was clutching.

10 RECOLLECTIONS

"Holy mother of Kali, are you weeping?" I was reading the last chapter of the fiction I was trying to finish when Jeevani found me. She mocked, noticing the tears sliding across my cheeks.

Pretty in her orange coloured long flared skirt and matching top, Jeevani's hair was braided into one long plait. The jasmine flowers chained to her hair were oozing freshness. Since her marriage, she dressed more like a young Tamilian in colourful attire and flowers in her hair that brought out her best.

I hugged her, breathing in the scent of flowers. "Well, it has a sombre ending written in such a lovely way." I grinned, knowing I was handing out free ammunition for her teasing.

"Gosh, you never change."

"Perfectly okay with me." I smiled.

"You don't have to find excitement in novels if you live a little instead of being confined to your Vanilla life!"

"Did you come all the way here to insult me, or did you find a helper?" I closed the book, turning to Jeevani with pretend anger.

"For both," Jeevani smiled triumphantly. "Devan found a boy who can help Aunty. You don't have to pay him much. Just give him a place to sleep and food to eat."

"Thanks so much, Jeevani." I was so relieved to have someone to support Amma with the chores around the yard and that she wouldn't have to lift heavy pots anymore.

"I brought the boy with me and spoke to Aunty. He is already helping her. Aunty told me I would find you here." Jeevani squeezed my hand and smiled. "Hiding away from the world and crying over fictional heroes." Her eyes were full of laughter, mocking me.

"My, my, it must be your hormones making you so bitchy today."

"Perhaps, or at least, that's the excuse I am using these days. Tell me, where is the castle?" Jeevani carelessly threw her jasmine wrapped hair over her shoulder, scanning the adjoining hill to locate Niranga Aiya's house.

"Oh, that is the real reason for your trip up here, then?" I teased Jeevani, pulling her up from the bench we were sitting on. Hand in hand, we walked towards the other side of our property to show the Senege's house, built on slightly higher land than ours.

"So, have you bumped into him again?"

"Yes."

"How was it?" Jeevani's eyes were searching for a clue to latch on to. "Have you two reconnected, resolved whatever is going on between the two of you?"

"Woman, don't you have enough things to worry about? What is this constant need to find drama in others?"

I didn't want to tell Jeevani what took place yesterday evening, as I am still grappling with the warm tingly sensation experienced being pressed so close to Niranga Aiya when he held my hand under the cold water.

"Hmm… he was extremely curious about you the other day."

I was debating whether I should ask Jeevani for details, but decided not to. I would not walk into her trap. In my experience, it didn't matter what response you gave; Jeevani would always say whatever she wanted.

"I could tell he was curious to find out more about you, but didn't want to show it. Much like how you are now." As I expected, she continued with her chatter.

"I told him all he should know about you!" Jeevani stopped strolling and grinned.

"Chill, no need to look so grim. I didn't split all your secrets, only the few I thought were important." I ignored Jeevani's comment, pretending I didn't care about what she had shared with Niranga Aiya.

"Tell me, how are you really? How was it to reconnect with him?" Jeevani's voice was laced with concern and interest. Then she gave me a thoughtful glance in her usual fashion, searching my face for emotional clues.

"Um… Bit awkward. It was like meeting him for the first time but having a vague memory of knowing him from somewhere."

"I mean about your emotions." Jeevani probed.

"What about them?"

"Honestly, Saku, why are you beating around the bush with me? You are struggling with your emotions!" I watched a small disappointment building in her eyes.

"I am confused." After a few minutes of silence, I confessed.

"Confused?" Jeevani squeezed her eyes, creating frown lines on her forehead.

"Yes, he is practically a stranger to me, a very sophisticated man. Sometimes he says things that remind me of the boy I grew up with." I didn't tell Jeevani that this boy was pulling invisible cords tied around my heart, dragging the pain and the affection I had buried deep inside me.

"So, you are avoiding him!" Jeevani was daring me to disagree. Without waiting for my response, she continued. "Saku, whatever happened between the two of you, don't let it become a barrier. Life is too short to hold on to grudges. At least try to salvage the friendship you had with him. He is a nice person."

Jeevani was the second one to give me the same advice. I didn't want to tell Jeevani or Akka that there is no viable way of salvaging a friendship when the trust was no longer there.

"It's okay. I will leave it for another lifetime. Let's have some tea." As I put my arm around her, leading Jeevani to the house, I could sense she was forming words in her head. I bravely waited for her to challenge me with one of her wisecracks when she gave me a sheepish smile.

"Hey, without trying to kill me, could you do me a favour after tea?"

"What?"

"I need to drop these documents at Niranga sir's place. Could you come with me?"

"Why can't you ask Devan to do it at work tomorrow? Isn't he working in the factory?"

"These are personal documents. Devan doesn't want anyone in the office finding out Niranga sir is helping us with the visa application," Jeevani was toying with her jasmine clad braid, avoiding my eyes. "Because I am here anyway, Devan asked me to drop them off."

"Leave the documents with me. I will get Malli to take them across when he returns from school." It was a relief to come up with a solution to avoid going to Senege's house.

"Please, Saku, come with me." Jeevani pleaded. "I made some vada for Meera. I brought you some as well." Jeevani smiled, trying to do her best to win me over with her culinary skills.

"Their house is only a few yards from ours. Just continue along the path."

"I am not a baby." Jeevani sat straight in the chair, sounding displeased and annoyed. "I can follow the driveway. It is just that I am not comfortable going there on my own. If Meera weren't their domestic helper, I wouldn't mind."

"So, you assumed going with me would be easier because I am their neighbour?"

"I need some support. Maybe it's my hormones that make me weak," Jeevani's eyes were filling up with helpless tears. "It will be a great help if you could come along with me, surely, something you would do for your pregnant friend?"

"This is how it is going to be for the next six months? You pull out the pregnant card every time you want something done your way? Unbelievable!" I shake my head in disbelief, giving in to her pleading.

"I love you too, hon." Jeevani squeezed my hand, grinning.

We made our way to Niranga Aiya's house after some tea and biscuits. I strolled, not to make it easy for Jeevani, but to prolong the visit. Jeevani talked nonstop about her pregnancy, filling the uncomfortable space between us. When I rang the bell, Aunty Nelum opened the door with a beaming smile. I breathed with relief, letting my tense muscles loosen, hoping to return home as soon as Aunty collects the documents from Jeevani.

"Aunty, this is Jeevani, my friend. She has brought some documents she wishes to leave for Niranga Aiya. Could we give them to you before she goes around to catch up with Meera?" Jeevani stood away with a nervous expression on her face. I could sense her uneasiness coming to the place her sister-in-law works as a domestic helper. Years of discrimination between the masters and the servants demanded forceful respect and obedience that traditionally got carried out by way one addresses or behaves in the presence of the master. This strong custom of capitulation had Jeevani standing deftly, pulling the edge of the envelope she was clasping too hard.

"Oh, you are Meera's sister? Please take a seat. This hill isn't easy on foot for anyone, let alone a pregnant girl." The way Aunty welcomed Jeevani surprised us both, making me smile with gratuity.

"Madam, my husband asked me to pass these documents to Niranga sir. Sir offered to check them before we submit them." Observing this subservient gentle persona of Jeevani was all new to me. I shifted my weight from one leg to another, wanting to flee back to my sanctuary when Aunty spoke.

"Sasoo, be a darling and go fetch Niranga. He must be in Uncle's study or his room."

I turned to Jeevani with anger, as this was one thing I was trying to avoid. Jeevani twisted her head away, but not before she could hide the guilty smile on her lips. If she wasn't already sitting in one of the veranda chairs they had for visitors, I might have pushed her down the steps, despite Jeevani being one of my best friends.

"Go on now, find him." Aunty lightly pushed me towards the living room, seeing I hadn't moved. I knew there was no way for me to get out of it without appearing awkward and silly. Although I haven't been to their house in over ten years, I wasn't unfamiliar with its layout. I knew where Uncle's study and Niranga Aiya's room were.

I dragged myself inside the house, fighting back old memories flying towards me like ghosts from every nook and corner. Niranga Aiya was not in Uncle's study, so I headed to his room. I knocked on the door, and as there was no answer, I slowly opened it. The smell of his aftershave came rushing past the door and hit the base of my nostrils. It was fresh and masculine, reminding me of the first night I saw him and last night when he held my hand under the running water.

The room appeared to be the same as when Niranga Aiya was a teenager. It still had the Brooke Shields and Madonna's giant posters he used to admire so much as a youngster. Although the bed was unmade, the room was tidy. A few computers were operating with a slight hum, as they were still running some sort of program for him. I turned around to leave when my eyes caught my Peter Pans drawing still on the wall. It had the marks from the day I tore it off from his wall.

***

The three-year gap between us didn't play a significant role until Niranga Aiya started preparing for his ordinary level exam. When he stayed up studying, I wanted to study with him. Fully aware of my stubbornness, Amma and

Thaththa let Niranga Aiya study at our place. I would sit across from him and would imitate him until I fell asleep.

When my eyelids got heavy as stone, and I could no longer hold them open, he would reach around the table, picking up me from where I sat and declare, "Time to sleep, sleepyhead." Then he would affectionately ruffle my hair and lead me to my room.

As the exam drew near, Niranga Aiya didn't come to play with me. It was also the school holidays, and Malli was visiting his grandparents. Akka stayed back as usual, and this time she had a genuine reason, as she was also studying for her O-level exam.

When the days grew into weeks, and then to a month, I lost my patience. I was lonely as I didn't have anyone to play with. It reminded me of the days before I met Niranga Aiya, except worse. The pain and hurt I was struggling with soon turned into anger. I was bursting with rage when I finally crossed the hedge that separated our lands, looking for Niranga Aiya, bruising the long leathery lush green leaves of purple and white Agapanthus bushes with my careless kicks.

"Sasoo, what brings you here?" What is the matter, honey? Are you bored?"

When I didn't answer her, Aunty Nelum stopped sewing her patchwork quilt and smiled kindly. I could hear the pity in her voice. She knew how close Niranga Aiya and I were. We were like Peter Pan and his Shadow and only separated when we fought, which was very rare. Being the one with a lousy temper, I was the one to storm out, threatening not to talk to Niranga Aiya and have him chase after, making me laugh. He was not seeking me out this time, leaving me to go after him after patiently waiting for over four weeks.

I sat beside Aunty Nelum and still said nothing.

"Come and learn patchwork. It will keep you busy until Aiya finishes his exam." Aunty stroked my hair and suggested with such kindness. Both our parents were gentle during that period, especially Amma, who conveniently ignored my acting out during those weeks.

Aunty's compassion made me feel heavy and uncomfortable. I couldn't stomach it anymore. I got up and went to Niranga Aiya's room, which was empty. The room was not as tidy as it used to be. Although the bed was made and the cloth rack was clear (thanks to their domestic helper), his study desk was cluttered. Many scrunched-up papers were on the floor, and a couple of books were open on the table.

I scanned the room with a heart full of anger and disappointment when my eyes caught the drawing on the wall beside his table. It was a picture I drew a few years ago in the art class. When we were assigned to draw our favourite fairy tale, I drew Peter Pan and his Shadow.

Peter Pan was on Captain Cook's ship, arguing with his shadow. I drew the shadow to appear as a silhouette of a girl with two pigtails. My teacher admired the painting's novelty, and when I showed the piece to Niranga Aiya, he loved it. He straight away knew it was a sketch of us, and though he didn't ask to keep it, something in his eyes made me tore up the page and handed the painting to him. I helped him to stick it on the wall beside his study table with some drawing pins.

When I saw the sketch, memories of our happy days rushed over me, shifting my anger into a feeling of deep sorrow. It was clear Niranga Aiya didn't love me anymore; if not, he would have sought me out as Peter Pan, who chased after his shadow. As I tore off the drawing from the wall and threw it into the pile of scrap paper on the floor, Niranga Aiya walked into the room.

He stopped in his tracks, frowning at me and again at the picture I discarded. He dashed across the room to stand in front of me, his eyes blazing with fury. I have never seen him that offended. Niranga Aiya always has been the cool one with laughing eyes.

"Why did you do that?" He was shaking my shoulders. I can't recall what scared me the most, the pain I had where he grabbed my shoulders, or the irritation in his tone. I did not have the guts to say, *'you are hurting me.'* When he heard my sobs, he looked at me helplessly. He let go of my shoulders and combed his hair with his fingers.

"Please don't cry, Cookie."

"I tore it because you are not friends with me anymore," I muttered in between my wails.

"Who said I am not friends with you anymore?" Niranga Aiya sounded more surprised than annoyed.

"You don't come to play with me anymore." I mustered helplessly. When Niranga Aiya started talking, I let him focus my attention on the floor and draw lines on it with my big toe. When he realised, I was not paying attention to him, Niranga Aiya stopped and made me sit on his bed. He opened his almari and took out a towel to wipe the tears off my face.

"Oh, what a cry baby you are." He knelt in front of me and ruffled my hair. Every time he did that, I felt a lot younger than I was.

"Hey, listen to me carefully, Cookie." Niranga Aiya held my hands. "I am still your friend and will always be your friend." He sounded very patient. When I glanced into his brown eyes, there was something else there besides the kindness and empathy that I saw. Like his voice, they were struggling to convey a message which I could not interpret.

"I only have a few weeks before the exam. I need to put in my best efforts. So, it is not a time for me to play, Cookie. I think when you come to my age, you will also understand. Look at it this way; once I become a successful engineer, we can build a better house than my cousin's house you admire so much in Kandy. I can take you anywhere you choose to go. I can get you all the velvet tamarind you want to eat. We don't have to wait for my pocket money."

Though he was kind of joking at the end, his tone was sincere. The seriousness in his voice scared me. I hunched, feeling small and childish. For the first time, the age gap between us loomed like an ugly giant. When we were roaming around the pinewoods, climbing trees and racing across the gravel roads, I assumed we were equals, and I never considered him older. But that day, sitting there in his room, having him kneel beside me, talking to me about his future, made me realise how young I was to him. I was a baby he thought he had to protect, someone he had to explain things to. I got embarrassed.

"Once the exam is over, I get a long holiday. We can go rowing in Lake Gregory. And if you stay out of trouble, I will take you to Maligawa. Okay? So, are we good?" When I didn't respond to his questions, Niranga Aiya lifted my face and peered into my eyes. "Hey, Am I still your friend?" He sounded concerned and worried, as if my response meant a great deal to him.

"Yes." I leaned forwarded and hugged him tightly. "You will always be my best friend." I never wanted to let him go. He hugged me back, and after a few seconds, pulled back and ruffled my hair.

Niranga Aiya got up from where he was kneeling and walked over to his bookshelf. After a couple of minutes, he came back with a few books in his hands.

"Why don't you read these books until my exam is over? If you finish these, you can come and get another from that rack."

That day, Niranga Aiya and I started a new form of friendship with different boundaries and expectations that I carried into adolescence.

***

The rush of old reflection was too heavy for me to bear; a lump formed in my throat, driving me to bolt back and nearly crashing into Niranga Aiya, who stepped into the room.

"Cookie, were you looking for me?" My presence in his room surprised Niranga Aiya. There was something between hope and happiness in his eyes. I panicked. He thinks I am there to see him.

"Yes…. Um… I mean no." I shook my head and tried to smile to hide my unease. "Jeevani is here to drop off some documents for Devan," I rushed to explain. "Aunty sent me to fetch you." I rattled away to hide my nervousness as Niranga Aiya kept quiet, keenly watching me.

It was awkward and strange, standing there as two strangers with all the history and emotions between and around us. I was wracking my brain for a witty ice breaker to change the uncomfortable silence building between us when I saw a bunch of cobwebs glued to his hair and on the base of his neck. Without thinking, I reached out and removed them. When my fingers touched the bottom of his neck, warmth started rushing through me, making me shudder. We glanced at each other with unease.

"Sorry," I muttered with embarrassment. "There were some cobwebs glued to your hair and neck." I tried to explain my actions, hiding my nervousness.

"Oh, I was in the storeroom, going through my old notebooks and stuff I left behind." Niranga Aiya quickly dropped the books he was carrying on his study desk and rubbed his neck with one of his empty hands.

It could be because he wanted to change the uneasiness we both sensed that he turned around and took hold of my hand. "How is your hand? Is it still painful?"

"It is good, thank you," I mumbled. We both stood there for a few seconds in silence. We were like two magnets attached, not making any attempt to move.

"Let's check out those documents". After some time, Niranga Aiya smiled and let go of my hand. I could feel the drop in my heart when a coldness replaced his warm touch. Despite the uneasiness we felt, I sensed Niranga Aiya also would have preferred to stay in his room, standing there listening to our breathing.

***

"Did something happen between the two of you before you joined us?" Jeevani asked me later on the way to the bus stop.

"What do you mean?" She studied my face and puckered her nose for dramatic effect. "It was clear neither one of you wanted to be there and preferred to be in his room!"

"You need to get off watching too many teledramas."

"There is something unresolved between the two of you! You can deny as much as you want, but even a blind man can detect it." Jeevani's voice was full of sarcasm. I shrugged my shoulders and pretended I didn't care while grappling with the sudden urge I felt to be near Niranga Aiya to experience the warmth of his fingers wrapped around my hand and to inhale his masculine scent. I shook my head, trying to erase that image, and turned to Jeevani with anger.

"Next time, do your visits without getting me involved. Now Aunty wants me to join their thirty-fifth wedding anniversary dinner." I didn't contain my irritation. "I can understand why you don't have many friends. You are such a pain in the arse."

Jeevani kept quiet for a change and let me walk with my anger and frustration all the way to the bus stand.

11 DEFLECTION

Despite swearing to Malli I wouldn't join his dance rehearsal, I caved in to get out of Saturday's lunch at the Seneges. I stomached the two hours of Kasun's drooling and unwanted admiration. Neither Thaththa nor Amma objected when they learned I was skipping the feast to go with Malli to his dance academy. But the moment Akka got to know this, she went on a rampage, scolding both Malli and me like the schoolteacher that she was. It was effortless for me to accept Akka's frustration than having to be around Niranga Aiya.

The last few days have been torturous. I was struggling with notions about Niranga Aiya dominating my thoughts. Yet, underneath the restlessness and apprehension, I was harbouring a wave of tingly sensation that was building inside. The shift in my physical reaction to Niranga Aiya's presence bothered me. I did not wish to bear any more of his intoxicating aftershave that lingered around hours after he left the room or his laughing eyes that caused my heart to do backflips. I couldn't choose what the worse was: his sexy Sri Lankan mixed Australian accent that appeared as he was caressing me when he spoke, or that touch burned into my bones, shooting a million nauseous sensations through my body.

Amid a workout, I had to stop myself from chuckling as the situation's irony struck me. Yet, there I was, subjecting myself to Kasun's obsession to avoid mine on Niranga Aiya. I left the dance academy full of empathy for Kasun. No one better than I could resonate with what he is going through- for crying out loud, I have had first-hand experience nursing such sentiments in the past.

"Sasoo, let's join the others for dessert." On the way back, Malli wanted to head over to Senege's house. I frowned at him, struggling to cover my urge to push him off the bus we were on.

"You go ahead. I got a splitting headache."

"Oh, I am sorry. Okay, you go and sleep it off. I will ask Amma to bring you some leftovers."

Malli's tone was filled with worry and a trace of guilt. His handsome face lost some of the brightness it had radiated from earlier. *'Serves you right,'* I thought to myself, *'Wanting dessert after making me dance with that psycho!'* Yes, the empathy I had been long gone by now.

It was easy to pull the wool over Malli's eyes, as he didn't have a suspicious mind. If it had been Akka, she would have not only inquired when and how the pulsating or throbbing started, but would also lay her palm on my forehead to check the temperature. Imagining Akka, I instantly touched my forehead, which Malli took as a sign of pain, and gave me a sympathetic nod.

I congratulate myself on coming up with a fake illness. This would support me to patch things up with Amma before I leave tomorrow. Since the night my hand got scorched, Amma had been giving me the silent treatment. When she needed to ask me a question or wanted to pass any information, she channelled them through Akka or Malli. It was as if Amma had me on solitary confinement, punishing me for a crime I was not aware of committing.

Amma's behaviour was hurting me. My heart was heavy and sad, but no one noticed the suppressed tears lingering in the depth of my eyes, nor could they hear the cry loitering at the base of my throat. Thaththa was rarely home, spending most of his time at Uncle Sarath's company. There was no point in speaking to Akka as all her topics revolved around Niranga Aiya and what a nasty bitch I have been to him. Malli was occupied with his schoolwork and dance practices, leaving me stranded with memories I wasn't ready to deal with.

I was careful not to be near Senege's family members. It was easy to steer clear of Niranga Aiya when he came to pick up Akka in the morning, as I always slept in. Having young Raju helping Amma with her plant nursery gave me room for reading during the day, the perfect excuse to avoid Aunty Nelum.

The evenings were the toughest, as I loved spending time with Thaththa and Malli when they returned home. The only way to keep away from Uncle Sarath asking for ginger tea when he turned up with Thaththa from their outings, and Niranga Aiya lingering over after bringing Akka home from work, was to pretend I was collecting photographs for an upcoming fictitious exhibition. Others in my family didn't have the technical savviness to notice that the lighting at that time of the day was terrible for photography or that my old camera didn't have a state-of-the-art flash to take any display-worthy pictures. So every evening, I left the house to wander around Lake Gregory until it was too dark to be on my own.

Whenever I sensed the wanting to be near Niranga Aiya, I reminded myself of the incident I had with finishing a bottle of French champagne once I was in Singapore. Although I knew that the warmth of its fine, well-integrated bubbles would make me drunk faster, I couldn't turn away from the most prestigious wine in the world. The terrible hangover the day after was the price I paid for not avoiding temptation.

My home had always been my healing ground. The place where I recharge my tired self, forget about the rest of the world and its troubles. But on this occasion, my visit not only amplified the frustration and weariness, but it also left me hollow. I couldn't wait to head back to Kandy.

When I returned home without Malli, the house was empty and silent. I welcomed the solitude and elected to sit outside on my favourite bench, facing Mount Pedro. I was trying to wrap up the last few pages of the novel I didn't get to finish the other day. Absorbed in my reading, I didn't notice until Niranga Aiya sat next to me. He has always been light-footed, having the ability to stroll in with little noise.

"It must be a good one." He spoke while working on reading the title of the book I was reading.

"A Stone for Danny Fisher. Wow, so you have moved on to Harold Robbins!" When Niranga Aiya chuckled, I gathered he was provoking me into a debate.

"What brings you here?" I questioned, still having my eyes glued to the book as I was not interested in starting a conversation about my tastes in authors. Whatever his reason to be here, I wanted to deal with it and get it over.

"You!" I saw him examining me from the edge of my eye. "Manoj said you had a headache?"

"Aney, it is gone now. I had a shower, and the cold air helped." I sighed, over-sharing to mask embarrassment and unease, caught in my lie.

"How is your hand?" Without waiting for a reply, Niranga Aiya took my left hand. Anxious he could catch the rise of my heartbeat, I willed myself not to pull my hand away to avoid awkwardness.

"Good as new. Thanks for checking." I chirped with a fake delight. *'Now you have, so please go back.'* I shushed the child, who was irked.

Though it seemed as he wanted to respond, Niranga Aiya let go of my hand without talking. We sat there in silence, both of us staring at the mountain. I tried not to move, not wanting to give a cause for a conversation.

"Do you remember the two stones we used as our stools before Uncle made this bench for you to read?" Niranga Aiya quizzed, dragging me back to our childhood. "This is such a serene place, quiet and calming." When he spoke again, I nodded in agreement, still not making any attempt to talk.

"What happened to us?" He turned to face me, watching me like a hawk, searching for clues.

"We used to be best friends. Now we hardly chat." I continued to stare at the mountain, pretending to be mesmerised by its sight.

"Did I do something to make you scared of me, Cookie?" Niranga Aiya asked.

"No, why do you think that?" My jaw dropped in surprise that he believed I feared him. Yes, I was afraid, but that was of my own emotions and reactions to his presence than of him.

"Okay, then tell me, if that isn't the problem, did I offend you?" Niranga Aiya was still watching me, and I noted how his eyebrows were drawn up as if he was sad. I shook my head as I was not planning on telling him how I was infuriated with my own senses that are hyperactive since the day he walked into our living room.

"Okay then, why are you avoiding me?" When he spoke again, one side of his mouth was raised with contempt.

"I am not avoiding you."

"Is that why you can't even look at me when you talk?" He challenged, still keeping his gaze on me.

"I hardly talked to you. So, that is not a rational conclusion." I twisted my head to glare at his face, trying to avoid blinking to cover the distress I felt.

"That is bullshit! How many times you have been dodging me, giving lame excuses? There can't be any building or mountain left in the town you haven't photographed!" I could feel my spine straightening with the realisation. '*So, he knew.*'

"You are keeping away from me." '*You bet I am!*' The inner child sneered.

"You are uncomfortable around me." He sounded disappointed than angry, voicing his observation.

"I am not," I lied. I would not admit how torturous it was to be near him. "Maybe you feel a difference because we haven't seen each other in ages. People change. We both have changed in the last ten years. We are no longer who we used to be." I continued talking, trying not to show my nervousness. It took all my courage to peer into his eyes.

"I don't buy it!" He declared with bitterness.

"There is something more. You are treating me as if I am a stranger." I was unsure how to respond without opening my heart and pouring its content kept locked away for years.

"I am sorry if you feel this way." When I said it, we both knew it was a lie.

"All right, say I believe you. Let us visit the stream. I am dying to go there since I came back." When I didn't respond, Niranga Aiya spoke again. "I didn't want to go without you." He paused and smiled, making his eyes glitter. "It was our place." When he lowered his voice with dilated eyes, I had to force myself to breathe.

"We wouldn't get another chance to do it. I heard you are leaving tomorrow." He continued to talk, not seeing my clenched fists, his eyes enticing. "Let's go, come on." He was on his feet as a spring and waited for me in anticipation. I had walked right into a trap.

"Come on, let us check out the place… it will be like old times." Niranga Aiya was daring me to stand by my word. I was reluctant, but could not refuse his invitation without admitting I lied.

"Let's go," I said, getting up from the bench.

As the sun was crawling to the west, Niranga Aiya's shadow was behind him. I stepped beside him, keeping inside his shadow, letting him go before me. He strolled in silence, hands inside his trouser pockets, deep in thought.

We took the abandoned trail that led away from where I sat towards the pinewood forest on the hill. It was clear that no one had walked this path in years. The weeds were knee high. Their skinny bodies could not bear the long thorny branches arching to the floor, creating a green tunnel of a lush canopy of weeds.

I knew the way like the back of my hand. It didn't matter I had not travelled this path in years; I could walk in blindfold. I was confident it was the same for Niranga Aiya. This path was an integral part of our childhood.

Every twist and turn had a conversation, a story, a memory bonding us together.

The closer we got to the stream, the more tiring it became to keep my memories suppressed. The pain in my heart was cumbersome; I wanted to run back home, leaving Niranga Aiya behind.

"Hey, why are you lagging? Don't tell me, are you still scared of Baba Yaga?" Niranga Aiya turned around with a chuckle. Of course, I used to fear Baba Yaga when I was a small girl. After meeting Niranga Aiya, whenever we visited the stream, he would hold my hand as I was so scared of the flying witch who ate children when they got lost in the woods.

Niranga Aiya made me promise not to visit the stream without him after my fall. I always honoured it more out of fear of Baba Yaga than anything else. Later on, when I was a teenager, I didn't tell him I was no longer scared and let him hold my hand. I liked the way I felt when his broad palm and long fingers wrapped around mine. I felt protected and cherished.

"Oh, come on, you can't still be scared?" I didn't expect Niranga Aiya to reach out and pull me to him. His unexpected tug threw me off balance, and I stretched my hand to steady myself, hitting it on his chest. I could feel the tight muscles on his torso and the rise and fall of his lungs. Being so close to him made me so uneasy and excited at the same time.

"Let go of me." When he instinctively put his arms around me to break my fall, I pushed Niranga Aiya away with a force that surprised us both. My outburst astonished him.

"Hey, I am sorry." He stepped back, lifting his hands, distancing himself from me. "I didn't mean to cross any boundary!" He sounded confused and apologetic. Saying nothing, I walked past him and continued the climb.

'You wanted to go to the stream, so let's go to the damn stream', I muttered to myself and got there before him. Niranga Aiya was not far behind me. He quickly caught up and stood in front, facing me. If I stretched my hand, I could push him into the stream. I was so angry and was seriously considering pushing him over. I hated Niranga Aiya for making me come to this place as flashbacks came crashing through, making my eyes water.

"What did I do to you to resent me so much?" Niranga Aiya spoke with a voice laced with anger. *'You made me fall in love with you,'* I wanted to scream. Instead, I lied.

"I don't resent you." It was surprising how well I have come to lie to him. Growing up, I never lied to him.

"Oh yeah, what was it back there? Your reaction was as if I was trying to abuse you." Niranga Aiya challenged, expecting an explanation.

"I am sorry." He was right. My reaction was way out of line.

"What made you react in such a way?" He was not ready to let it go so easily.

"I am sorry," I said again, peering over his shoulder, noticing the afternoon sun fading away through the pinewood trees. "I got annoyed with you for making me visit this place."

"Why don't you like this place anymore? This stream used to be your favourite place, our place." He sounded hurt, more than angry now. I sensed the pain in his voice.

"Exactly, it used to be!" I could feel the anger building inside me, making my cheeks and ears warm.

"What changed?"

"What is the point of it now?" I lift my shoulders with desperation, wishing to be anywhere but here.

"I want to know what made you resent me and despise this place!" Niranga Aiya was determined to get an answer. He had a stubbornness written across him; I am familiar with. My experience reminded me he would tire me with his questions until I satisfied him with the answers.

I wanted to end this conversation and head back home. Maybe there was still time to leave for Kandy today. It was a bit after three o'clock. I could say I have a work emergency and pretend Sula wanted me to take over one of his tours. I took a deep breath and frowned. His keen eyes were following my every movement.

"You were the one who changed it from our place to your love nest!" I could not hold it in anymore. The fury and pain I had suppressed for years came out with an elevated voice.

"What on earth are you talking about?" I saw the unexpected tremor run through him as his head snapped and his eyes filled with concern.

"This was our place, and I didn't bring any of my girlfriends here! Believe me. What girl are you talking about?" He asked, appearing startled.

'Why are you lying to me? Why can't you recall being with Akka? Was Akka not that important to you?' I didn't ask him any of those questions going through my mind at the speed of light.

"Seriously?? You want me to give the exact date and time?"

"Okay....... okay, let's get this over with. I saw you hugging a girl here........" It was hard for me to bring myself to talk about the incident. I took a deep breath to compose myself and continued. "It was on that week I finished my O-level exam. To be exact, it was the week you promised to take me on a boat ride on Lake Gregory!" What I said made him lose his balance, and he was going to fall into the stream. Instinctively, I stretched my hand and grabbed him, breaking the fall. For a few seconds, we were staring at each other's eyes, mine full of mockery and Niranga Aiya's with shock. If I let go of his hand, Niranga Aiya would fall into the stream, which would satisfy my anger. As he could sense what I was contemplating, Niranga Aiya quickly tightened the grip he had on my hand and pulled himself up. He stepped away from the edge, frowning at me in disbelief.

Harming someone was not in my nature. But the angry urge I had of wanting to let him fall into the stream scared me. *'I would not have let you slip.'* I wanted to tell Niranga Aiya, but I did not. Instead of apologising, I turned around and walked past him.

"Hey, wait, we need to talk." Niranga Aiya stropped my stride, grabbing my hand. I stopped and glared at his hand and then at him. *'When are you going to stop touching me? I don't want you to touch me.'* As if he could hear my inner scream, he quickly let go of my hand and started running his fingers through his hair.

"What is there to talk? What is done is done. Let us just leave it at that."

"So, you would wipe away years of friendship we had because you saw me with a girl?" His question stopped me from walking away. He sounded disgusted and disappointed, and I felt nauseous and frustrated with myself. *'What sort of person would turn her back on her best friend for one fault?'* A tiny voice asked me.

"Friendship? What friendship would that be? When you didn't tell me you had a girlfriend?"

"I told you already, I didn't bring any of my girlfriends here!" Niranga Aiya's jaw was in a tight grip, and he was puffing. His voice was oozing frustration. "Are you sure you did not imagine it in the same way you believed that crazy witch was real?" He asked.

Did my mind record the incident incorrectly? Did I imagine a story to distance myself from Niranga Aiya because I couldn't accept him choosing Akka over me? I was no longer sure what happened ten years ago. Am I holding on to something I created in my head? If I doubt this memory, how reliable are other recollections I hold on to so dearly going to be? I could doubt my memory as much as I wanted, but I couldn't forget how I felt that day. I felt rejected by the person I adored the most. I felt betrayed because he didn't tell me he was in love with Akka. He used to share everything with me. Akka has already denied any romantic liaisons with Niranga Aiya. Should I confront him? How can I do it without giving away the biggest secret of my life? So many questions were passing through my mind without waiting for any answers.

"Okay, let's say my memory is vague," I said, opening myself up to consider a different perspective of past events. I watched Niranga Aiya's shoulders relax. "Are you telling me you didn't keep any secrets from me?" When I asked, Niranga Aiya tensed again, appearing uncomfortable. He combed his hair with his fingers, avoiding my eyes. Even before he spoke, I knew he would not tell me the truth.

"I didn't get a chance to share." He spoke as if it was my fault. "You went to Kandy."

I crossed my arms across my chest, speechless. Surely, he will not pin that on me. He is the one who made me flee to Kandy.

"Why are you so angry? You knew I had girlfriends. You knew most of them. What was different at that time?" Niranga Aiya asked in frustration. *'Because she is my sister, you moron.'* I kept my mouth tight to restrain the anger.

"Why did you have to bring her here? This was my place!" The moment the words slipped from my mouth, I realised I sounded silly and comical, resembling a child who had lost her favourite toy. This never was my place; this land belongs to the Seneges. I was trespassing from day one. Niranga Aiya had all the right to bring any girl here as he pleased.

"You sound like a spoiled brat." Niranga Aiya chuckled, turning his face into the adorable little boy I knew. I wanted to lash out and wipe the smile off his face. He was right. I was behaving like a cry baby. I assumed, like the stream, he too would be mine. I expected him to wait for me to become a woman, the same way the stream waited for me to visit.

"All this cold shoulder business is over a stream?" Niranga Aiya raised his eyebrows, showing surprise, as though that was the last thing, he anticipated from me. "Gosh, I will happily give this plot of land to you if it means that much!" He laughed.

"I don't want your damn land!" I glanced away with annoyance. I was more irritated at how my heart was pounding in response to his laughing eyes than what he suggested.

"Why don't you tell me the truth, Cookie. Was it the stream? Or did something else bother you so much?" When he spoke again, his voice got soft but deep, making me gaze at him. He was observing me with the same intensity as I was watching him. I contemplated my response.

I could not tell him I was in love with him or tore me apart when he chose Akka. I was planning a smarter response when he squinted his eyes and asked, "Were you in love with me?" His words came out slowly, a whisper sounding happy.

Is he mocking me? I bit my lips with frustration.

"What?" I was horrified. *Did he guess?* I shuffled my feet in unease.

"Were you in love with me? Is that what got you so upset?" His eyes were laughing, and his voice was thick with confidence.

"Oh, please, why would I fall for a Casanova when I was after a Gorky?" It pleased me when I sounded malicious. If I hurt Niranga Aiya, he didn't show it. But the light he had in his eyes disappeared. His jaw lines got tighter. He glanced away at the pine trees, trying to contain a fit of anger, struggling to respond.

"What was it then? What did I do that was so unforgivable?" Ten years have not changed him much. He was still relentless.

"You betrayed my trust."

"How did I betray your trust?" Niranga Aiya stood there watching my every move, letting me contemplate how much I was going to share.

"You promised this was our place, my place, and you made this to be your love nest! Isn't it a betrayal of trust?" I dared him to say I was wrong and fabricate a story I could latch on to. Deep down, I would have believed anything he said. I was after salvation and no longer wanted to hold on to this anger that was burning me, hurting me, consuming my sanity. *'Please give me a reason to make this pain go away.'* I sobbed inside, tears pooling at the base of my eyes.

"Hold on a second. I never betrayed your trust. I didn't bring a girl here, but you are right. I was in love. I didn't have time to tell you." His words push me into a bottomless abyss, a dark, horrible place. It confirmed he chose Akka over me. I have been invisible and irrelevant.

"You mean you didn't have five minutes to tap on my window and tell me, guess what, Saku, I am in love with...." I nearly said *'your sister'* and luckily stopped myself.

"With who...?" Picking up the hesitation in my fragmented speech, Niranga Aiya asked in anger no different from mine. He was panting, and his cheeks had turned red. He was shifting his feet.

"The flavour of the month... you didn't have any problem of sharing about other countless flings you had!" He was watching me intensely. I bet he was trying to understand why I was sarcastic. I wish I could ask, *'I was your friend, your confidant, your wing girl? Why did you choose Akka over me?'*

"I am surprised you even noticed me." Niranga Aiya gave me a thoughtful look, but his voice was still full of anger. "As I recall, you never had time for me." There was a trace of sadness in his annoyed voice.

"I was preparing for the O-level exam. You should remember, you did the same when you sat for yours." I put my hands on my hips, daring, *'Tell me I am wrong!'* He was silent, his eyes trying to pierce through me. "You didn't speak to me for weeks. I had to bury myself in those stupid novels you gave me until you finished your exam."

I still remember how I bruised those long green leaves of Agapanthus on my way to his house one evening filled with rage when he shut me off during his study period. How he kneeled next to me and explained his focus was on his exam. I watch his facial expressions transforming from confused to realisation. Something that made little sense to him before was no longer a puzzle. He has found the last missing piece. I had seen that expression millions of times on his face when he finally resolved a mathematical dilemma that bothered him.

I ebbed over to one of the nearby rocks and leaned on it to rest. Niranga Aiya slouched next to me. *'Where to from here?'* I asked myself. We both have antagonised over the past, having our own justification. I am realistic enough to know he was not sharing everything, just as I was.

"Is there any salvation for us?" When Niranga Aiya finally broke the silence, he asked the same question that crossed my mind earlier. The pain in his voice made me turn to him. I thought I saw a trace of tears in his eyes, but then he blinked, and they were no longer there. I felt dejected seeing him appearing defeated, a sight that was foreign to me. Could we go back to who we were to each other ten years ago? I was not sure. Even now, we are not truthful to the other. My account of that day may be fuzzy, but I couldn't ignore how I felt. The pain and betrayal I lived through were real. My heart still nursed those raw feelings, housing a big black hole glued with a web of draining emotions.

"I am not sure. We are now two strangers with screwed up memories. Maybe we are better off not trying to rescue the past." I heard the defeat and sadness in my voice and felt the contracting pain in my heart. I wanted to put my arms around me and hug myself, tell me not to be miserable; it would be all right.

"Let's reset."

"What?" I turned to Niranga Aiya, not following what he meant.

"Sorry, occupational hazard." He smiled sheepishly. He ran his fingers through his already messy hair. "Let us start over. We can pretend to be two strangers meeting for the first time. Let's forget the past." There was optimism in his tone. *'Is he for real?'* my facial expressions must have been transparent as Niranga Aiya's face changed from hope to concerned despair.

I didn't want to start over. Nor did I want to bury the history I cherished so much. I didn't want to erase those beautiful moments of my youthful days shared with him.

"What else is there to do?" When I didn't respond, Niranga Aiya spoke again. "Would you rather keep on avoiding me?" *'Yes, I just have to weather it until I head back to Kandy and not return home until you leave.'*

"Is that your grown-up solution?" As if he heard my internal struggle, Niranga Aiya confronted me. We both sat there glaring at the tall pine trees as if the answer hid in one of those thorny branches.

"Surely the bond we shared is worth fighting for, don't you think?" His high-pitched voice cut through the long, uneasy silence we had between us. I didn't turn to look at him as I feared what I would find on his face, although I was not clear what I was expecting to see, either. I didn't want to point out that ten years of separation outweighed the six years of childhood friendship we shared.

"What do you say?" When he didn't get a response, he peered into my face with a hopeful smile.

"Yes, I think we should try to reconnect." I gave him a weak smile, not believing in what I had just said.

"To a new beginning!" Niranga Aiya got up from where he sat and stretched his hand across to me. I didn't expect him to make it formal. I stretched mine reluctantly and let it slide between his palm and fingers. Niranga Aiya gripped mine with a solid, firm handshake while grinning.

His hand felt warm, making my body tingle with unease. We could pretend all we wanted, but deep inside, I felt there was no escape from what I felt for him, reminding me of the consequences of finishing that bottle of French champagne when I was on tour. I was better off staying miles away to let my heart heal. I slowly withdrew my hand from his warmth that I so much wanted to wrap myself in.

"So, Saku, what should we do first?" He rolled my name in his mouth as if it was an exotic food he tasted for the first time and gazed at me wistfully. He shifted his feet with unease while trying to hold my stare. The whole situation felt wired and artificial, and I couldn't stomach it anymore.

"I have to go; I am expecting a call," I murmured in a choking voice, holding back tears. "Let me get back to you with something we can do." I threw over my shoulder as an afterthought and left Niranga Aiya at the stream and ran down the rolling hill until I reached my room and closed the door. I wanted to pack my bag and get on to the next available bus to head back to Kandy. I would have done it if any buses were going to Kandy at the hour. Because of the mist, no one would leave the town until morning.

A sudden weakness came over me. My knees gave way to my body, and I slipped down, crouching on my bed. Tears I had pushed back for ten years started sliding down my cheeks onto my chest.

12 COMPOSED

Our commute to Kandy didn't begin smoothly. Niranga Aiya looked as if someone hauled him out of his bed when he showed up to pick me up.

"Seat belt!" He barked and put the car into drive. Though I am not accustomed to wearing a seatbelt, I buckled up feeling embarrassed about overlooking it.

Niranga Aiya was agitated or disoriented. I wasn't clear if it was because he was sleep-deprived or he, too, didn't wish to share this long drive with me confined to the small space of the car. *'Guess what? Neither did I choose to be here.'* I muttered to myself. The atmosphere in the car was not pleasant. I became tense and uncomfortable, as if I was sharing a passage with a serial killer.

When Amma announced earlier that I would share a ride with Niranga Aiya, it annoyed me. I contemplated smart ways to pull out of it, arousing no suspicion and could not see of any. If I had come up with an excuse, they would have questioned me. It was logical to share the drive with Niranga aiya, heading to Kandy to run an errand for Aunty Nelum.

In the end, I gave up. I accepted I had to endure a four-hour journey trapped. I coaxed myself to deal with the situation with a positive affirmation: I could handle the drive ahead of us.

Ten years ago, when my world fell apart, I never permitted myself to ponder. When I moved to Kandy, I bottled everything and let it plunge into the depth of my heart, not allowing it to surface. I buried myself in studies and let myself get dazzled by Channaka, not giving my younger self the closure I should have given.

Yesterday, the house was empty and silent except for my teardrops and the sound of my heavy breathing. I said goodbye to a chapter of my life, releasing sixteen-year-old me to shed bitter tears over the first love she thought she had. After a good cry, I realised I was not that girl anymore, not a sixteen-year-old naïve believer. Now I am a strong and mature woman who won't waste any energy on a man who did not desire her. The last thing I was going to do was pine after a man. Even though if that man was Niranga Aiya, the hero of my childhood.

"Do you have any water with you?" Niranga Aiya's gruff voice jolted me back to the moment, making me reach for the water bottle I carried with me in my backpack. I unscrewed the lid, being careful not to brush my hand with his when I handed over the bottle to him. He drank a potion of water before handing over the bottle back to me.

"Thanks." He grumbled, forcing himself to be polite.

"Are you all right, Aiya?"

He frowned at me before responding. I sensed he was debating if to tell me the truth.

"I got a hangover and a splitting headache." He uttered with disgust, as if I was the one to course it.

"And you decide to drive?" If he expected any empathy from me, he did not get it. The best he could have done was to sleep it off- not get behind the wheels on a narrow windy road. The road was challenging, even for experienced drivers, and needed more than usual attention. I wonder how a sleep-deprived, hungover holidaymaker is going to negotiate the hairpin bends on crumbling edges.

"Have you met my mother?" Niranga Aiya took his eyes off the road to glare with annoyance. *'Who are you kidding? When was the last time you did something you didn't want to?'* I bit my lips to keep the child quiet.

"You are a grown-ass guy! You should know better!" The contempt in his eyes suggested he didn't appreciate what I said. *'Why put two lives in danger because he feared his mother?'*

"So much for choosing the lesser of the two evils." I heard him muttering to himself while applying last-minute breaks to give way to a man who ran across the road.

"What?"

"I didn't expect you to bicker. I thought you would pretend to be sleeping until we reached Kandy." Niranga Aiya chuckled. "You have been pretty good at coming up with excuses not to talk to me." I noticed he was striking, even with ruffled hair, a full day of stubble, and crumpled clothes.

He was referring to last night when he came looking for me, and Malli told him I was still sleeping off a headache. At least then, it was true. After all that crying I did in the afternoon, I ended up with a pounding headache. I didn't leave my room to avoid others noticing my puffy eyes.

'I was not pretending. I really had a headache.' I wanted to tell him. Instead, I ordered him to pull over, pointing to a broader stretch of the road. A bit bewildered, Niranga Aiya brought the car to a halt and turned to me, squinting his eyes.

"Get out," I point him at the door. "I will drive." He glared as if I was speaking in a foreign language.

"You can drive?"

'No, I was going to ask that man!" I pointed to a random passerby with frustration. *'Why is he surprised that I can drive?'*

"Thanks, I'll take over after some sleep." Niranga Aiya was relieved and happily changed sides with me. It stunned me when he did it with no further persuasion. Even when he was tired, Saman Aiya didn't allow me to drive. He would swap with Thaththa (yes, with his tremors) or with Malli, although Malli doesn't have a driver's license, but never with me.

"Here, Aiya, take these." I grabbed some Panadol from my backpack and gave it to him with some water once he settled into the passenger seat. He snatched them with no questions, threw them down his throat and flushed them with half of the water I had in the bottle.

"Stop calling me Aiya. My name is Niranga."

Ignoring his command, I adjusted the seat and the mirrors before starting the car. I changed the radio channel to my favourite music station and slightly wound down the driver's side window. The car was reeking with Niranga's aftershave. I wanted to avoid it creeping into every cell in my body.

Niranga had placed my backpack on the window as his pillow and had his head resting on it. His arms were across his chest, and his legs stretched out in front of him; he was already sleeping.

I always enjoy the drive to and from Kandy, as it is one of the best scenic roads in Sri Lanka. My heart typically feels sad each time I leave the colonial town and begin the 1400-meter descent to Kandy. Today, I didn't notice the familiar heaviness I usually carry with me. I assumed it was because I was leaving the claustrophobic unpleasantness I harboured over the last few days.

The hairpin bends were challenging to navigate, with cowboy drivers trying to race up and down the narrow road. I always drive slowly, not because I feared the demanding road, more because I was afraid of some idiots on the road. I also wanted to enjoy the spectacular view. There was something exciting about mastering a steering wheel on the narrow windy highway, changing my mood from heavy and anxious to relaxed and happy.

I relished the cool mountain breeze and the friendly call-outs from young kids running between the main road. They were taking shortcuts to the mountain slope to sell wildflowers and homegrown vegetables to passing vehicles.

Usually, I stop to buy some from two or three kids. Amma always scolded me for doing that, saying the products were not hygienic enough. But I considered it as supporting the local ecosystem and putting some food on their table. I give the flowers and vegetables I buy to my landlady, who enjoys organic produce.

Today I didn't want to stop and disturb Niranga, who was in a deep sleep.

The road was busy, with many vehicles returning to Kandy at the end of the weekend. Occasionally, I had to line up in long queues to give way to commercial vehicles running in low gear. As some parts of the road had been washed away in the recent monsoon rains, I was vigilant and focused on the road, which allowed me to be present with no space for my mind to wander about the past or future. I didn't realise how long I had been driving until Niranga stretched his arms and yawned loudly.

"I am hungry." Niranga declared, reminding me of the little boy I used to know. He would have had us stop at least twice by now to satisfy his urges for snacking when we travelled on the same route as when we were kids. In my opinion, Niranga had an eating disorder when he was young. However, for the Senege parents, it was a healthy appetite, and Aunty Nelum adored little chubby Niranga. Memories made me smile fondly. Glimpsing it, Niranga squinted his eyes.

"There is a place in Pussellalwa town with some facilities and good food." By this time, I was also in need of a toilet break and a stretch of legs. I didn't feel the two hours it took us to get there when I pulled the car into the restaurant's car park.

"Let us go and get something to eat." There was some excitement in his voice when Niranga got out and started walking towards the restaurant. The outside temperature was much colder than I expected, making me dash behind him.

"Hello, miss, only one guest today?" Raju, the resident waiter who knows me from my frequent visits, greeted me with a warm smile.

"Yes, Raju. Bring us two strong ginger teas, short eats and some coconut roti with chilly jam." After placing the order, we both went on our way to freshen up. When I returned to the seating hall, Raju was waiting for a chat.

"Raju, how is Nadan?" I inquired about his seven-year-old son.

"He is doing well, miss and likes his school." Raju bent his head to a side, looking down and muttered respectfully. "He is going to be sad when he finds out you came by today. The boy was here earlier and just left." Raju's voice was loaded with regret and sadness. Little Nadan enjoyed my visits, sharing his details about his school and teachers, trying to impress me with random foreign words he had picked up from tourists stopping over the buy flowers from him.

"I am glad he enjoys it. Hopefully, I will see him next time I come this way."

"Yes, miss, I think my son has some talent and loves learning. I hope…"

Raju paused his chatter, eyeing over my shoulders, and headed to the kitchen after a slight bow of his head in respect. I guessed he was returning to bring our tea, as the food was already on the table. I turned my head and watched Niranga strolling towards me with a bounce on his step. He had washed his face, and his cheeks had turned pink.

"Did you have a shower or what?" I asked, spotting the water droplets stuck on his stubble.

"My god, the water was icy." He shook his head in disbelief.

"There was no hot water!" Niranga's groaning made me laugh out loud.

"Why are you laughing?" He pulled out a handkerchief from his pocket and started wiping his face, his voice full of disapproval.

I raised my eyebrows, mocking him. "Look at you, Mr Australia, expecting hot water taps at a restaurant in a small town!"

He tucked his damp handkerchief back in his pocket and scanned the seating area, and said, "I have to wait until summer to thaw myself now." Then, after a few seconds, he pulled the chair opposite me and plunged in with a dismissal look on his face.

"Oh well, eat up to hibernate." I pushed the tray of food closer to him.

"Aren't you going to eat?" He grabbed a few cutlets from the try onto his plate.

"Nah... I had a big plate of rice before we left. It will do until tomorrow morning."

"Come, eat something." Niranga pushed the food tray across. "It is odd to eat alone."

"I am not hungry. I am going to wait for the tea."

"Do you have a weight complex?" After a few minutes of silence, Niranga stopped chewing and studied me.

"What?"

"You must be so concerned about your image. You hardly eat." Niranga ran his eyes over me with a critical stare. I was disappointed that Niranga's foreign education hadn't abolished some of the bad habits he had picked up growing up.

"I eat to live, not the other way around." I leaned across the table, trying to contain the irritation.

"You look like a teenager." When he addressed me as a kid sister, the pain of disappointment settled in my heart. *'Who is he to dish out his opinions willy-nilly?'* Niranga aggravated my inner child. *'As if I would give a shit about the way he sees me!'*

"Wow, these are so good; try this one." Oblivious to my internal chatter, Niranga placed a cutlet on a side plate and pushed it across to me.

"Excellent choice to stop here." He said between a mouthful and grinned. To shut him off, I pulled the plate towards me. I continued to watch him eat in silence until Raju brought the tea.

"You still eat like the Cookie Monster." I realised I had voiced my thought out loud when Niranga lifted his eyes with surprise. I used to call him 'Cookie Monster' when we were kids. He had a voracious appetite, similar to the Cookie Monster on Sesame Street, the kids' television program we used to watch religiously.

Niranga used to chase after me, saying, *'Me want a cookie,'* imitating how Cookie Monster on the show used to chant, pretending to eat me. He did this a lot when I was not talking to him to get me to give up and give in to him. That was how Niranga started calling me *'Cookie.'* I was his *'Cookie'*, and he was my *'Cookie Monster.'* I loved the way it sounded in his voice, as it made me feel unique and cherished. Niranga's eyes held the earlier smile as if he also remembered those innocent and carefree days we shared.

"You drive well, not like most here. They drive as though Rome is on fire." Niranga uttered in between mouthful. I wanted to tell him, *'Don't eat too fast, you will get indigestion,'* but I didn't.

"Thanks, I had a wonderful teacher."

"Gorky?" I ignored the irritation bubbling in me, having Niranga's reference to Sula as Gorky and nodded my head.

"You enjoy driving," Niranga said, while sipping his tea. I wonder if he had slept at all. How else he would notice my love for driving.

"You are in a much better mood than before." He explained. *'Interesting, the pot calling the kettle black?'* And Niranga saw me rolling my eyes.

"I was sleep-deprived and hungry." He gave me a sheepish smile to justify his earlier foul mood. We continued for a few more minutes in comfortable silence. The tea was refreshing with a strong ginger flavour and just enough sugar to sweeten it. When we finished, Niranga left some money to cover the bill. I wanted to add extra for Nadan, but I had left my purse in the car.

"What's wrong? Didn't I leave enough?" Quick to pick up my hesitation, Niranga eyeballed the money he left on the table.

"Um.... Oh, no, it's just that I always leave some extra tip for his son's school material. Um...... I don't have my wallet with me." I shrug off his concern, deciding to make it up to Raju the next time I stopped over here.

"Here, take mine and give whatever you want." Niranga pulled his wallet from his back pocket and handed it over.

"Are you sure?" I clutched his wallet with unease. "What if I take all of your money?"

"Well then, I would have to think you are not the wise woman you appear to be." I felt a warmth running inside me. I was unsure if it was the tea, or I gave more weight to his compliment than I should have.

"Thanks. I will return it later." I laid a few more notes on the table for Raju.

"No need, I will figure out a way for you to repay me."

Niranga gazed over, showing he already had a few ideas on his mind. My cheeks were getting warmer, noticing his provocative tone and evocative stare.

'Get a grip on yourself, girl' , the adult schooled as I hurried ahead of him towards the car park.

When we returned to the car, I headed to the passenger side when Niranga stopped me.

"Why don't you continue driving if you don't mind?" When Niranga suggested, I turned to him uncertainly. Allowing me to drive when he was asleep differed from willingly choosing to be a rider.

"I have been driving around since I came back. It is time for me to be a tourist and enjoy the view."

Intuitive to my hesitation, he explained. I went to the driver's side and settled in. Maybe he saw the thrill I had sitting behind the wheel, or perhaps he was tired of having to drive all the time; whatever his reason, I was glad I got to continue with the task.

13 ENTRANCED

"So, how do you know Raju's family?"

I shared the history of how I met Raju on one of my many visits to the restaurant where he works. Raju, who was in his fifties, has five children. A few years ago, when things got more challenging, his wife left him for another man. He lives closer to the restaurant, working as a server, and his income is inadequate to run a family.

Raju's eldest son is a 20-year-old young adult who works as a garbage collector. The second one is 17 years old and dropped out of school to work as a farmhand. His third child is a fourteen-year-old boy who works as a domestic helper in a house in Colombo. Raju is barely caring for his two young children, a nine-year-old girl and a seven-year-old Nadan.

When I saw little Nadan selling wildflowers to tourists running between the roads, I wasn't aware he was Raju's son. I always bought flowers from him as he had the cutest smile and was the cheekiest kid amongst the lot. It was a mere coincidence when I came across both of them one evening selling vegetables when I was on tour with some clients.

"Aren't you like the Pied Piper? Kids following you around wherever you go." I draw my eyes off the road to peer at Niranga, not grasping his comment. "I mean, with your travel around the island, you must support kids all over the country!" Niranga chuckled and continued on explaining.

"You are delusional." I jeered, ridiculing his remark. "Do you think I am a bloody millionaire?"

"Are you telling me Devan's kids and Nadan are the only kids you care?" Niranga turned in his seat to face me, finding a comfortable posture as if he was ready for a long-lasting debate.

"I wouldn't say I am supporting any of them. I don't have the means to do that."

"Well, you sure seem to do a lot more than the average." With a reflective glare, Niranga dismissed my comment.

"I wish I could do more, at least support them with their education." It troubled me when I lay eyes on children who suffer from poverty, not having the right to basic needs. But if Niranga caught the pain in my voice, he didn't show it.

"Do you like children?"

"I do." I felt the warmth spreading through me, recalling the radiant smiles of kids I have encountered in the past.

"Planning on having any?" I glanced at Niranga with irritation, not appreciating the directness of his question.

"Why do you look annoyed?" Niranga chuckled. "Is that too sensitive to ask?"

"It is too personal." I faced the road to focus on the big passenger bus descending the mountain at a snail's pace.

"I am honouring the Sri Lankan culture." Niranga was mocking me. I caught the subtle laughter in his voice.

"And I thought you went to Australia to learn a refined way to interact with people!" I said while trying to push away the irritation bubbling up. He is not the first or the last to ask that question. I live in a country full of intruding strangers who disregard personal boundaries as part of its culture; at least Niranga is someone I grew up with.

"They say when in Rome do what the Romans do." He winked, disregarding my displeasure. "Anyway, why beat around the bush and waste time asking questions about things I already know." Niranga boldly declared with a condescending voice. I pondered what information Niranga assumes he has on me and rolled my eyes.

"I got the basics covered: who you are, your family, your education, job and marital status." Niranga saw me and started counting his fingers, daring me to contradict him. When a silence stretched between us, I realised Niranga was waiting for my response to his earlier question.

I gazed outside the window, trying to gather my thoughts. Do I want kids? How many? Is it strange for a girl to be twenty-six and not be well-versed in what she wanted with marriage or children?

"Um...... Maybe... Don't know....... Not given much attention to it," I told him the truth.

"What if you can't have any?"

'What the fuck?' The directness of his question shook me. "It wouldn't be the end of the world." I sneered.

"Would you consider adopting?" This conversation was getting weird by the minute.

"If I desperately want to have a kid on my family tree, I might."

"You don't sound confident. " Niranga was not ready to end his line of questioning.

"I am not sure if I possess the same qualities Amma and Thaththa have to treat every child the same way."

"What do you mean?"

"Majority of us still haven't learnt that a child doesn't have to be yours to love one."

"Why do you say that? Your family wasn't like that. I don't think anyone would know Uncle Rajitha isn't your father or Manoj isn't your biological brother unless you tell them."

"Yep, we were different. I admire our family, all in one melting pot… then again, our circumstances were unique. We didn't have any extended family or family friends who poisoned the water." I took my eyes off the road to have a quick look at Niranga's face that watching me with a thoughtful stare.

"But I've seen a lot of families where adopted child or the kid from the first or second marriage get ill-treated by the mother, father, siblings or relatives often. Some things I have seen are so immoral. It makes me wonder if some of these people are even human." Niranga was nodding his head, listening with interest. So I continued.

"Your experience must be different living in a western country where kids from different marriages live amicably. Or at least those countries got child protection services that are active and work for kids. We are not there yet."

"You have a point there… surely, not all are bad."

I didn't tell Niranga some ideas are woven into the fabric of a society that may take aeons to change, and I believe adoption is one of those concepts that would take its time to grow.

"What if you were living in a foreign country? Would you adopt?"

"Where are you going with these questions, Niranga? What exactly do you want to know?" He eyed me oddly. It could be because it was the first time I called him by his name without calling him Aiya. Something shifted between us, and I couldn't put my finger to identify what it was.

"No reason."

"Okay, so tell me, what would you do? Would you adopt?" I asked. He smiled, noting he was under the spotlight.

I learned Niranga wanted a large family. He missed not having any siblings. Some days, he envied Akka, Malli, and me for having each other to support, love, and even have occasional fights. Children were important to him, and if he didn't have any, he would adopt, as Amma and Thaththa had been his role models. He said he wanted to have more than one kid as he didn't want his child to grow up as a lonely only child. I never considered him a lonely child. He was always with us as part of our family. Perhaps he experienced loneliness when he moved to Sydney. It must have been hard to be on his own in a big city.

I wanted to reach across and squeeze his hand to let him know I was there for him, and he was not alone. *'That isn't true, is it?'* I asked myself. We haven't spoken for years, and even today, I wouldn't be in this car having this conversation if Amma didn't corner me.

"How long have you been friends with Devan's family?" I gathered Niranga wanted to change the subject.

"Jeevani, since our OL classes, and Devan after they became a couple."

"You were not a supporter of their marriage." I looked at him with surprise, and Niranga continued to talk. "Devan talks a bit when he is nervous. The other day he got uneasy when he realised we were neighbours." It reminded me of how intuitive Niranga has always been.

"It is so nice of you to help them. Jeevani and Devan need a lucky break. I hope this will be it." Niranga glanced at me with a bit of amusement.

"Maybe I have an ulterior motive."

That shocked me. I was not sure if Niranga was sharing his true intentions or Jeevani has shared our inside jokes. *'Can't be Jeevani, she wouldn't. Could it be Akka?'* I pondered.

"Don't worry, Meera isn't my type. She is very submissive. My preference is someone with a fighting spirit." Niranga was enjoying my discomfort when he gave me a sarcastic smile.

"Why the hell does everyone have to tell you everything?" I was irritated and embarrassed at the same time. I should not have doubted Niranga's motives.

"Because I am a nice guy. You will know if you just get to know me." Niranga smiled, making his eyes glitter. He had always been a good person who constantly watched out for others, even when he was a kid. I didn't have to have to learn it. I just had to remind myself it was not Niranga who hurt me. It was I who dragged myself through the pain.

"So, tell me, what keeps you awake at night?" Perhaps, because of the change in my mood, Niranga turned to me with an inviting grin. I pulled my eyes off the road and glanced at him.

"I thought we were trying to get to know each other!" Picking up my hesitation, Niranga chuckled. *'He is delusional! As if I am going to tell him any of that!'* Both the adult and child in me agreed unanimously.

"Too soon, Niranga. It is too intimate." I explained when he turned to me with dilated pupils. "We are not that close for me to share my dreams with you." I mocked his enthusiasm.

"Yet!" Niranga stressed in his usual stubborn way, making me smile. I focused my attention back on the road, finding solace in the rolling hills full of lush green tea bushes and sweeping sunrays.

We settled into a comfortable conversation zigzagged between us, what we do and what we believe in. It felt strange to share a part of my life with him. When we were climbing trees and running in the pinewood forest, searching for each other, I never imagined we would end up being strangers in the years that passed.

"So, how long are you going to be in Sri Lanka?"

"A few more months."

"Wow, how come? I thought you only get around four weeks of paid leave."

"Yes, that is the standard. I am taking some extra time off."

"Are you planning to spend the entire time in Nuwara Eliya? Wouldn't you get bored? There isn't anything much in the town. Most of your friends must be in Colombo or overseas?" I knew the questions came from the fear of facing him again the next time I visit home. I wasn't keen on being confined to my room or taking walks around Lake Gregory when it was icy cold in the evenings.

"To be honest, it doesn't feel like I am not on holiday." He sounded tired. "I have been working most of the days. I am trying to revamp Thaththa's business. Thaththa needs something to work on after I leave so he doesn't get into a rut now that he has retired."

I need no explanation. Since my parents retired, I have witnessed the lack of purpose eroding the spark in Amma and Thaththa. Amma at least tries to keep herself occupied with her plant nursery, but I haven't seen Thaththa engaging in anything except reading the daily newspaper.

"I know what you mean. Since Amma and Thaththa retired, they have been rapidly ageing. So they need something to give them a meaning in life."

"Exactly. I am making some changes in Thaththa's business, so it would be easy to manage it. Creating employment and helping a few along the way will keep him happy and give him a purpose than visiting that damn golf course each day."

"What you are doing is great, Niranga. I wish Thaththa can do something like that." A lump formed in my throat, remembering the struggle my parents were having.

"I forgot about it. Uncle was an accountant, wasn't he?"

"Yes, he was." I gaze across as Niranga pondered. *'Should I ask his help to find Thaththa a job?'*

"I am looking for an accountant. Do you think Uncle would mind doing some part-time work?"

"Mind? He would love it." I tried to hide my excitement, but I wanted to hug Niranga. If I were not behind the wheel, I would have done just that. What a great opportunity it would be for Thaththa to work again. "Honestly, Niranga, that would do good for Thaththa."

"Excellent, I will talk to Uncle when I get back home. It would be great for Thaththa to have Uncle working with him."

"So, when do you return to Sydney?" I asked.

"Not for a while; I am taking a gap year."

"What is a gap year?"

"It's time one takes to discover their intention in life... normally some take it before going to university... I worked my arse off for the last ten years... so I am taking a gap year now" I wish I was sitting in front of Niranga to read his expression as it was hard to peek sideways while I was trying to navigate hairpin bends. I wanted to pick up the emotions on his face to understand his deeper sentiments.

"What inspired you to take one?" When he didn't answer me straight away, I thought he didn't want to, or he had not heard me. After a bit of silence, he turned to me with a thoughtful look on his face.

"Over there, when you are an immigrant, you work harder to make it. Nothing is given freely. You survive by proving yourself repeatedly. That is what I did from the day I arrived in Sydney. I worked hard, became the best, if not great, in my field. Now I can comfortably say I made it!" There weren't any traces of arrogance or overconfidence in his voice. Niranga was sharing his journey with me, being open and honest.

As he paused to collect his thoughts, I let the silence stretch between us, processing what I just heard, trying to gauge how rewarding it would be to be content knowing you have achieved your life goals. I felt a subtle sadness pressing on me, questioning when that day would come for me.

"Have you ever sensed a loneliness or emptiness even when you are amongst people?" When Niranga spoke again, he appeared pensive. I knew straight away he was reflecting on some of his private thoughts.

"How about pangs of hunger even after your belly is full of food? The notion of poverty when your bank account has enough to live comfortably? That suggestive thought comes out of nowhere, making you realise that something is missing even when you have everything?" His profound insights enchanted me.

"I am in search of that thing that would make me whole."

Since the day I seized responsibility for my way of life, I have been on a high-speed passenger bus that travels from one destination to another. I was too busy chasing my life goals to sweat on what I hadn't achieved, to stop and ponder on erudite observations about life. Yet strangely, I could understand him; still, I couldn't come up with a single thing I thought was missing in his life.

"Do you believe being in Sri Lanka will help you with your quest?"

"Not sure…… I will not spend my entire time here. As soon as I settle the business, I am heading back. I haven't decided how long I am going to stay. I might hang around until the Europe trip I have planned with two friends."

I remember Uncle Sarath commenting about an upcoming Europe trip, and I was keen to find out details. But my inner child was too quick to pipe in.

"Perhaps what you are missing is a woman by your side" Both Niranga and the adult in me agreed such a comment was beneath their expectations. Niranga pursed his lips showing his dislike.

"Why does everyone think having a woman solves all my problems?" He alluded to his disappointment in receiving a similar response to his dilemma.

"Maybe they all want to share what had worked for them!"

"So, is Gorky your solution? Do you feel whole?" Niranga peered with dilated eyes.

'Oh no, you are not going down that rabbit hole.' The adult warned me to stay away from this line of conversations. I knew the consequences of having an in-depth discussion of my happiness would not stack up well for me.

"Hey, I am not the one complaining."

"Fair enough.... You are lucky to find happiness at such a young age." There was sadness in his voice that made me want to reach out and squeeze his hand to give him some comfort.

"I could be chasing a ghost... because even when I had the perfect woman by my side, I still had that niggly notion that something was missing." I watched my mind clutching on to *'had,'* and inquisitive if it means Niranga is single now. *'Why do you care?'* the grown-up was curious.

"I guess I am trying to find me or that thing that makes me stop searching." I realised Niranga had just shared some of his intimate thoughts, as if he was opening up to one of his closest friends. The idea of us being friends again entranced me as if I was under a magical spell, making fireworks in my heart.

We talked more in between listening to songs playing on the radio and took turns to increase the volume when one of our favourite songs came up. Both of us effortlessly fell into our childhood habits and mocked each other for song choices when the other didn't appreciate it and made fun of the radio presenters and their comments. Unintentionally, we had our own mini-debate about what they were broadcasting on air. We talked about his work, his life in Sydney and his friends, places he has travelled (which fascinated me the most) and places he is planning to visit (which made me full of envy). I got a glimpse of the man he has become.

It took us over four hours to cover the 100km journey from Nuwara Eliya to Kandy. We were not in a rush. I drove slowly, maybe because I wanted to avoid making silly driving mistakes, or perhaps I had a secret desire to prolong my time with Niranga.

By the time we got to Peradeniya, my coldness toward him had faded away in parallel to the warm breeze that grazed my cheeks as we descended from the mountain.

"Do you still live with your Loku Amma?"

"No, she migrated to Canada. Once her son, Waruna Aiya, got married and had kids, she joined him. I have a little annexe."

"You live alone or sharing it?"

"I used to share it. My friend got married two months ago and moved out. I am keeping it. When Malli starts university next year, he can stay with me."

"Isn't that putting too much pressure on Manoj?" Niranga sounded disappointed.

"Malli doesn't know I am holding on to the annexe because of him." I haven't shared my plans with anyone except Reshani and Sula. I have kept that hidden from Amma and Thaththa, not wanting them to worry about the extra expenses. It was interesting how easily I parted with this piece of information with Niranga without a second thought.

"Do you think he will go to a local university?"

"Why wouldn't he?" I sensed the panic building inside me.

"Oh, I am just curious. Manoj is pretty advanced for his age. I thought the logical choice would be for him to attend a foreign university to specialise in IT." I could feel the swelling of my heart and the smile that beamed across my face. I have always believed Malli was a gifted kid, way smarter than his age group. Still, it was great to receive validation from an equally talented person.

"I am hoping he will get admission to Peradeniya University, although I hear Moratuwa University offers more advanced courses. It all depends on him getting through his A-level exam and then his first-year performance at the university. Malli is super talented, so I am pretty sure he will get through. I wish I could have him come to Kandy for his AL studies. The tutors in Kandy are far better." I was rambling to hide my discomfort. I wanted to keep the overseas study option off-topic. Though it could be the best for Malli, I didn't like to acknowledge we could not afford such luxury.

"You are heavily involved in Manoj's stuff, aren't you?" Niranga sounded like he was not pleased about it.

"That's what big sisters do, be a pain in the bum."

"Why didn't he come to Kandy for his AL studies?" I glance outside to gather my thoughts. I was contemplating what to share. Maybe Niranga has already picked that underneath our facade of an upper-class family, we are a family of counting rupees for our survival.

"We couldn't afford the additional expenses, with Thaththa and Amma being retired and with Akka's wedding. It was too costly to have Malli study in Kandy. Amma and Thaththa didn't want me to chip in as I only started working full time." Although I saw thoughtfulness on his face, I was not sure if Niranga understood the gravity of weighing the monetary value of decisions. Having been born to a wealthy family, he wouldn't have a clue about our daily struggles.

I kept on driving until we came to my place. When I parked the car in front of my annexe, I invited Niranga in to have a cup of tea.

"Are you sure?" Niranga sounded worried.

"Yes, of course, I am not that clumsy. I wouldn't burn myself again." I reassured him, assuming his concern came from the hot water scalding incident.

"Oh, not that. I thought it wouldn't be nice to come inside as you live alone." His sensitiveness touched me, as it was a kind of him to consider our backward culture and its prerequisites.

My landlady suspects am a high-end call girl. One more man visiting me after dusk wouldn't make any difference to my already tarnished reputation. I didn't dare tell Niranga this, as I didn't want to shock him.

"If you would like to have some tea, you can come in. We are a bit more modern in this part of the country." I said, as if it did not bother me either way, yet I didn't want Niranga to leave. I was enjoying his company, and I was grasping for ways to delay his departure. Niranga needed no more reassurance. He undid the seatbelt and jumped out of the car before me.

My annexe was a compact unit with a bit of sitting area, kitchenette, two bedrooms and a shared bathroom. The sitting area only had a small sofa, a bookshelf, and a coffee table. Thank god, I have left the place in a clean state. When we walked inside the house, it was so warm after being closed off for a week. I switched on the lights and opened the window to let some fresh air flow through the room.

"Have a seat. I will make some tea." I pointed to the sofa and headed to the kitchen to drop off the food containers Amma gave me before I left. It's hard for me to say no when Amma gets up so early in the morning to make my favourite curries to take back with me, assuming I can't cook for myself. I don't understand why she insists I bring the containers back when they are not containers at all but are reused ice cream tubs. As I stuck them in the tiny fridge in the corner, I knew I would get into trouble again for not taking the empties back with me.

"This is neat. How long have you been living here?" Niranga had followed me into the kitchen and was curiously scanning the place.

"After I became a lecturer in the university.... Um... Almost three years now."

"Is it close by to your work?"

"Yes, it is about a 10-minute walk to university and a 20-minute drive to Kandy town. I can shorten the journey when going home. Most of the time, I catch the bus from Peradeniya town." Niranga was leaning on the counter next to me and was watching my face while I was talking. I felt claustrophobic standing so close to him.

"Let me prepare that tea." I moved to the sink to fill up the kettle with some water.

"I will stay for tea on one condition." When Niranga stopped me, I stared, doubting what he had planned.

"You go and have a shower first. I am going to duck outside and make a phone call to a friend. I saw a communication centre on the way here."

When he left without waiting for my response, I knew it was to give me privacy and time to have a shower. I recalled telling him nothing gets me off the weariness of a long journey, like a cold shower and a warm cup of ginger tea.

★★★

Niranga returned carrying two bags and headed straight to the kitchen.

"What is all this?" I followed him with curiosity.

"I was starving, so I stopped at the café you pointed out on our way here and bought some short eats."

"Oh, you went to Benthota restaurant? My god, how can you be starving? You finished the entire tray of food only a few hours ago?" His ability to eat and keep his shape genuinely amazed me.

"That was an appetiser, and for your information, I don't have an eating disorder."

"Neither do I." I spattered with annoyance, not bothering to hide my anger.

"So, prove it and eat with me, get some plates out."

He was bossy and demanding. I got us some plates, and we carried the food and tea to the coffee table in the sitting area. My annexe was not big enough to have a dining table, so I did all the eating at the coffee table. Niranga didn't have any problem sitting on the floor to have the meal. We sat cross-legged across from each other; the food and fruits he brought spread on the table with two cups of tea. I was hungry after the long drive and the refreshing shower, so we began eating.

The room was no longer warm, with fresh air circulating through the open window. We ate in comfortable silence, with the hum of busy mosquitos and the sounds of passing vehicles keeping us company.

"Oh, I forgot to ask you, do you have a place to stay tonight?" As it was getting darker, I was curious where Niranga was going to spend the night.

"Why? Are you going to offer me to stay?" I felt uncomfortable when Niranga stared at me over the rim of the cup he was holding.

"If you needed a place to stay, I have a spare room." I was making polite conversation. Offering a person outside the city a place to stay for the night was something that came naturally to me, given most of my friends, Sula's friends and my family treat my annexe as an Amballama, a communal house.

"Do you want to give a heart attack to your landlady?" Niranga inquired with a mischievous glitter in his eyes.

"Nah, after two years of putting up with me, she got a strong heart. She already suspects I am a high-end call girl. Having you stay over wouldn't even make a dent in her mind." I didn't realise I had said that out loud until Niranga choked on his tea. He had tea dripping all over his chin and on his t-shirt. I rushed across and patted his back to ease the choking, feeling terrible for speaking out loud.

"Are you okay?"

"Yes, thanks." He dragged a handkerchief out of his pocket and wiped his face and chest to clean himself.

"You don't mind about your reputation?" When we settled back, Niranga regarded me with some concern. The disappointment I heard in his voice made me feel sad. His question reminded me of the struggle I went through to fight the rumours spread through the university when I became a part-time tour guide. Each time I came out of a hotel with a tourist, I got treated as if I had slept with a guest. Initially, I fought back, struggling with anxiety, anger, bitterness, and self-pity. I tried to explain myself to others, aiming for their approval. Then, one day, Reshani confronted me.

"Why do you need others' approval? They are not the ones who are going to walk in your shoes. So what if they say you sleep around? They are jealous that it's not them on top of you, girl. The only person you need to be honest with is yourself."

I still remember the warmness of the day and the mechanical hum of the table fan trying its best to cool down Reshani's living room. I was in tears, trying to contain my anger more than the pain I had in my heart. Reshani was holding on to my hands tightly when she glared at me. "By the way, if you want to sleep around, it is your business. I would advise you to take precautions. Be careful. I may not like it, but we will still be friends." We both cried when I hugged her.

It took me many more months to stop crying myself to sleep with self-pity. And more years to understand I can't control how others regard me and judged me as they do it with their own experience and expectation. People have a habit of projecting their own weaknesses and fears onto others. After understanding this, I learned to stop living my life in fear of others' judgement.

It allowed me to focus on what I wanted to do with the rest of my life, an opportunity for self-reflection and transformation. It shaped me into who I am today. I was not sure if I wanted to share my journey with Niranga. There was no point in sharing the pain I endured.

I was worried about how it would affect my family. The constant struggled I had for years, choosing the path I love or giving up because of the fear of words like daggers that plunge into the depth of my heart, damaging my confidence. Running against the grain of the culture and my parents' expectations of me required a lot of courage. My eyes got teary with memories.

"A long time ago, I chose not to let my happiness rest on those who hardly know me. Unfortunately, people are too quick to judge you without understanding your journey."

If Niranga saw the tears in my eyes or heard the sadness in my voice, he said nothing. Instead, he stretched his hands and took mine. I have gathered Niranga is a touchy person, so I didn't pull away when he squeezed my fingers with empathy. The old familiar comfort of being protected by his firm, broad hands came rushing into my mind from the days of roaming in the pinewood, fearing Baba Yaga, the flying witch.

"It must have been so hard."

"Actually, I wouldn't have been able to cope if it was not for Reshani, my soul sister," I said.

"If it means anything at all, I am so proud of you." Niranga leaned forward and peered into my eyes.

"I know I am just getting to know you and have only seen a glimpse of the real you. But, from what I have seen, I think you are pretty amazing." He squeezed my hand again and smiled. I was pleased and uncomfortable at the same time. I withdrew my hand and picked up my empty tea mug, pretending I was drinking, not paying much attention to the warm glow spreading through me.

"How would Gorky take it if I stay over?"

"It has nothing to do with Sula."

"I would be deeply disturbed having a good-looking man like me spending the night with my girlfriend." Though Niranga was attempting to joke, his voice was high pitched. I could sense a bit of uneasiness underneath his smile. He hasn't realised; when he pretends to smile, it doesn't reach his eyes.

I studied his face, debating if I should tell him Sula is way more handsome than he is, and I wouldn't classify taking up a spare bedroom as spending a night with a man. I pondered this for a few seconds before I responded.

"Either you have trust issues, or your girlfriend can't be trusted."

"Ouch, that hurts." He said with an intense glare, pulling me into the dark depth of his brown eyes.

"Come on. It is almost nine, and you better leave now. I have an early morning class tomorrow." I got up from where we sat, wanting to get away from the uncomfortable tension around us.

"Yes, I should go. Let us get this cleaned up." Taking the cue, Niranga got up from where he was sitting and helped carry the empty plates back to the kitchen. Instead of stacking them in the sink, he started washing them.

"Just leave them; I will wash them later." It felt odd watching him dominate the kitchen space with his formidable presence.

"That's okay. Why don't you put those leftovers away? I will take care of this." It was as if he was searching for a reason to stay longer, and I didn't mind it at all. I enjoyed making secret glances at him while I put away the leftover food and fruit he bought. I watched him efficiently washing and drying the plates and cups. "Your girlfriend has trained you well." I teased him, hoping he would reveal any love interest he had. *'Why would you even care?'* The wise one questioned. I watched him, considering his response, before he turned to me and smiled.

"I had a part-time job as a kitchen hand in a restaurant when I was in uni." He said nonchalantly. He had least bit care on admitting doing domestic work that was left for the servants to. They dared not let him attempt such chores in Sri Lanka because that would be against the cultural norms in a society where males are favoured and dare not step into the kitchen. *'So this privileged boy has experienced a hard day's work.'* Instead of mocking him, I told him the truth.

"I never thought you would work in a place like that."

"Things are costly there, and I could not expect my parents to finance my lifestyle. I went to Australia to learn from them, so I learned to be independent and earn my own way." He sounded proud of what he had achieved. And I understood what he meant.

"Right, I better go now," Niranga said, rubbing his palms together

We both moved to the living area and lingered around the door. Niranga didn't leave, and I said nothing, as it was already awkward. Noting the photo collection taken at various times in my life that was precious to me on the bookshelf, Niranga crossed over to the other side of the room. I stood there watching him, taking each photo frame for a close-up view: me standing in front of the Maligawa after my first solo guide tour, as the bride's maid at Reshine's wedding, one with Jeevani and Devan, with Sula in front of our tour agency, one at Akka's wedding.

He picked the one that was most important to me last. It was our family photo on my graduation day. I was in a white Kandyan saree, and my hair pulled back in a ponytail. All of my family was around me with beaming, proud smiles. It was a victorious day for all of us, and the photographer has done an excellent job capturing it.

"This is a beautiful photo. It must have been a wonderful day."

"It was."

"It looks like you had a bit of flesh around your bones." If he said that to irritate me, it didn't work.

"I think the entire batch put on a kilo or two after the finals." I laughed off his remark and crossed the room to open the front door, pretending I wanted him gone. He walked past me, picking up the clue, and before he stepped out, he turned back with hesitation.

"Hey, will you be free to join us on a trip? A bunch of us are going around Sri Lanka. Perhaps you can be our guide?"

He suggested the days when they were on tour. When I checked my diary, my schedule was full; I had lectures at the university and tours I had to lead. As the hope on his face quickly got replaced with disappointment, I rechecked my calendar to find out if there was a way for me to accompany them. I wanted to do it, not because of the discontent I saw on his face, but because of the plunging discomfort I felt in my heart. There was this bubbling desire to spend more time with Niranga, the need for this evening not to be the last time I saw him.

"I can join you for one day on your Sigiriya trip. But it has to be from Kandy. After Sigiriya, I have a trip to Galle coming up on next day, so I have to return that evening."

"Could you?" Niranga was pleased as hope returned to his face; his eyes got brighter, and his smile wider.

"My Friday is free, so we can visit Sigiriya on Friday morning. However, that means you will have to come to Kandy on Thursday night."

"That is not a problem. I can rally the troop to do that. So let us lock it in." We agreed on the date and time to meet in a week.

"Okay, I will get going now. Thanks for having me. Catch up with you in a week."

We both stood there in awkward silence. I was waiting for him to hug me - I wanted to press my cheek against his and feel the warmth of his skin on mine. *'Get a grip, woman. What sort of Bollywood movie are you trying to act out?'* The wise one cracked.

A few seconds later, Niranga clumsily stretched his hand and ruffled my hair as if he had changed his mind midway from hugging me.

"Goodnight, Cookie." He left in a hurry without waiting for a response while I stood there until the sound of his car engine faded away into the night.

The annexe was empty when I walked back to my room. I went to bed with a nagging feeling inside me; I was missing something. Then, moments before my eyes caved into sleep; it dawned on me: I missed Niranga.

14 DESPERATE

"Oh, how I missed you!" I hugged Reshani, holding on to her longer, filling my lungs with her gardenia scented talcum powder scent.

"Why didn't Sula keep you entertained?" Reshani laughed off and closed the front door. It was Wednesday morning, and I didn't have a teaching class in the morning. I visited Reshani as she returned from her holiday on Sunday and was not planning to work until Monday. Reshani works in the same faculty as me, but she teaches literature.

"I haven't seen Sula in a week now. He is in Vilpatthuthu National Park with this big group. They are going around the national park for wildlife photography. I went home instead."

"How come you missed it? Isn't that your thing?"

"I had to go home before I got into trouble for not visiting for three months. And I couldn't take time off from uni. If I missed another lecture, the Dean would kick me out." I barely manage my conflicting priorities, but somehow get away from a lot of disciplinary action from the head of the department. If it was not for the high standard of assignments, I set up for students and the practical skills they develop completing those, the faculty head would have had the grounds to end my employment due to my disgraceful attendance record.

"Tell me all about it, from start to finish. Leave nothing out." I invited Reshani to talk about her holiday, her experiences travelling across France, Italy, and Greece: my dream destinations. I settled on her sofa, ready to absorb every word and expression Reshani would share about their Europe trip.

"Hey, thank you for planning the entire trip. Ravidu shouldn't have got you to plan it." Reshani complained. Ravidu wanted to surprise her for their anniversary, so we planned the trip in secrecy. Knowing the places on Reshani's bucket list, it was easy to work on the itinerary.

"Why are you annoyed with Ravidu? He has been an awesome husband!"

"Stop taking his side. What he did was cruel! They were your dream destinations too, Saku. It wouldn't have been nice to plan a trip for someone else when you are dying to visit those places yourself." Reshani mentioned with a sense of genuine sadness.

"You are silly, woman. Do you think a bank teller breaks down each time they come across a fat bank balance on a customer account? I work as a tour planner; I can't afford to get sentimental every time I have to plan a trip to one of my dream destinations!" I shrugged off her comment, changing the subject.

"When do I get to see the photos? ". There was no point in dwelling on things you can't do much about it. I always try to mind the gap between what my life is and what I dream it to be.

"Ravidu has dropped the negatives off yesterday. We will get them back next week."

"Is Ravidu back at work?"

"Yes, he started on Monday. I don't know how he does it with jetlag. I am still struggling a bit."

"Everyone reacts to it differently! Going to Nuwara Eliya gives me jetlag and makes me want to sleep in."

"You will find any reason to sleep in, you lazybones." Reshani shoved my shoulder, mocking my sleeping habits.

"So, tell me about you, anything interesting happened while I was away?"

***

"Aunty must have her menopause, or she could be bipolar to treat you like that," Reshani said with a displeasing tone after listening to my venting in the last half an hour.

"I don't know. Sometimes I think Amma becomes spiteful as she ages. She was very mean to me last week with no reason."

We were in Reshani's kitchen preparing lunch. I finished chopping the vegetables for the curry Reshani was planning on cooking and washed my hands. I watched the corners of her mouth drawn down in response to the defeat she heard in my voice.

"Akka isn't aware of anything?" Reshani turned to me with concern in her eyes.

"She was only interested in Niranga. Anyway, even if she knew everything, she wouldn't share it unless she wanted to." I felt a sadness gripping my heart, accepting that Akka and I would never be close to each other like I am with

Reshani and Jeevani. I was closer to Malli than to Akka, and our relationship was confined to mere siblings.

"Niranga sounds like a nice guy." Observing the tears ebbing into my eyes, Reshani was quick to change the subject.

"He is," I admitted. "One of the few good guys I have met, and I am not just saying that because he is helping Jeevani."

"How come you didn't tell me any of this before?" Reshani's voice was heavy with much more than disappointment.

"When I came to Kandy, all I wanted to do was forget about Niranga. I was angry and hurt. And I was with Channaka, so I didn't want to talk about Niranga. Plus, I was kind of looking for a new start."

"But you were comparing all the guys to him!"

"What do you mean?" I asked, while slumping on the nearby kitchen chair.

"You have always been so critical of guys, too quick to find fault, being a typical *praying mantis* . I was always curious why no one was good enough for you."

"What are you talking about? I love Sula and Ravidu." I asked, letting her passive-aggressive reference to *praying mantis* passed without latching onto it.

"Yes, we all know why you feel safe around those two!" Reshani said.

"I wouldn't have survived the first few years of Nuwara Eliya without Niranga's friendship. Niranga was not only my best friend; he was also my big brother who always protected me."

I tried to conjure my reflections of young Niranga, that chubby little boy with laughing eyes and a whiff of the strawberry flavoured bubble gum smell. It annoyed me that a desirable, formidable-looking man with the scent of pinewood and mint mixed aftershave had replaced those memories.

"Nice way to appreciate him by being a total bitch to him!"

Reshani had a point. I have been ungrateful. Niranga's small acts of kindness not only made a massive difference in my life but altered the lives of Amma, Thaththa and even Malli. In the last ten years, I have been self-centred, focusing only on my sentiments.

There was never a rule that said Niranga only belonged to me. Maybe I have been too hard on him, punishing him for a thing he didn't do. It was not his fault that my feelings for him crept outside the friendship. Niranga never gave me any sign that he ever considered me to be more than a good friend.

"If I knew all this before, I would have put some sense into your head. I can't understand why you were so pissy about something that happened ten years ago?" Reshani stopped chopping onions, quenching her eyebrows, and frowned. I avoided her eyes because I was not only ashamed but also disappointed in myself.

"I am glad you let go of the past. Whatever happened isn't relevant to anyone now...." I sat there and didn't respond to Reshani's comment as I grappled with the new revelation. As if she could sense the space I needed to mull over my selfish behaviour, Reshani continued cooking, leaving me to my thoughts.

"I don't think you were in love with him, Saku." After a long stretch of silence, Reshani addressed me with a solemn voice.

"If it wasn't loving, why did it hurt me so much?" The despair I felt ten years ago was still raw in my heart. I stared at Reshani as if she could demystify it for me.

"How can there be love when you have so much anger?" Reshani's eyes were filled with empathy; I stared at her, feeling small and weak.

"My take is that you have been in love to be in love, or maybe it was a misguided obsession." When I didn't respond, Reshani continued to talk. "I think it was your ego that got bruised when Niranga didn't pick you. Admit it; you always have this *'standing on a podium above Akka'* thing going on." Reshani stopped stirring the curry to air quote *'stand on a podium above Akka.'* The challenge she had in her eyes was so strong, I glanced away quickly.

"You couldn't accept it when you assumed he picked her. Do you believe you would have got so worked up if Niranga took a random girl to that stream or had an affair with someone you didn't know?" I stared at Reshani, speechless, as I never considered it.

"I thought I loved him for years, and then I hated him." The sorrow and defeat in my voice saddened me. I felt the burning sensation in my eyes when I tried to hide the tears welling up.

"For a person who harps on simplicity, you sure have outdone yourself, haven't you?" Reshani laughed.

"I was not planning to have any connection with Niranga after Saturday. But that all changed. It felt as if we were picking up things from before the incident at the stream, which was the reason I left Nuwara Eliya."

"Enlighten me," Reshani said.

"I could talk to him. I could laugh with him."

"That is good. But are you sure you have let go of the past? There is not a trace of resentment in the back of your mind?"

"I don't know." Reshani raised her eyebrows, picking up the uncertainty in my voice.

"Maybe I do. I can't stop questioning if Akka and Niranga are both lying to me." I voiced the question that was turning in my head in the last few days.

"What purpose would that serve either of them? Even if they lied, does it matter now, Saku?" I felt confused, and Reshani saw that on my face. "Does it matter now if they had something going on between them ten years ago? Maybe they both are not proud of it." Reshani stopped her cooking and eyeballed me. "They are not with each other anymore. Akka is married, Niranga seems to be over whatever he had with Akka, and you have not been truthful to them either." Reshani was right. Who was I to throw stones at them from a glasshouse?

"I never thought of it that way," I told Reshani the truth. Now that I have immersed myself in the past, I have to re-evaluate the situation in today's context to determine what kind of relationship I want to have with him. Do I let him be the neighbour I hate because of something that happened ten years ago, which does not matter today, or do I salvage my childhood best friend and redefine our friendship as two grown adults? I sat there grappling with Reshani's point of view and my inner thoughts, trying to decide.

"Does Sula know?" Reshani broke the silence, handing me a glass of juice she had just prepared.

"No, I didn't have time to talk to him yet."

"You are going to tell him." Reshani made a statement, giving me a stern glare. If I were a child, her gaze would have made me pee in my pants.

"When he gets back," I assured Reshani. Keeping things from Sula was not an option; it may not be a tale he would want to listen to, but I had to share.

"He will be hurt."

"He shouldn't. It is in my past." I had to be very careful about what I shared with Sula. I didn't want to damage our relationship because of my feelings for Niranga. Unlike Sula, Niranga will leave in a few weeks or months, and I don't want to end up bearing the loss of not one but two important people in my life.

"So, you are excited about the Sigiriya trip?" I was glad when Reshani changed the subject, as I was not too fond of the heaviness that started creeping in me.

"I am, more than I should be," I admitted.

"It is good to have you excited, Saku."

"Aney, yes. It would be great to show Sigiriya to Niranga and show off some of my skills as a guide. He will see how great I am at my job."

"It is good to see you alive."

"What do you mean, I am alive? Was I dead before?"

"Admit it. You don't have any passion outside of your work. You float between uni and touring. The only time I saw you beaming like this was when you talked about doing your PhD in Greece, even that you have placed on the back burner to support Manoj."

While Reshani was finishing up in the kitchen, I recalled some conversations I had with Jeevani. She always teases me for leading a mediocre life. So why do two of my closest friends see me as having a run-of-the-mill lifestyle? I was deep in thought when Reshani spoke again.

"Can I give you some advice?" Reshani sounded ardent. She came and sat opposite me, peering deep into my eyes. When Reshani had something to share, she was a force to reckon with. "Can you please try to live in the moment? Stop replaying the past, stop worrying about the future, and be in the moment. Just let bygones be bygones. Let the day unfold. Expect nothing. Just let it happen. Can you do that?" I nodded my head. I heard what she said, but I didn't know how to stop thoughts about Niranga from consuming my mind.

***

After lunch, we sat outside to watch the sun scrolling down the Hanthana mountain range and catch up on our reading. Reshani and I love reading and have our own book club group to share thoughts about our latest book. No matter how hard I tried, I couldn't focus on my reading today, as deep nagging thoughts in my head were disruptive and weighed me down. Finally, I placed the book aside and turned to Reshani, giving in to the urgency to confide in my best girlfriend.

"Resh, there is something else I wanted to talk to you about."'

"What is it, Saku? Is everything okay?" Picking up the worry in my voice, Reshani closed the book she was reading, giving me her full attention.

"The tour agency is going under. There is no money in the bank." Reshani's face turned pale with alarm. She has been with us since the day I met Sula and has witnessed our journey. She knew what that meant for both Sula and me.

"How is that possible? You two are always busy. I can't remember a weekend you have been unoccupied."

"I really don't know, Resh. I have been super careful with my quotes and handling expenses like a penny pincher." With that simple admission, I felt a hundred times lighter, making me want to share more. "When Sula didn't pay me the last couple of months, I didn't bother to check with him. I have always left managing books to him. Our van was ceased two weeks ago; that's when I knew how bad it was."

"Oh shit, I am so sorry to hear this, Saku." Reshani squeezed my hand, her eyes filled with worry and uncertainty. I was familiar with what was on her face. I had seen the same expressions on mine in the last couple of weeks when I looked in the mirror.

"What is happening?"

"I do not know. I tried to talk to Sula about it. Each time I approached the matter, he shuts me off. He is like an ostrich with his head stuck in the sand. He must think if he pretends it doesn't exist, this will go away."

"What did he tell you about the van?"

"For the first time, he lied to me and said Ashini hasn't paid the instalments on time. It is not Ashini's job to manage the outgoings. She is there to support inquiries when neither one of us is in the office."

"What does Sula do with the cash you two bring in? I remember him saying your trips to India and Thailand bring good profits."

"Yes, we make more profit than my university salary from one overseas trip, which is why I don't understand. We had a great run this year, and we planned to pay off the van and spend some capital on developing a website for marketing." We both were silent, mulling over the situation. I wish I didn't have to unload my worries on Reshani, as her face was pale with concern.

"Did Sula say anything about it?"

"Nothing other than telling me not to worry. He got it under control. It is not the truth. I can go on without getting paid for my work. But I can't put more money into the agency. I don't have to tell you how bad my home situation is… I am scraping the barrel."

"Oh, honey, I am so sorry… you don't deserve this… I feel sad you had to struggle with this while I was away." Reshani leaned across and hugged me tight as if she was trying to pass on some of her strength to me.

"I want to solve this, but I don't know how to correct it. I don't have any money to recover from the debts."

"Is there is more? Not just the van?" Reshani's eyes widened. She is reacting the same way I did when I discovered the depth of our despair.

"Yes, he hasn't paid a lot of bills either. Two hotels we run on credit terms declined to accept any booking until we settled the outstanding payments."

"Oh, shit. It is that bad!" Reshani was pulling invisible threads on her skirt, not liking the situation any more than I did.

"Last time I tried to talk, we fought. I told Sula I would work out if he didn't fix it. I have invested all my savings in the agency. If it goes under, I wouldn't be able to support Malli with his studies. If that happens, I am going to kill Sula!" I turned away to wipe the tears sliding down my cheeks. I didn't want Reshani to be sad and worried more than she already was.

"I wish Sula would talk about this. At least we could come up with a plan. There is no point in sweeping it under the carpet."

"You know how Sula is, all macho and wanting to be a saviour for all of us. It must hurt him more than we think. Let me talk to Ravidu. Maybe he could have a chat with Sula."

Our friendship has thrived on strength sharing, as we have been at each other's corners. While Reshani has been our compass for emotional matters, Ravidu has been the sounding board for anything to do with commercials.

After a long time, I breathed with some calmness, though I have not got an immediate solution to my financial problems, merely talking about them with Reshani shred kilos of weight I have been carrying around. I didn't know how long we could operate with no money in our bank or what would become of Sula if the business went bankrupt. I knew I would not get much sleep the next couple of days and weeks, not only because of Sula, but also because of Niranga.

15 ENTICEMENT

Niranga was very attractive in his casual clothes. He was wearing knee-length denim shorts with a white Ralph Lauren polo t-shirt. The collar was turned up in the same way Malli usually wears his t-shirts. The matching loafers he was wearing completed his outfit. He smiled and waved when he saw me walking towards the bus parked beside the hotel entrance. I couldn't tell if his smile reached his eyes, as he had oversized dark sunglasses on. My heart leapt, pounding fast with the excitement of being near him again.

In the last few days, I tried to keep control of the brewing uncomfortable yet exciting emotions that had crept into my thoughts about him. Luckily, lectures and translation work kept me busy, not allowing me much time to pursue those daydreams.

"Hey, how have you been?" Niranga indicated I should get on the bus with a wave of his hand.

"I am impressed; you all are here on time."

"Amma warned me if I was not on time, you will push me down the citadel like King Kashyapa." He reminded me of my conversation with Aunty Nelum when I called to confirm our meeting's timing and location. Aunty was so pleased I was joining him and promised me she would pass him the message to be on time to pick me up so that I didn't have to hang around waiting. I told her I would push him off Sigiriya if he came late. She had passed it on to him.

"Hope in; I will introduce you to the gang." Niranga moved to the side, making room for me to stand at the front of the tour bus.

"Oh my god, Sakunthala Ranaweera, is that you?" As soon as I dropped my bag and turned around, one of Niranga's friends jumped up from where he was seated and came to the front. He grabbed my shoulders and pushed me back, studying me. "Oh my god, how come you look the same but more gorgeous?" He reeked of alcohol and sounded drunk. I had no memory of knowing him from somewhere. I would have remembered his attractive face and cheerful voice.

"Hey Nadee, check this out. It is not even nine in the morning, and Janaka is already hitting on ladies." One guy sitting in the front row shouted.

"Let go of her, Janaka. You are scaring her." It must be Nadee who came and stood next to the man who was clutching my shoulders.

"I am so sorry, dear. He is still drunk from last night." Nadee said, trying to drag Janaka away from me by pulling him from his waist. "Let go of her Janaka, you are alarming the poor girl," Nadee warned him for the second time.

"Oh, why would she fear me?" Though he was responding to his wife, his eyes were on me. "Hey guys, meet Sakunthala, my first crush in school." Instead of letting me go, he draped his right arm around me and pulled me closer to him. He turned to the back of the bus, introducing me to the rest of Niranga's friends. There were about eight adults and six kids curiously staring at us. While I was trying to get a grip on the situation, I frantically searched around for Niranga.

I only felt a hand going around my waist and pulling me towards a tight chest. At the same time, the driver applied brakes to stop the bus from colliding with another vehicle. I saw Nadee holding on to the top bar of the bus, wrapping one of her arms around Janaka to keep him safe.

"Are you okay?" I turned my head, following the sound when I heard Niranga whispering into my ear. My lips nearly brushed his lips as he was so close to me. I inhaled his aftershave and felt him breathing heavily through the thin layers of our clothes. He was still holding me tight while the inhale and exhale of his chest was pressing on my back.

"I will be if you can tell me what's going on!" I was not sure if the irritation I felt was because of how my body reacted to Niranga's closeness or because of Janaka's melodrama.

"Meet Janaka and Nadee." Niranga slightly turned me towards his friends. "You remember Janaka from my school?" He turned his head, expecting me to remember him. "He was a couple of years junior to me."

"Oh, this is that Janaka?" Then I realised he must be the Janaka who gave me my first love letter when I was not even in my OL class. "So sorry, Janaka, I couldn't recognise you," I said, as I never expected to meet him.

"Oh, I am guttered. How could you not? I gave you one of the most poetic love letters in the entire history."

"That's enough, mate." Niranga pushed Janaka onto the nearby seat, making him sit down. "One more word out of you; I am going to throw you off the bus." He sounded firm, reminding me of the time he scolded Malli for having me in a headlock. Nadee gave a grateful glance and sat next to her husband.

"Once a bully, always a bully." Janaka gawks with a hurtful voice. I thought calling Niranga a *'bully'* was strange, as I couldn't recall him acting tough. Back in the school days, Niranga was more of a reserved, bookish type. I would even call him a bit of a shy one. However, he came out of his shell as we grew and became one of the popular boys in his high school classes.

"Come, let me introduce you to the rest of the gang." Niranga let go of my waist and guided me towards the back of the bus, holding on to one of my elbows. He took the time to introduce me to his friends and their kids, who were all under ten. His friends were around a similar age as was he, who all came from overseas. The kids were congregating around the back of the bus playing some weird game, while the adults were in front engaged in conversation.

By the time we crossed the Polgolla Dam to head towards Wattegama, all were settled in, and Janaka was dozing off. Niranga sat next to me and explained that the group got together last night in Kandy and that their drinking session didn't end until dawn. Janaka had a bit more to drink than the others, hence the drama. There was easy chatter amongst the group. They were sharing stories and jokes the way only a tightly knitted group would.

I had a quick glance at Niranga sitting beside me and having a conversation with two friends seated opposite us. I was relaxed and happy to be near him. It reminded me of the times when we used to go on trips as kids.

"Hey Sakunthala, what do you think about the theory that Sigiriya was built by aliens?" Seneka, who has gone to the same university as Niranga in Sydney, came and stood next to us, grinning.

"Oh no, we don't want to listen to your alien theories Seneka, we had an earful of that last night." Tharushi, one of the wives, made a face. I drank half of the water bottle I was holding, preparing for a long conversation.

"That is always a possibility. One thing is for sure, Sigiriya was not built in 17 years. There is historical evidence of its existence before King Kashyapa." I survey Seneka, trying to read his face. He had a definite lean facial expression and a calm disposition. He had thick eyelashes and laughing eyes with an inviting smile. Seneka had an openness about him that makes you like him.

"Okay, you two carry on with your debate. I am going to sit with the kids." As there was no sign Seneka was prepared to move from where he stood, Niranga got up from where he was seated and moved to the back of the bus. As Seneka sat next to me, occupying the space Niranga took earlier; I noted the immediate change in the atmosphere. It was not charged up and electrifying as it was a few seconds ago.

"So, what is the earliest evidence we have?" Seneka half turned to me, settling in for a long conversation. I loved these chats. Sigiriya, being one of the greatest monuments of our history, most got their own opinion and theory about when it was built and what it represents. My personal favourite relates it to Alakamanda, the beautiful celestial city ruled by the mighty King Rawana, dating back to the 8th or 9th century

After a while, I watch Niranga walking past us and joining Nadee in the front. I saw him checking on me from time to time from where he sat at the front of the bus. Once our eyes met across the floor, and I could read the question in his eyes. I nodded and smiled for reassurance.

I liked it better when he sat next to me with his shoulder and hip barely touching mine. I miss the excitement I felt when his naked arm stretched in parallel to mine, gripping the railing of the seat. We both knew there was no need to hold on to it. Perhaps we both secretly enjoyed having our flesh brushing each other randomly with the twists and turns in the road.

To ground me and keep things pragmatic, I focused all my energy on my conversation with Seneka. The chat with him lasted a while. Seneka was well read and had done his own research, so it was easy to logically argue with him on the theory's pros and cons.

When we reached Sigiriya, it was a bit after eleven o'clock in the morning. Luckily, it was not a very warm day. Although the sun was shining, there was a cool breeze that made the climb effortless. The group was physically fit, and the kids were energetic, so it didn't take us long to pass through the fountains, boulder and terrace gardens to the mirror wall. The kids enjoyed trying to overtake the adults and each other on the rocky staircase. I happily observed the group's astonishment when they stopped to catch their breath at the top of the mirror wall, marvelling at the spellbinding scenery.

"Aunty, why is it called a mirror wall?" One of the young boys inquired with curiosity.

"Because at the time it was built, the King used this as a mirror."

"Oh, cool.... So, they have polished a rock to make it into a mirror?" The same kid exclaimed with awe, his mouth open and neck stretched, admiring the ancient ingenuity.

"So, how did it got damaged and doesn't look much like a mirror anymore? A young girl was curious.

"It got damaged pretty much because of the graffiti that you find on the wall. The majority of those are folk poetry scribbled by visitors to the fortress. Today we study them to understand the culture and the literacy level related to the era." I could see kids were getting impatient, wanting to explore further up. Having seen millions of travel photos of Sigiriya, they were more interested in taking the stairs through the couchant lion's mouth to the summit.

"Now, kiddos, no running on the spiral staircase. Hold on to the handrail for safety." I stopped to advise before we headed towards the narrow spiral staircase that leads away from the mirror wall to Sigiriya frescoes.

"What is on the top, Aunty?" One of the young girls looked towards the sky, shading her eyes with her palms from the sun.

"On top of there, you will see the famous Sigiri frescoes. That means paintings of elegant ladies in colourful clothing and jewellery. There are many stories about who they were, as some think they are the paintings of King Kashyapa's wives. Some suspect they are paintings of dancers and singers that used to entertain the royal court. Those painting are over 1600 years old. Though you will only see about twenty images today, this whole place had been one of the world's largest galleries and probably the world's first gallery. To protect what is remained, we are not allowed to take any photos." As with everyone who came to visit Sigiriya, they were surprised by the display of gorgeous ladies in colourful jewellery and flowers in their hair. Not being able to take photos, they all spent a lot of time gawking at the painting, seeking to imprint them into their memories.

When we walked away from the gallery, the group took their time to cover the lion staircase leading to giant lion paws. I lead them slowly, not demanding to hurry them across the very steep marble steps. Once everyone reached the open ground, their focus became taking photos standing between the giant lion's paws. I happily accommodated their wishes until Seneka called out.

"Hey Sakunthala, can you please ask someone to take a group picture and come and join us?" When I handed the camera to a fellow tour guide to snap a group photo, Niranga's friends made space for me to stand next to him.

Through the climb, Niranga and I had little chance to be close. It must be the reason I found my heart raising when he put his hand around my shoulder, drawing me closer to him for the photo.

The unexpected closeness made me look at him, and I wished I could read what was in his eyes underneath his oversized sunglasses. He smiled and stroked my shoulder as if it was the most natural thing to do while my heart was fluttering like a kite in the open air.

"Hey, you two, shall we make a move?" I quickly stepped away from Niranga to grab the camera from the tour guide in response to Janaka's call out. The group slowed down, blending with fellow tourists, taking their time to climb the most challenging part of the fortress. Both Nadee and Varuni marvelled at some elderly ladies returning to the ground barefooted when they claimed they had jelly-knees.

Before the last few steps, I stopped to catch my breath, letting others go past me when Niranga took a few steps down to lend me his hand. Though I felt odd, I let my bony hand slide between his large palm and fingers, leaning on his strength to cover the last few steps.

Once we reached the top of the rock, the group spread out, appreciating the ruins of the Sky Palace in the citadel. Inhaling the crisp air, standing on the 8th wonder of the world, I knew I had made the right decision to become a tour guide. I felt so proud of my heritage and culture and wanted to share them with others.

As I explained how hard it would have been for the ancient labourers to carry raw material up the same pathway, we took to reach the summit when building the grandeur palace, kids listened in awe. As they were only exposed to about a 200-year-old colonial history in Australia and modern technology, their tiny brains were exploding with wonder with their jaws open wide. I was just about to share some facts about Sigiriya and Indigenous history in Australia when a group of men approached me.

"Excuse me, Miss Ranaweera, how are you?" When a young man came and inquired, at first, I couldn't recognise him. After few other men joined him, and when they removed their caps, I realised they were my students from the second-year class at the university.

"Hello, Savidu. Are you all working on the assignment?" It appeared they all were on a field trip as they had notebooks and pens, and some had cameras and tape recorders in their hands.

"Yes, miss, the assignment you gave us is very challenging." One student chipped in from the back. I smiled, as it is the tradition to complain about assignments.

"So, how is it progressing? Last time I checked, this was an individual assignment, not a group one." I reminded them of the criteria.

"Yes, miss, so can we ask you some questions?" I noted Niranga and his friends were now listening to the conversation and felt it was inappropriate to spend a lot of time with the students. I was their guide for the day, and my time and attention should be given to them. They have already been kind in sharing my time when one of my tour guide colleagues stopped us near the mirror wall earlier to have me translate some details to one of his German guests, as he could not follow the explanation in English.

"Five minutes–that is all." I turned to respond to their questions.

"To us, Sigiriya feels more like a palace than a fort. After today's visit, we agree it could be considered as being like Alakamandawa." Savidu started the dialogue by evoking my interest in the ancient city, Alakamandawa. I have a secret fascination with the city; I dream of running an excavation programme to discover the lost palace one day. In my mind, it would be for a more significant discovery than the Atlantis.

"The book Ravana Watha describes these frescoes differently, not in line with the common belief. Ravana Watha doesn't believe topless ladies were paintings of King Kashyapa's favourite wives in his harem. It says they could be ladies from different tribes: Yakka, Naga, and Deva, reflecting the unity of the tribes under King Kashyapa, whose mother is believed to be a Yakka. So, he had the birthright to Sigiriya from his mother's side!" They have done a bit of research and were excited about their line of thinking.

"Is there a question somewhere, Savidu? As we have limited time, maybe you want to ask it and leave your justification for your paper?" I suggested softly, getting them back on track. Though it would have been wonderful to discuss the Rawana Watha, what it implies, and other historical evidence discovered to date, I wrapped up the conversation quickly and joined Niranga and his friends.

"Tell me again, what is your actual job?" Nemantha was curious when I joined them. "Let's see, you are a tour guide, a translator, and now, from what we gathered, you are also a university lecturer?" He listed out his observation, folding his fingers one by one so he wouldn't miss anything. Although it appears to be three different jobs, for me, it was one significant role with slight variations, each interconnected.

"I was a volunteer translator when I was in high school. Though I didn't get paid, it refined my Japanese language skills, and I enjoyed the challenge. When I was in my second year at the university, I began touring work, covering Kandy town and the Maligawa. Once I finished university, I worked as a full-time lecturer and a tour guide taking any translation work that came my way." I said, sharing a bit of my journey.

"Becoming a guide helped me financially when I was in university. It also made learning easy, as I visited most archaeological sites and learned from the diggers and museums' curators. So, becoming a lecturer was a natural progression for me when I got good scores in the final exam." Seeing their interest, I continued.

"Which one do you enjoy the most?" Nadee was inquisitive.

"Touring. I get to visit places, and I love spending time in Sigiriya, Maligawa, Anuradhapura, Pollonnaruwa and Yapahuwa. It also allows me to share our rich history with the world."

"My god, you seem to be passionate about history as Niranga is about his gaming!" Seeing my excitement, Janaka tested. He wasn't wrong; I am always in my element when I visit those towns with their rich history and endless learning opportunities. I caught Niranga's eyes staring intensely and looked away, distract butterflies in my stomach.

"Which one is the most challenging?" When Seneka also chipped in, it felt as if I was at an interview.

"Touring is a strange career for a woman in Sri Lanka. I live in a country where most people easily judge you. I am part of a culture where people jump to the conclusion the only reason men and women go to a hotel is to sleep with each other." Noting the kids were occupied chasing each other, playing cops and robbers, I explained. "Working as a guide is difficult. Even after five years, I am still struggling. I repeatedly prove that females have a right to be in this field. Each day I survive, I am making it a bit easy for other girls who may want to choose a similar career." It was effortless to be open and honest with them. Like Niranga, his friends were also broad-minded, genuinely interested, so sharing came naturally.

"Oh my god, where do you get time to do all that? Do you get a chance to rest? What does your boyfriend think of you doing all this? Do you make time to see him at all?" When Janaka started rattling on with a list of questions, I automatically glanced at Niranga and noted he was watching me.

"What is with the hundred and one questions? Have you had enough of Sigiriya?" I deflected the question with a joke.

"You clearly are interesting as the Sigiriya is, if not more!" Seneka said with a smile." It is not appropriate to ask personal questions, Janaka, although you have given Sakunthala a love letter ages ago." He turned to Janaka, shaking his head with disapproval.

"Seneka is right. Let us head back. I am hungry." Nadee nudged Janaka's shoulder, pointing to the steep stairs leading to the ground below.

***

Niranga and I were the last two to descend as others had already gone past us. We walked side by side, way too close. His hand would accidentally brush mine from time to time, and when that happened, I felt a strange sensation going down my spine. His aftershave mixed with perspiration filled my nostrils. The smell was intoxicating.

I was craving for all - his smell, his touch, his voice, the Australian Sri Lankan accent I adored. I was waiting for the next accidental brush with such excitement that I had not felt before.

We spoke aimlessly, nothing extraordinary, while I secretly wished for the descent not to end and we wouldn't run out of topics. I didn't want an uncomfortable silence to build between us. The space between us was exciting and enticing, and I heard myself screaming, *'Don't go there.'* I was oblivious to what it meant.

We both were in a daze, as neither of us noticed the time when we reached the ground that all of Niranga's friends were gathered around, waiting for us to join them.

"Oh, by the way, what happened to you two?" As soon as we got closer to hearing distance, Janaka asked, throwing me off balance. I assumed he was questioning why we took such a long time to join them. I felt embarrassed and nervous, so I nearly lost my footing and would have fallen if Niranga didn't grab my hand.

It was the second time he saved me today with his quick reflex. Same as in the morning, he was not ready to let go of my hand. He steadied me and held on to it longer before letting go.

"We stopped to take some photos." This was not exactly a lie. Niranga patiently waited for me to take pictures and posed for a few with little of a fuss.

"I didn't mean what is happening now." Janaka brushed off, making others grin.

"I meant when we were in school. All this time, I thought you broke off with him. Niranga never wanted to talk about you. Have you two patched up? Is that why, after so many years, you are back?" I was baffled, not knowing why Janaka believed Niranga and I were a couple back in school. I eyed Niranga, wondering if he could enlighten me.

"What on earth is he talking about? Is he still drunk?" I hissed, taking a step closer to stand next to Niranga.

"Ignore him." Niranga casually brushed it off, appearing uncomfortable. His hands were in a fist, and his face was darker. He was swaying from left to right, and I would always recognise that move, as that is how he would react when he was angry and couldn't control it. It didn't take long for Janaka to grasp I was not aware of the incident. He eyeballed both of us, trying to understand.

"Oh my god, Niranga, did you lie to me when you said Sakunthala was your girlfriend?" Janaka turned to Niranga with utter horror on his face.

"Are you drunk again, Janaka? What on earth are you rattling on?" I was perplexed by Janaka's question and tired of the conversation that was not making any sense.

"Oh, you don't know how we became friends, do you, Sakunthala?" Janaka's comment made me wonder. Janaka was in a junior class, and I couldn't recall Niranga hanging out with him when we were in school. I still remember how angry Niranga was when I showed him the letter I got from Janaka so many years ago. It was fascinating to find out how they became best friends.

"Leave it, Janaka!" Niranga commanded, sounding furious. Janaka pretended not to hear.

"Didn't he tell you the next day after giving you that letter Niranga bashed me? He punched me and said if I go near his girlfriend, he would have my hands broken so that I couldn't write a single letter ever again."

"Niranga is the one to blame, Nadee." Janaka turned to Nadee with a sad and defeated face. "He is the reason I can't write anything poetic these days. That man scared the life of me that day when he punched me in front of my classmates! He told everyone in my class I went after his girlfriend. I should be in lifelong therapy. That is why I can't write anything other than test manuals these days. He robbed my creative juice." The tension building between Janaka and Niranga put the others on edge. None of them found humour in what Janaka said to laugh.

"Holy mother of Kali, Niranga, when I asked you to whack him, I didn't mean it. I was only joking. But thank you." I glanced at Niranga to warm him as I lied.

I was in shock; yet, I pretended it was all fun and games. Inside, I was struggling to cypher the mystery about why Niranga would do such a thing. Was he trying to protect me? Then why didn't he tell me? We used to share anything and everything. I saw Niranga calming down a bit. His hands were not in a tight grip anymore, and his facial expressions had softened.

"So, it was you who sent him to bash me? Not cool Sakunthala, not cool." Janaka was pretending to be hurt. I ignored him, walking towards the car park, trying to get away to process what I had just learned when I was stopped in my tracks.

"Give me your hand, my precious; I can read your future like a newspaper." One of the elderly Gypsy women loiters around in the car park, grab my hand for a palm reading.

"I am not a believer, Kanmali." I laughed off and kept on walking, ignoring her.

"Mark my word, my precious; your stubbornness is going to harm your love. Don't doubt his love. Your prince will love you more than his life." She spitted some excessive saliva from beetles she was chewing and wiped her red mouth in the fold of her sari with an intense star.

Like a broken record, Kanmali said the same thing repeatedly, trying to tempt me to read my palm. When that fails, she shouts out a random burst of her insights to convert me into a follower. Not bothered by my disinterest, the other four females in our group stopped to have their palms read.

"Don't try any voodoo tricks on these ladies, Kanmali. They are my friends," I warned the Gypsy, knowing how manipulative she can be, charging exorbitant fees from innocent believers.

"My precious child, one day you will, believe me, so don't be so hard on me; I only tell the truth." I ignored Kanmali's hostile stare and crossed the car park to stand under the shade of the tall neem tree. Standing under its cover, I pulled my camera out to take a few pictures. I got a perfect frame of Kanmali surrounded by ladies with their palms stretched, waiting for their future to be revealed.

I pondered if this illiterate, unexposed Gypsy who didn't even know the existence of cities outside of Sigiriya, let alone countries outside of Sri Lanka, would be apt to capture the dreams, fears and hopes of modern women within her trance. Can Kanmali be good at picking up the challenges these women navigate daily, their inner demons and the threats they face dealing with a society full of discrimination, bullying, harassment and inequity? Maybe, despite all that, at the core, we all are the same: hope to be loved, cherished, successful, and happy. Perhaps that is what Kanmali taps into; maybe that is why she keeps telling me I will be loved and goes far in life. But do I have the same dreams? I was secretly wondering when my thoughts were interrupted by Seneka.

"Is she a fake?"

"Not sure. I have never allowed her to study my palm. Some say she is gifted."

"You don't want to consider what she just said?" He sounded curious.

"I rather read Mills and Boon." I smiled.

"You don't suppose you are worthy enough for your boyfriend to love you more than his life?" Seneka asked.

"I don't believe one could love another more than oneself." I turned to face Seneka, watching his expression. "That is fundamentally flawed. It is a concept created by poets and novelists to romanticise people doing stupid things in the name of love."

"You are a cynic."

"No. I am a realist."

"How are you a realist?"

"Why put so much pressure on someone you claim to love and set up for failure?"

"You are a strange one." Seneka shook his head, as he was not clear about what to think.

"Aren't we all in our own way?" I challenged.

"You, my dear, are absolutely correct," Seneka laughed pleasantly.

"So, how well do you know our Niranga?" He nodded towards Niranga, who was in deep conversation with Varuni, Seneka's wife, a few yards away from us.

"I knew the boy, not the man." I captured a couple of photos of the group before I responded to Seneka.

"What do you mean?" When Seneka gave me a piercing look, I thought he was too slow in grasping things.

"Exactly what I said. I knew Niranga when he was a boy before he went to Australia. I know little about the man he has become."

"You would know him more than I do." I turned to Senaka to see if he would disagree with me. I would not tell Senaka, the boy I grew up with, was tugging invisible cords in my heart. But the man he has become, in many ways, is a stranger to me. And I was learning to admire and respect that man and leave the boy I once knew behind.

"So, how was he as a boy?" Senaka asked.

"He was soft, caring, and jovial. And responsible and focused. He would make friends with anyone; class, creed, wealth...... they were immaterial to him. Niranga was a boy who could easily sell ice blocks to Eskimos." Refreshing my memories about the Niranga I knew, the one I admired and loved, made my heart expand with warm happiness.

"Then there is no change between the boy and the man. He is exactly as you described him." The way Seneka spoke about Niranga showed he had great admiration and respect for his friend.

I was curious. Why is it I sensed a difference if Niranga had changed little? I have always been attracted to Niranga, although the emotions I am experiencing these days are different, more intense, more demanding. When I was a teen, I was happy to be on the sideline and be content. Not anymore; I want to be there in the middle, sense it, inhale it, and touch it.

"I am curious why Niranga didn't tell us about you at all?" Seneka was eyeing me as if the answer to his question was written on my face.

"Why do you think that is? No one knew he had a punch up with Janaka until today," He said. *'Yes, I am also interested in that punch up.'* I wanted to tell Seneka, yet I didn't.

"Does he know all about your neighbours?" When I asked Seneka, he turned to me clueless. *'Gosh, this guy's brain must have been in a freezer.'* I was running out of patience.

"Do you normally share stories about your neighbours with your friends?" The second time around, Seneka got my drift and laughed with amusement.

***

It was time for me to head back to Kandy; Niranga walked with me towards the main bus stop near the café, where others enjoyed a late lunch.

Walking side by side towards the bus stop, we were too close, yet also apart. I was eagerly expecting his hand to brush mine, waiting for that warm vibe to engulf me. I was happily breathing in the dry air filled with his body, adore with nervous excitement that he was there beside me. If I stretched my fingers just a little, I could intertwine mine with his. I wanted to relive what I felt in the morning when my back was pressed against his chest and the emotion I felt when he held my hand earlier to save me from falling. My heart was pounding fast. I didn't want this moment to end.

I did not want to leave him and get on a bus in a few minutes. That sudden realisation that I may not cross paths with him again, I wouldn't feel the warmth of his skin brushing on mine, made my heart contract with an emptiness.

I wanted to stay. I want to stretch my hand and hold his, feel the weight of his fingers on mine. I wanted to lay my head on his chest and listen to his heart beating. I wanted to find out if it was also beating unusually faster as mine did. I wanted to stand on my toes and kiss him, feel the softness of his lips. There was so much I wanted to do; just imagining them had a warmth rush through my body.

I nearly stopped in my tracks with a shock. I could not believe how I was enticing my mind, stepping into unknown territory. I never felt this intense yearning to be with someone; the strength of my thoughts was scaring me.

"Do you have to leave?" When Niranga spoke, I barely heard him. I felt a rush of warmth spreading across my heart, grasping the want in his voice.

"Yes, I have to." Even though I didn't want to, I couldn't stay. I have to take a group to Galle tomorrow morning. There was no point in talking about it.

My days were locked in. He already knew this, as I could only join him for this one day.

"Why did you do it?" When I asked, Niranga knew what I was referring to. He drew his fingers through his hair.

"I think you know why." After a deep breath, he murmured with his signature smile, melting my heart. I thought I knew what it meant; I'd rather not speculate. Deep down, I was scared to consider that possibility. To acknowledge the hope that he, too, had wanted me the way I did.

"You own me a few love letters; you robbed me the chance of getting any with your stunt." I thought a joke would ease the tension that was building.

"You could have had many if you didn't run off to Channaka." I couldn't read his eyes, as they were covered with his dark sunglasses. I noted his jaw was tight, and his voice sounded bitter and angry. I didn't understand the correlations between Janaka's letter and Channaka. Being a mathematician, he should know those two were mutually exclusive events.

"Stay. We need to talk." Niranga saw my anger and grabbed my hand with an intense look.

"I can't." I glanced away, avoiding his glare, and murmured with helplessness.

"You can't, or you won't?" He broke the silence with a voice loaded with exasperation.

"I need to be in Kandy. I can't break my promise. I made a commitment to Sula." No matter how much I wanted to stay with Niranga, I couldn't go back on my word. Sula needed a break after being on the road for three weeks. If only Niranga knew how badly I wanted to stay with him here, how hard it was to keep my fingers from stretching and intertwining with his. How desperately I want to reach out and wipe away the traces of sweat building on the side of his temples because of the harsh sun rays shining sharply above us.

"How strange is it you will keep your promises to all others except me?" When Niranga spoke again, sounding bitter, I was not sure what promise I was breaking.

"What are you talking about, Niranga?" I couldn't contain the annoyance I felt, and he could hear it in my voice.

"Remember the boat ride we were supposed to take on the weekend you finished your exam? If only you had the decency to keep your promise!" I couldn't understand why he got the right to be angry when he was the one who made me break my promise.

I saw the anger, disappointment, and heartbreak that I thought I had nicely buried lifting their ugly heads. My heart sunk when I realised just like that, I lost the euphoria I was enjoying a few minutes ago. I thought we were on a new beginning!

"You are still carrying the past with you." I was angry. I wanted to pull him by the collar of his t-shirt and shake him until it hurt. I wanted to scream: why do you always pretend that you got hurt when I was the one who got burned?.

The timing was perfect. I saw the Kandy bus heading towards the bus stop, and without waiting for his response, I pulled my hand away from his grip and quickened my steps towards it.

"Saku, wait." I ignored Niranga's call and got on to the bus. The bus was not crowded, so there were few empty seats at the back. I trudged towards the end and purposely sat opposite, where I wouldn't see Niranga anymore.

When the bus moved, it was then that I admitted I had been holding my breath, waiting for him to get on it, somehow stop me from leaving. I was hoping this wouldn't be my last memory of him I would carry around with me.

'Why did you ruin this beautiful day? Why couldn't you give me this day for a keepsake?' I wished I could have asked Niranga, but he was not on the bus stopping me from leaving. Tears silently fell down my cheeks and dropped onto my hands. It felt like Déjà vu.

16 SALVAGE

Ten years ago, I made a similar trip; although it was a short one from our place to Jeevani's, I recall my emotions that day was not that much different from today.

I can't pinpoint when things shifted between Akka and me. Maybe it began when we moved to Nuwara Eliya, or perhaps when she returned home after finishing high school. Even though we both tried, it was hard for Akka and me to get back to the same simple relationship we shared when we were kids. I could not shake off the abandonment feeling loitered in me since she stayed in Kandy when we moved to Nuwara Eliya. By the time she returned, I had filled up the void she had left with Malli and Niranga. I had no intention of welcoming her home and left her to her device, focusing on my studies.

Akka came home ready to accept the changes in our lives and Thaththa and Malli as her own family. She slowly started mending her bridges with both. Thaththa, in his usual fashion, was very accommodating and kind, welcoming her with open arms. Malli was not that easy to win over. Akka's obsession with keeping the house tidy didn't help her battle with him, as Malli was at an age where he was behaving like the Speedy Gonzales, leaving marks of disruption in every room he had been in. They always had fights that went on for days. Still, Akka was relentless. Slowly and steadily, she claimed her rightful place as the oldest sibling in the family.

Akka was a younger, more refined version of Amma; soft, beautiful, and vulnerable. She had laughing eyes, and a soft musical voice was intelligent enough to hold a conversation with anyone and was charming enough not to threaten their intellect. She had a striking personality that attracted and kept anyone's attention effortlessly.

I was too busy with my studies to notice Niranga was slowly showing more attention to her. They both were at the same age and were waiting for their AL-exam results. By this time, Niranga was a mini-celebrity in Nuwara Eliya. He had money and his own car and became Akka's chariot, escorting her around the town, showing her its secret beauty, taking her on her trips to find material for her patchwork projects, and sometimes even to hang out with his friends.

As my exam got closer, all these things passed through my mind without making many impressions. I didn't have time to dwell on them. I expected everything to get back to normal when I finished my exam. After all, Niranga was my friend, not Akka's.

I was used to Niranga's parade of girlfriends. He had his first girlfriend when he was about fourteen. I used to be his wing girl as she was from my school. He was a young Casanova, always having carefree fun and none committed relationships that never lasted. He got bored too soon. Girls he was hanging out with were too clingy, demanding, too dull or too much fun. There was always a reason to break it off after a few weeks or months. I had no grounds to get jealous. I never considered them a threat, as I naively assumed I had the power to win him over when I was ready and wanted. I believed we were inseparable and was mine to be taken when I was ready.

Niranga still turned around seeking my company and brought me Mills and Boons when he came across a new book. He also bought me bags of velvet tamarind that I loved so much. And teamed up with me when we played badminton or carrom or debated on some silly topics.

I have always known about what was happening in Niranga's life. So, if he was having an affair with Akka, I didn't expect him to keep it from me. But I should have noted something was amiss when Niranga didn't hug me as before. He stopped sitting close to me and sat opposite me. And Akka started watching Niranga's every gesture as if she would miss a critical movement if she turned her eyes away from him. It was as if they were conversing in a secret language, glancing at each other over the badminton net or a cup of teas and having their own hidden coded jokes.

Niranga promised to take me on a boat tour on Lake Gregory to celebrate finishing my OL exam that weekend. It was something that he knew I always loved doing. On the last day of my exam, I came home after school with joy. After months of slavery, I had finally finished the ordeal and was free for a few months until the results were released. In my rush to find Niranga to make holiday plans, I didn't find it strange and paid little attention when Lechchami, our domestic helper, told me Akka had gone to the pinewoods. It was unusual as Akka hardly goes there on her own. She was not an outdoor person, a homemaker: good at patchwork, cooking, and dressmaking.

I ignored the nagging feeling as I headed to Niranga's place. He was nowhere to be found. Aunty Nelum suggested checking the pinewoods. Again, I disregard the uneasy feeling I felt at the bottom of my stomach. Too distracted by the excitement of the freedom, I mount the pinewood in search of Niranga. As I got closer to the stream, his silhouette was visible through the tall pine trees. I almost called out his name, but I decided against it as I wanted to creep in and try to push him into the stream, get him wet and laugh out.

I didn't get to take more than two or three steps when I stopped in my tracks, seeing Akka and Niranga sitting way too close to each other, their heads touching.

What happened after that point is a blur. I can't recall how I got home. However, I can remember the pain that pressed on my chest seeing Akka at the stream. *'How could Niranga do that to me? The stream was ours. It was mine, and he promised it will always be our place a long time ago.'* I was screaming inside.

I didn't expect Niranga to fall for Akka. I couldn't understand why I thought it was not a possibility. Akka commanded attention from the opposite sex in the same way Niranga did. *'How did I miss it?'* I asked myself repeatedly. It was natural for them to be attracted to each other. I returned home and visited Jeevani, pretending it bore me to stay home as I didn't dare to face either.

Despite how hurt I felt, I didn't cry. No tears fell from my eyes. I was too young to understand my emotions. Yet, I knew I had to stay away, so I didn't return home that day and spent the weekend at Jeevani's. Her parents loved to have me, so we called home to let Thaththa know I was going on a trip with Jeevani's family.

I mastered my avoiding tactics by carefully orchestrating not to be around Niranga when I returned home. When he came knocking on my bedroom window, I pretended I was not in the room or asleep. After a couple of days, I convinced Amma and Thaththa to let me visit Loku Amma for a couple of weeks. I left without saying goodbye to Niranga.

Loku Amma lived in Kandy, close by to where my annexe is now. She has only one son, Waruna Aiya, who was in the engineering faculty at Peradeniya University. That is how I met Channaka, my first boyfriend. Channaka was one of Waruna Aiya's batch mates who also lived close by. I attracted Channaka to me from the early days. He used to come to Loku Amma's place to hang out with Waruna Aiya. After our encounter, his visits became more frequent.

It was usual for us to talk about books we had read for hours. Waruna Aiya was not into reading and didn't find the conversations entertaining, so he left us to our devices, giving us the freedom to talk to our heart's desire. Channaka was an erudite and a poet. His musical voice and ability to make even the most unadorned word sound romantic and sincere mesmerised me. Channaka not only made me stretch my two-week escape, but he also convinced me to consider sitting for the A-level exam in Kandy. When Amma demanded I come home after staying away for more than a month, I reluctantly returned.

I didn't wish to go home, not because I didn't prefer to leave Channaka, but because I didn't want to face the truth that Niranga no longer considered me his favourite person in our household. Although Channaka added excitement, and no matter how strongly I tried to convince myself that he had an iridescent persona, he couldn't replace Niranga.

On reflection, it was Akka's involvement that shattered me into pieces. Akka was family, and I could not fight for his attention to rob it from Akka. I recollect Reshani asking me a few days ago, would it be different if it involved a random girl? I guess now I know the answer to that question.

Niranga was pleased to have me home. He used to come searching for me at every opportunity he got. I pretended I didn't care. And I purposefully avoided him. I wanted to show I was not alone; I had Channaka. I started talking more and more about him.

"Channaka is like Maxim Gorky. He is such a poet, and his writings are so uplifting and romantic; it gives me goosebumps."

"Oh, our Sasoo is in love for the first time Niranga." When Akka teased, I didn't deny it. Channaka had asked me to be his girlfriend and declared his love before I returned home.

"Channaka sounds like a loser to me… Why would he waste time with a child when he is at university? I bet all the girls in his batch must have turned him down." I still recall the way Niranga arrogantly mocked and ridiculed Channaka and the attention he had for me.

That was the tipping point. I was so enraged by Niranga's comment because I felt he belittled me, not worthy of being loved. So, I said yes to Channaka.

Now I know all I did was use Channaka to drive a point. I was not in love with him. I cherish the attention I got from him and was thrilled I could prove Niranga was wrong. Despite what Niranga thought, I was no longer a little girl; others saw me differently. In retaliation, I bravely pronounced Channaka as a grown-up, while Niranga was just a boy pretending to be a man. That widened the rift between us, reshaping our interaction.

No one could believe it when I demanded I wanted to go to a high school in Kandy for my AL studies. When Amma refused profoundly, unable to fathom my reasoning, I cried for two days and went on a hunger strike. I was determined to do anything in my power to leave home and get as far away from Niranga as I could. Thaththa had to step in to support my decision. Maybe I should have stayed as everything changed once they released the advanced level exam results. Niranga won a scholarship and migrated to Sydney for his studies. Akka got selected to study business administration at Colombo University.

Though I was with Channaka, I was heartbroken, so I purposely didn't bother coming home to say goodbye to Niranga when he left the country. I pretended I had a class that I couldn't miss.

Channaka and I didn't last long. Soon, Channaka's possessiveness and his romantic poems tire me and their ability to cause butterflies in my stomach passed. Despite what Niranga assumed, Channaka didn't make a dent in my heart when we went our separate ways after six months.

Niranga was clueless. Even after ten years, I still carry the pain of rejection that I felt on the day at the stream. He is in the dark about how he ruined it for all the boys and men when he pulled me out of that mud pile that rainy day. I was in love with that chubby, bubblegum flavoured boy from the very first moment our hands touched. I am enraged he blamed me for breaking a promise when he was the one that made me run away.

There was no relevance in rehashing the past now. Our relationship has gone through too much; the rift has stretched beyond mending to start over. And it was seemingly unlikely that we would meet again.

***

"Saku, it's me." I was preparing a quote for an upcoming tour at the tour agency when I received Niranga's call. Hearing his voice unexpectedly on the other end of the phone made me sit up straight. As a few days had already passed since the Sigiriya trip, I was not expecting to hear from him ever again. I felt an electrifying sensation crawling down my spine, hearing his husky voice making me gasp for air.

"Oh, hello," I tried to sound natural, pretending my heart was not battering against my ribcage.

"How are you?" After a brief pause, he inquired.

"I am well, thanks."

"Um…. Are you busy now?" Niranga sounded nervous.

"Yes, got a bit to do."

"What time do you finish work?" It felt strange talking to him over the phone as if nothing had happened. I was still nursing a disappointment, more than a fit of anger over our last exchange in Sigiriya.

"Don't have a fixed time whenever we finish the work."

"Oh…." He was disappointed.

"What do you want?" I was arrogant and rude, and I didn't care. I had enough of getting hurt by him.

"Well, I am hungry. I thought if you are free, we can have some of those yummy short eats you were raving about from Green Cabin." His voice sounded hopeful, referring to one of the famous local eateries.

"You are in Kandy now?" I swallow the enormous ball of saliva pooled in my mouth. Hearing he was in Kandy made me sweat with the anticipation of seeing him.

"Yes, and just a few minutes away from Green Cabin."

"You know where it is?"

"Why? Are you impressed?" I sensed he was smiling at the other end.

"Maybe…" He picked the softening in my voice, and he grabbed the opportunity quickly.

"Impressed enough to meet me in a few minutes?" He sounded excited and hopeful. Although our last conversation ended badly, the possibility of being next to him made my body shiver, and I could feel my cheeks hurting from the cheerful grin spreading across my face.

"I am not sure if we should! You are pretty hung up on the past." I was honest. I didn't want to live through another fight with him. Seeing him, not being with him, was hard enough without going through old, painful memories.

"That is why I need to meet you; I want to apologise," he said.

"Sometimes, some things can't be salvaged," I muttered in disappointment.

"I screwed up; I am sorry." Niranga's voice was thick with remorse.

I thought about what he said. *'Would we be able to reclaim our childhood friendship if we give it another chance?'* I was not convinced.

"Saku? …… Are you there?" when I didn't respond immediately, Niranga called out with worry. "Please, Cookie, just remember, how many times I have sneaked in Mills and Boons for you? Do you know how badly I got teased by the boys? They thought I was reading them. You should see me for the sake of those." He was highly knowledgeable about my weak points and knew all he had to do was remind me how adorable he has been in the past to melt my heart.

"You deserve the teasing. You made me summarise the plot for you."

"Hey, come on, have some sympathy. I got bullied because of you. Not only that, I had to make sure Aunty didn't catch me in the act……. So, what do you say? Will you come?" When he didn't get a response, he asked again, sounding hopeful.

"I might if you hang up the phone so I can get there." I sighed, conceding.

"Yes, ma'am." I imagined him straighten up as he said that. I forgot to ask where he was when we agreed to meet in ten minutes. My hand was shaking when I replaced the receiver. When I lifted my head, Sula was staring displeased.

"Niranga?" He raised his eyebrows, watching my face. "You are grinning from ear to ear."

"Oh, shut up," I shrugged off his remark. "Could you wait for me before you lock up? Be back after some tea." I asked Sula while tidying up my desk, as there was no point in concentrating on the quote anymore. I was so distracted by the anticipation of seeing Niranga to focus on my work now.

"Are you sure it is a good idea?" Sula asked, a worried look in his eyes. When he saw me on my return from Sigiriya, I was in a mess. Sula held me, allowing me to cry and listened to my story with such patience that was foreign to him. If I disappointed him, he said nothing. Sula just sat there, letting me rest my head on his shoulder, not demanding that I shouldn't wail. Once the sobbing started, I didn't have a clue how to stop it. Tears were falling as the Dunhida falls, one of the largest waterfalls in Sri Lanka, rushing down after the rainy season, heavy and uncontrollable.

It was the first time Sula had seen me break down in such a manner. He had always regarded me as the stronger one on many fronts, too busy to succumb to emotions. When he got me some Panadol for my headache afterwards, he was tactful not to comment on my bloodshot eyes or puffy eyelids.

It didn't matter if it was not a good idea. I had a compelling urge to hurry and meet Niranga. I smiled and stood up to leave.

"Then don't forget to take an umbrella." Sula stopped me from rushing out of the office.

"Why?"

"It's going to rain. I don't want you to get sick." Sula pushed a folded umbrella into my hand. I accepted it with no arguments and headed to the toilet downstairs to freshen up. I checked the mirror to see if my saree was in order and wished I had worn something more appealing for Niranga. It surprised me as I rarely gave much attention to my attire than its convenience. I finger-combed my short hair and applied some lip gloss on my dry lips. 'This will do', I told myself.

Though Green Cabin was about a five-minute walk from the agency, I purposely followed the longer route. I didn't want to show up early in case Niranga got wind of my eagerness. I observe the bubbling excitement and nervousness, happily grinning to myself.

When I got to the café, Niranga was already waiting, sitting at a corner table away from the crowd. I watched him taking a few seconds to recognise me before he waved me over to his table. With each slow step I took towards him, my confidence dropped. I noted his eyes settling on my mid-drift, where my skin was bare, peeping through the saree. It seemed as he wanted to hug, but he didn't. I sat opposite him, clutching my saree in nervous hands.

"You look regal in a saree."

"So, have you ordered something to eat?" Not wanting to let my heart expand with that small compliment, I inquired.

"Yep, I ordered for both of us. I hope you don't mind. They said they were closing up soon." I couldn't understand why he sounded worried about ordering for both of us. It was not like he was taking away my freedom by placing an order for me.

"So why did you want to meet?" I was restless. There was no patience left in me to play the game of beating around the bush. I jumped right in with no safety net, no harness, not bothered how deep I was going to drown.

When he glanced at me, I wanted to reach out and remove his sunglasses that were masking his eyes. I tried to catch my image in his eyes and read them. Instead, I only saw my bony reflection in his dark shades.

Before he could talk, the waiter came in with a platter of food and two cups of tea. Although neither one of us was listening to anything, the waiter continued explaining the platter of food he laid on the table. We both pretended we were hanging onto every word that came out of the waiter's mouth. My inner desire to hear Niranga's response was so much so that I felt a scream building in me. I gulped some water to flush it down.

"To apologise for being a jerk the other day." I blinked, but said nothing. "To give you this." He passed me a bag. I picked it with curiosity. When I drew the contents out, there were two old copies of Mills and Boon's books. I bet he had gone to Cindy's, one of the famous old book stores in Kandy town, to buy them as a peace offering. It made me smile, but I suppressed it, not wanting to show any leniency.

"I don't read these anymore." I pushed the books aside with disregard. I would not make it easy on him.

"I thought you might say that. So that is why I got you these as well." Niranga slid another brown paper bag across the table. I gripped it and silently took the two books out. They were the latest releases of Wilbur Smith and Harold Robbins. I wondered how he knew these two authors were my favourites now. Maybe he saw what was on my bookshelf when he came to drop me off a week before. I contained my happiness. It was a thoughtful gift.

"Thanks," I muttered indifferently.

"Third is a charm." This time, he slides across a smaller bag. There was a strange twitch on his lips when he glanced at me. I was inquisitive about what he had in the bag. *'What could he buy to impress me, to make me forgive him?'* I was curious to find out what was inside. When I opened the bag, I screamed with pure delight.

"Holy mother of Kali, where did you get these?" The bag was full of velvet tamarinds, the little sweet and sour fruit I loved so much. They were dark brown and were oozing with flavour. My mouth was watering, anticipating its sweet taste. I could feel my cheeks hurting with the stretch of my grin as I was in pure heaven. He remembered how much I craved them.

When growing up, Niranga used to buy me bags and bags of velvet tamarinds during the season. He got into trouble with Amma, as I always end up with a split tongue suckling too many sweet and sour fruits and dropping shells all over the house. Niranga didn't mind the scolding as he always claimed he was paying in advance to compensate for the rest of the ten months they were not in season and kept a count of favours I owed him, although I don't believe he cashed in on them.

Niranga was quiet. I lifted my eyes and caught him watching me. He had taken off his sunglasses; his eyes were full of laughter and relief.

"Thank you." I felt so happy; I automatically reached out and touched his knuckles with gratitude. His skin felt warm. Niranga turned his hand and grabbed my fingers. They felt smooth and firm. We were peering into each other's eyes; I couldn't capture the depth I saw in his brown eyes with any amount of words. I let my fingers rest on his grip, being happy and content before dragging them away.

"Am I forgiven?" He asked softly, giving me a pleading stare.

"Maybe…" He smiled happily, filling his plate with short eats from the platter. I was not hungry. I sipped my tea, watching him enjoying the food. Niranga sunk his teeth into the puff pastry that was more puff than savoury. He continued to eat it, having no idea how the flakes were stuck around his chin and had fallen onto his t-shirt.

"Gosh, why do you always eat like the Cookie Monster? You are making such a mess!" I shook my head and grabbed a paper napkin from the table to dust off the flakes on his t-shirt. Niranga smiled softly, showing no regard for the mess.

"There are some flakes stuck around your chin." I ignored the crazy thought that came to my mind to lean across and pick those bits. Instead, I gave a napkin to him, showing he should tidy himself up.

"So, is it a good time to ask you for a favour?" After rubbing off flakes from his face, Niranga asked softly; though he sounded doubtful, I gathered he would still ask, anyway.

"Unbelievable! You bring some books and a bag of velvet tamarinds and expect me to forget what a jerk you have been?" I pretended I was angry, although I wasn't. If he asked, I would easily give him one of my kidneys.

"Tell me, what else can I do? You name it, and I will do it." He sat up straight with worry. I turned my head aside and gave him a sly glance; I wanted to drag this if I could.

"You are loaded, aren't you?"

"What do you mean?"

"I mean, you have money to spare, don't you?"

"You want money, sure, if that's what you need." He leaned forward with concern.

"Okay, here is what you are going to do if you choose to make it up to me for being a jerk. I am going to suggest that you do something, and if you do it with no 'ifs' and 'buts' and 'maybes', you will be forgiven."

I sounded stern, purposely in the authoritative voice I use in the lecture room. I watched him process the information, trying to figure out what I was planning. I had an internal chuckle visualising the wheels of his thoughts moving.

"Um…… Okay, got it. Now tell me, what do you want me to do?" After some contemplation, he asked with curiosity.

"I am going to save it for a later date. You better remember that you made a pledge to honour it no matter what and when I call for it." His arms were crossed, and he was studying my face, trying to understand what my intentions were. Maybe he was expecting me to borrow money from him. He is intelligent, so I am sure he had figured out that I am struggling with my finances, though I juggle three jobs most of the days.

"Okay, done!" He bounced back quickly from his concerned, curious status to a contended one, stretching his hand to close the deal. I clutched his hand in disbelief; I didn't expect him to accept my challenge that easily.

"Now, can I ask for the favour I was going to ask earlier?"

"What do you want?" I drank a bit of tea before I peered into his eyes.

"Come to my parents' anniversary dinner on Saturday." He already knew I was not planning to attend the party they were hosting, despite my promise to Aunty. I kept on drinking tea in silence, watching him, trying to read what was going on in his mind. *'Why does he want me to show up? Is he experiencing the same invisible pull, wanting more? Is he also burning from the warmth of the heat building between us?'* I was having my hands out on a giant bonfire, letting them burn, though I knew it could eventually reduce me to ashes.

"Why do you want me to come?" He didn't answer me straight away. He was weighing his thoughts, having a monologue on what he should be saying. I was impatient, but I didn't show it, so I quietly waited, watching how nervous he was when he ran his fingers through his hair.

"Um…. So that Amma wouldn't blame me for your absence. She believes the reason you are so distant from us is that of me. It would devastate both if you didn't turn up." Aunty Nelum's intuition impressed me. Niranga was the reason I kept away and was planning on not attending the event.

"Could you please come? I can't bear not having you there." There was hope in his eyes. He wanted me there, and I wonder if it was powerful as the desire I felt wanting to be there.

"I will try." After some silence, I muttered, I would not make it easy on him. I will pretend I am not going to hastily drop all my plans to be near him.

"You used to do anything for me." Niranga had an adorable look on his face; I remember he made the same pouty face when we were kids, when he wanted me to go along with many of his crazy ideas.

"I grew up."

"Yes, I am fully aware of that." He gazed over at me appreciatively. A warm rush ran through my body, and my cheeks were on fire. I didn't want to read what was in his eyes, so I glanced away.

"My god, how do you keep up your six-pack with all that junk food?" I said, to overcome the uneasy nervousness I felt.

"There are a lot of ways to burn calories." I am not sure what triggered it, but his comment immediately projected him shirtless in a bedroom. If I had fair skin, he would have been able to pick my cheeks turning red. The temperature change I felt internally was not visible outside.

"One of those would be to leave before we get kicked out. They are closing." To shake off that disturbing image, I gathered my umbrella, got up from where I was sitting, and collected the bags he gave me. Niranga took my cue and finished up what he was eating, and settled the bill.

"Oh,… nooo…………. It's raining." Sula's prediction was accurate. When we came out of the café, it had turned dark, and the rain was pouring down. City lamps were on, and you could barely make out the silhouettes of buildings, people, and cars amongst the neon lights.

"I will walk you back to your office." Niranga took the umbrella from my hand and opened it to protect us from the rain.

"Let's take a long way." I was debating which way would be the easiest when Niranga whispered in my ears. I turned around, hoping to read what was in his eyes. As it was dark outside, I couldn't. It felt as if we were back in Sigiriya descending the citadel, the anticipation of his hand brushing against mine awakening the butterflies in my stomach. Not bothered with responding, I followed the same long path I took coming here.

As we started walking towards my office, Niranga crossed over to walk on my right side to keep the oncoming traffic away from me. It was such a subtle motion of protection and care, which I would have missed if I was not in tune with his gestures.

I have noted Thaththa and Amma doing the same when they walk with anyone of us. Even though I have been independent and fully capable of managing myself for years, I felt a warm appreciation for him. With a simple act, he made me feel protected.

We walked in silence. Rain was beating heavily. Both of us were half soaked as the small umbrella Sula gave me was not enough to cover us both. The hemline of my saree was soaking wet. I shivered as the icy wind blew across us.

"You cold?" without waiting for my response, he put his arm around my shoulder and drew me closer to him. I could feel the warmth of his fingers warming up my arm that was already soaked by the rain. Part of me wanted to resist and pull away, and the other part of me wanted to put my arm around his waist and melt into his warmth, seeking the shelter of his body heat.

"Hey, this is not Sydney." I brushed off his hand and moved aside from the excitement I enjoyed, letting my sensible side win.

"I thought you were a liberated woman," there was sarcasm in his voice.

"Exactly…" He doesn't know my deliverance comes from not giving in to that desire. He gave me a puzzled look and dropped his hand. Though we were stuck on the long path, it was a brief journey. When we got there, most of the other offices were closed. There was light in ours as Sula was waiting for me.

"Here we are. Would you like to come up?"

"Maybe another time……. Um…. Is Gorky going to drop you home?" Catching Sula's silhouette through the window curtain, Niranga raised his eyebrows.

"Don't be rude. He has a name." Niranga unfolded the umbrella and gave it back to me without even noting my comment.

"You take it, it is still raining," I pushed back the umbrella, worried he would catch a cold.

"No, it is okay. I am already wet. I will have a shower when I get back." Niranga stuck his hands inside his trouser pockets, refusing to take the umbrella back. There were so many things I wish I could ask him, like where is he staying, what if he gets sick, when is he going back to Nuwara Eliya? I shuffle my feet, hoping that will sweep away those inquisitive thoughts from my mind.

"Will you come on Saturday?" Niranga broke the uneasy silence between us.

"I will have to try these and determine if they are worth travelling 100kms." I pointed to the bag of velvet tamarinds he gave me with a wicked smile, brushing off the hopefulness he had in his voice.

"You can bring Gorky with you." Niranga didn't sound overly pleased with the proposal.

I blinked. "Why should I?"

"Wouldn't you want to dance with your boyfriend?"

"And have Amma planning my wedding next week?... Um..... No, thank you." I told him the truth, which would be the case if Sula came. Niranga appeared concerned, thinking, processing what I said.

"Go now. We need to lock up and head home." Before his thoughts turned into a lengthy list of questions, I shoved.

"I'll see you on Saturday. " He would not give up easily, or maybe he knew me better than I did. Without waiting for my response, Niranga turned around and left. When I returned to the office, Sula was waiting for me.

"So why has he come in a rush to see you?"

"To give me this." I showed him the bag full of velvet tamarinds. Knowing my obsession with the fruit, he chuckled.

"Is he that hard up that he couldn't get you something expensive? I thought he is loaded," Sula teased, snatching a hand full of fruit from the bag. "Seriously, what was he after?" Sula asked while sucking on a fruit.

"He wants me to come to his parent's anniversary dinner on Saturday."

"Which you were planning to avoid." Sula was gently reminding me of my earlier decision.

"Yes.... Um.... I changed my mind. I am going now." I was not sure when I had concluded, but I felt so happy and excited.

"Of course, you are, especially when he comes bearing a bag full of velvet tamarinds." I ignored the sarcasm in his voice and locked up for the night.

"He invited you as my plus one." Sula was surprised as I was.

"Didn't you tell him you don't want Aunty getting worked up planning our wedding?"

"Yes, he doesn't see the irony in that."

"So I gather you still haven't told him the truth?"

"Serves him right for jumping to conclusions. I am sure one of these days, he will figure it out."

I gave a wicked grin, and Sula joined my laugh.

***

"Do you know? Sex is overrated!" Reshani, Sula, and I stopped eating, staring at Nilush in astonishment. It was our usual Thursday night dinner to catch up. As Ravindu was on the night shift at the hospital working on his rounds, so it was just the four of us having dinner at my place. Thursday night catch-ups have been a ritual for us since the early days at the university before Sula dropped off. When Ravidu and Nilush became members of the trio (Reshani, Sula and I), we changed the venue from the university canteen to a more centralised location. We started gathering at Reshani's or my place as both Sula and Nilush still live with their parents.

We were sitting cross-legged in my small living room, using the coffee table as our dining table; happily sharing the two packs of kotthu roti, Sula got us. It began as another ordinary evening with the usual banter, carrying on a meaningless chit chat without an agenda. Everyone was taking a turn whining about their challenges of the week, so no one expected such a bold declaration from Nilush.

"What I mean is, our culture gives it much more prominence than it should be." Noticing our bewilderment, Nilush continued to explain. "Wanting to have sex is the natural order of life. It is like drinking and eating. We are the ones who have established parameters around it and have made it complicated and more important than what it actually is, a biological need!"

None of us uttered a single word. I picked the same concern going through my mind on the faces of the other two.

"Who are we to say we should only limit our affection to one person or that one can't have sex before marriage or one shouldn't have casual sex?" Still, no one of us talked, not having any clarity where Nilush's stream of thoughts was leading.

"Tell me, Resh," Nilush turned to Reshani, glaring at her with piercing eyes. "If this damn culture allowed you to have sex before marriage, would you and Ravidu have married when you did?" Sula and I also swung to Reshani, eagerly expecting her response.

"Let me reflect." Reshani stopped eating and got up to grab a cup of ginger tea from the nearby book rack. We all followed her movement with curiosity. I felt a jittery uneasiness swirling in my tummy.

"Hmm... Now that you mention it, you are right Nilush," After taking a few sips of tea, Reshani returned to where she sat before and spoke with lucidity.

"The only reason we got married when we did was that it gave us the license to sleep with each other without being judged. If we had the guts to have a relationship outside the cultural expectations, we might have not married."

In the years I have been friends with Reshani, she has never spoken to us about her marriage this way. She was the first closest friend I made after moving to Kandy. I was there when she got married to Ravidu when she was just twenty-one years old. I could have sworn to the growth of their love from a tiny thread to a thick rope over the years that kept them bound to each other. I have witnessed the evolution of their affection from jealous possessiveness to an undemanding acceptance. But this piece of the declaration was new to me.

"Now when I think back, five years ago when we got married, we barely knew anything at all about sex, love or life." Taking our silence as an invitation to explain, Reshani continued to talk.

"We were kids. I was in my second year in university, and Ravidu had just graduated. He was my first boyfriend. After that, I had not been with any other man other than Ravidu. Now, I can never!" Reshani signed with a defeated voice.

"Do you want to?" Not being able to keep quiet anymore, I uttered in disbelief. I was not sure why I felt so scared. Maybe because I was worried my best friend was contemplating a divorce. Or perhaps this entire conversation forced me to admit the invisible thread that keeps pulling me towards Niranga is more physical than an emotional need to be connected with him.

"Fuck, no! I can never find a man who would put up with me the way Ravi does." Reshani shrugged off and continued eating as if what she said earlier didn't matter at all. I didn't notice I had been holding my breath, hands clenched with concern, until I heard Reshani's affirmation.

"What you are saying? That it is okay to sleep around?" Sula asked in disgust. His face had turned darker, and I guess that must be because he was annoyed. I glanced at Sula in horror. *'Does Sula know?'* My heart sank with the fear of facing Sula; I could not comprehend how to explain myself to him. If Sula gasps at what I have been keeping from him, he will never forgive me.

"Pretty much so. What is wrong with that? You eat not only rice and curries all the time. You try other dishes too, don't you?" Nilush straightened his torso and spoke with gusto.

"What sort of decent person would be involved in erotic contacts and short-term lust without a romantic attraction?" Sula drew his eyebrows, clearly showing his disagreement.

"Casual sex doesn't rob one's human decency, Sula! One can still be decent and have their values and not be in a committed relationship." I wondered why there was heavy stress on *'relationship'* and the reason behind the dark, gruelling stare Sula threw at Nilush. I sense there is a subtle conversation between these two that I was not ready to translate.

"Hey, can you two stop your pissing contest and help with an idea for an anniversary present," I said to avoid this exchange turning into something ugly and unpleasant. I had a hasty impulse to stop their dialogue. Though both Sula and Nilush look like they want to punch each other, they both give in, turning to me with their full attention.

"Why don't you give them one of your photos? Surely, there are a couple of good ones that you can pick one have it enlarge to hand in one of their room." Sula suggested.

"Saku, bring out your photo collection. We can help you select one." Reshani nudged me towards my bedroom to fetch the box full of photos I keep underneath my bed, agreeing with the idea.

I brought out the collection of photographs I had held over the years. I have kept them all in order with their negatives. We went through my clicks going down the memory lane, recollecting the trips we took as a group and my tours with guests, revisiting locations and background stories we had of each other.

We all fancied the photo I had taken of a silhouette of an elderly couple against the sunset in front of the Galle Face beach. The elderly gentleman was helping his wife (I assumed), who was in a saree, to step onto the edge of the stone he was standing on. His hands stretched, holding her by one and pulling her up by the other. There was such admiration and love on the lady's face. The backdrop of the gold and orange mixed sunset above the dark blue shades of the rolling waves was just perfect. We agreed it would be an ideal gift for a couple celebrating their thirty-fifth wedding anniversary if we enlarge it to a sizable frame. They could hang it in their lounge if they wished.

We had little time to prepare. Sula had a friend working at Luxman Studio who could get it ready by midday on Saturday; it would give me enough time to take the afternoon bus home. I also picked a couple of photos for Niranga from many photos I took on the day we visited Sigiriya for printing.

One of Niranga's photos I have taken had captured the best of his facial expressions, highlighting his smiling eyes and sharp cheekbones. His shades were off, catching the laughter, his brown eyes sparkling like stars. The White t-shirt he wore that day had made his mahogany colour skin tone more prominent. The backdrop of Sigiriya and the green leaves of the big neem tree on the side of the frame had given it a refreshing natural take.

"No wonder women go nuts over this guy. I wouldn't be able to keep my hands off him either." Nilush muttered, admiring the photo seductively. Though Sula didn't seem pleased, he said nothing.

"He sure is handsome, Saku. You haven't exaggerated." Reshani said, taking it for a closer look.

"Don't you wonder why is he single?"

"We are not sure if he is single!" I ignored the subtle resentment in Sula's voice and shared something I had been speculating about lately. It is unusual for Niranga not to have a girlfriend, so someone could wait for him back in Sydney.

"Oh, wow, who captured these? You look gorgeous, Saku". Reshani was going through some random photos Niranga took of me after grabbing my camera.

"Niranga."

"Hmm… He has captured your best side." Reshani said, comparing my face with the image in the photo.

"Resh, can I borrow a dress from you to wear to the dinner?" I changed the subject as I was not comfortable watching my friends glaring at my photos and commenting.

I was planning on begging for a dress from Reshani later, but the awkwardness I felt made me use it as a distraction.

"Why? Can't you buy a new dress? Don't tell me you don't have any money with all the hours you do!" I knew Reshani's contempt was directed at Sula when she turned to me with disappointment on her face, hands on her hips. She already knew I didn't have enough money to spend on a new dress.

"What good is it doing three jobs if you can't afford to get a new dress when you want one?" I wished she would stop, as speaking about our dire financial predicament made my eyes tear.

"Why do you need a new gown? Why are you so worked up about this party?" Sula turned with irritation, trying to understand why I was unusually interested in dressing up.

"I want to feel confident." I glared at Sula with annoyance because he made me feel embarrassed having to explain myself. *'I can't seduce him in my jeans and t-shirt, can I?'* Inner child screamed, admitting for the first time why I was so worked up about the anniversary dinner and wanting to look attractive.

"You don't need a pretty little dress to be confident. You are born confident! Just dazzle everyone with your gorgeous smile." Sensing my discomfort, Sula immediately lifted my spirits with reassurance.

"Awe, that is so sweet. You can paralyse the entire world with your smile like a Black Widow then!" We all sensed the jealousy in Nilush's voice when he referred to the deadly spiders that kill their prey with their venom. After all these years, it was amusing to see Nilush still feels threatened by me. Reshani winked and raised her shoulders to say, *'Someone is jealous?'* and I saw Sula glancing away, looking pleased.

17 TEMPTATION

By the time I got home for the anniversary dinner, it was dark. Malli came to pick me up on his bicycle as usual. Amma and Thaththa were already at the Senege's house, helping them prepare for the celebration. It has always been that way; those four adults treated each other's affairs as their own.

The driveway to Senege's house was illuminated with colourful lights. Their house reminded me of the Water Palace in Rajasthan, India, at night. Akka said the Seneges expect many guests, the *'whose who'* in Nuwara Eliya, was to grace the event.

Uncle Sarath used to be one of the town's most prominent business executives respected by the community. Aunty Nelum also had her fan base at the church. I expected nothing less from the Seneges; ten years ago, the town lived to attend their parties. Although, I was curious why this celebration was not being held at the Grand Hotel in the city centre.

When Malli, Akka, and Saman Aiya and I arrived, the party was in full swing. There were many people in small groups in the garden engaged in lively discussions. Seneges always had a well-kept garden. Even when they were overseas, they had a permanent gardener up keeping the lawns and landscape. There were tables and chairs in neat arrangements underneath the garden trees, decorated in the same colourful lights as the driveway.

"Wow, these guys are loaded." Saman Aiya exclaimed as we approached the Senege's house. Saman Aiya was back from his business trip in time to escort Akka to the party. It shouldn't have surprised me his first observation was Senege's wealth as his previous encounters with Aunty and Uncle been brief and years apart.

"Yes, the Seneges are one of the wealthiest families in town," Akka was too eager to volunteer.

"So, what do they do for a living? Do they have a local business?" I was not interested in lingering around and take part in that conversation. Malli and

I left Akka to respond to Saman Aiya's inquisitive questions and went to the house.

The live band had already begun, and joyous music was flowing across each room through open doors and windows, synchronising the beat of my heart. I started swaying to the rhythm as I navigated through the guests to find Aunty and Uncle. We saw them standing in the living room, welcoming their guests.

"You look gorgeous, Aunty," I hugged her and Uncle, congratulating them on their anniversary. Both Akka and I grew up admiring how elegant Aunty Nelum always presented herself. While Akka picked up her dress sense, I remained a passive admirer. Aunty had a natural talent to pair colours with her skin tone. Today was no different. She was in a neatly cut olive-coloured cocktail dress, accessorised by a pair of pearl earrings and a necklace complimenting her outfit. Her makeup was subtle, not as loud as I saw on a few other ladies I just passed by.

"What about Uncle?" Smiling happily, Aunty winked at Uncle, who was standing nearby.

"Uncle is born handsome. Aunty, you are so lucky to have him," I grinned, giving a cheeky smile.

"That charm will not work on me today! I am cross with you, young lady!" Uncle wagged his index finger, shaking his head with disappointment.

"Oh, dear, what did I do wrong? I wasn't even here to offend you, Uncle."

"Stop teasing her, Sarath! Look at her; you got the poor girl worried now."

"Don't pay any attention to him, Sasoo," Giving Uncle a dismissing glare, Aunty patted my cheek to console.

Akka, who joined us a few minutes ago with Saman Aiya, eagerly quizzed. "What did Nangi do, Uncle?"

"Aney, it is nothing, no big deal, Amali." Aunty shook her head with indifference. "Niranga was going to take Uncle on a deep-sea fishing tour. He has changed it to whale watching because of Saku's lecture on the ethics of fishing." Aunty laughed. Akka didn't have to mutter, *'You will get it thick from Amma.'* as I already expected Amma's disappointment and scolding tomorrow. I remember the warning I got from her on the night we talked about fishing.

"Please don't worry, Sasoo." Noting my apprehension, Aunty grabbed my hand to comfort me.

"I am so glad Niranga stopped fishing. I hated it. Don't pay any attention to Uncle; he doesn't know what is good for him, even if it hit him in the face." Aunty Nelum put her arm around my waist, hugging me to cheer me up.

"Uncle, you will love whale watching much more than fishing. So tell me, what can I do to make it up to you?"

"Your punishment is to convince Niranga to get married soon." Uncle wagged his index finger again with a stern look on his face. *'Why would I do that when I don't believe in it?'* I was so relieved that he couldn't hear my thoughts.

"I love your confidence in me, assuming I could attempt something even the God hasn't been braved enough to try!" I smiled innocently, ignoring the laughter Aunty and Uncles were trying to hide.

"Then you have to convince your boyfriend to marry you." Uncle Sarath was not ready to stop. He pinched one of my cheeks and peered into my eyes, expecting acceptance.

"Now, that is something I can work on." I smiled happily.

I saw Saman Aiya watching our exchange with the irritation of an outsider who could not get the subtlety of the conversation. Not acquainted with our relationships, he couldn't follow our banter.

"You little possum, go join others." Uncle laughed in his pleasant way and nudged me away from him.

I felt a bit left out when Akka and Saman Aiya walked away with Malli to have their own conversations with groups of friends they knew. When I moved to Kandy, I purposely shred all my ties with the town and many people I knew to wipe off my memories of Niranga. The only friendship I maintained was with Jeevani because she never crossed paths with him at that time. When I returned for visits, I was too busy spending time with my family to form new friendships or acquaintances. Looking around the room, I hardly knew any of the guests.

I picked up a glass of wine, surveying the room for Niranga. I was eager to see him. When I couldn't find him in the room, I felt disappointed and relieved at the same time. I was not prepared for how to respond to his presence. I plodded to the other room, trying to find a familiar face, wishing there would be someone I could strike a conversation with.

"Hello, my precious, looking for your Prince Charming?" Nadee stopped me, imitating Kanmali, the Gypsy palm reader from Sigiriya. She was sitting at a nearby table with a couple of other friends.

"Hey, you two, how are you both doing?" I was so thrilled to be around two familiar faces.

"Nice to see you girl, you are stunning in that dress." Nadee hugged me. I beamed, knowing the extra effort I put on today to dress up was being noted. I wanted Niranga to notice me as a woman. Tonight, I want him to experience the same emotions I grapple with; have butterflies in his stomach when he eyes me. I want him to note an allure of craving to stand close to me. And I want to catch his eyes light up with desire when he gets sight of me across the room, wanting to hold me.

I was wearing a bright orange Bohemian dress I borrowed from Reshani. It suited my skin tone perfectly. The free-flowing long sleeves and short flared skirt gathered at the waist were a perfect fit for me and did the occasion. The black tights I wore underneath with my heels made me appear lean and tall. I came to the party with confidence tonight, carrying myself as one of those African models than an overgrown tomboy.

"Hey, come and join us." When Nadee invited me, I quickly pulled out a chair and sat next to her.

"Where are the kids?" I glance around, trying to find Nadee's twins, expecting to spot them running around the house.

"Oh, we left them with our maids. This night is for us adults to enjoy." Nadee laughed off, giving Janaka a suggestive look. I joined her laughter and settled into the night, joining their friendly chat, catching up from where we left off the other day at Sigiriya.

After a few minutes of a conversation, Janaka leaned in and spoke with a bit of regret. "Hey Sakunthala, I want to apologise for teasing you the other day. I am so sorry if I had offended you or hurt you."

"Yes, we are truly sorry, Sakunthala. We are clueless about what happened between you two. I hope Janaka didn't open up any old wounds." I felt awkward when Nadee, too, remarked. I stomped down the urge to share not only them, I too was in a mystery about what eventuated in the past. But as I pressed on a new beginning with Niranga, it seemed churlish to harp on the past, and I was unsure if I really wanted to continue with the conversation.

"Oh, don't worry about it. I should be the one to apologise. When I asked Niranga to whack you, I didn't expect him to act on it. Growing up, he was like an older brother, so I didn't want to admit how much I enjoyed reading your letter." I maintain the white lie I fabricated in Sigiriya, filling my voice with gusto I didn't have.

"I am glad you two are friends now," I added in for reassurance.

"It truly tested our friendship last week. Niranga was in a foul mood after you left." Janaka took a sip from his wineglass, glancing away, recalling the incident.

"I wasn't sure if Niranga was angry because you found out about the bashing or because you left." He turned, staring at me as if he could find the answer to his dilemma on my face.

"Sasoo, come on, they are all waiting for you," Malli barged in, interrupting the conversation. He dismissed my attempt to introduce him to Nadee and Janaka, saying he had already met Niranga's friends and dragged me back to where Aunty and Uncle were to take a family photo. I focused on not bumping into anyone accidentally while Malli was paving the way, pulling me along behind him.

The living room was filled with guests in small circles, chatting, eating, and drinking. Senege's second living room was converted into a photo booth where the photographer had his lighting and camera ready. The atmosphere resembled more of a wedding or a homecoming party than an anniversary dinner.

When I finally lifted my eyes, I saw Niranga standing there with a broad grin. His eyes lit up when he saw me behind Malli. I watched his eyes travel from my head to toe with an appreciative gaze.

I felt the butterflies in my stomach, happiness inflating into an enormous balloon bursting with anticipation. I nervously wiped the sweaty palms on the side of my dress, trying to contain the wide grin I knew was spreading across my face. Niranga looked striking in a white shirt, black trousers and a slim fit dinner jacket.

"There you are. Where have you been hiding?" Before I could respond to Niranga, the photographer started demanding we stand closer for the photograph. It was the perfect excuse for me to stand next to Niranga without giving away my desire to be near him. It felt like a lightning strike when Niranga draped his arms around my waist, pulling me closer to him. I was giddy, leaning in, getting as close as I could; I have been craving this proximity ever since we shared the umbrella on that rainy evening.

"Even with your heels, you are still short Saku, move to the front with Amali." As the photographer was still demanding us to get closer, Niranga slightly pushed me to stand before him, still holding onto my waist.

"You smell so nice." When he leaned forward and whispered in my ear, I thought my heart would burst through my ribcage with excitement. I felt his lips brush past my ear ever so lightly, sending a million and one electric sensations down my spine, making me wonder if it was an accident or was he purposely flirting with me.

"You too." I stretched my neck to glance at him sideways, intentionally lowering my voice, making him lean forward. I felt his hands tightening their grip on me as if he was trying to contain something that was struggling to get out. The thrill I felt of being alive and excited was like a half-boiled egg, soft and wobbly inside, waiting to be cracked open.

After the photo was taken, others went on their separate ways, leaving me standing there feeling lost and awkward, yet excited that I had Niranga's attention to myself.

"Where were you?" I asked, breaking the silence.

"Why?" A mischievous smile spread across his lips. "Did you miss me?" His voice was husky, eyes loaded with laughter.

'Of course I missed you. I have been missing you since the last time I met you. My heart skipped with joy when I saw you.' I bit my lips to keep my thoughts. He doesn't need to know my nights were filled with too many erotic dreams about him and days with sensual thoughts. I gazed into his eyes and pealed them away to hide my nervousness.

"Did you?" I wanted to find out what he felt for me.

'Does he feel the same pull I have for him? Does he get the same insane rush of blood, the tingle in his spine? Does he also feel crazy, short of breath with lumps in his throat?' I wondered.

"I was too busy to look for you," When Niranga said with unexpected indifference, I turned to walk away to hide the rejection I felt clutching my heart. That invisible balloon filled with happiness floated beside me earlier when I stood near him, smiling at the camera burst into pieces with his careless shrug.

"Hey," Niranga's voice sounded earnest, making me stop. "I was lying. I couldn't wait to see you."

"Where are you going?" Niranga questioned with urgency when I didn't respond.

"To Janaka's table."

"He is married!" I heard the subtle warning in his tone.

"Are you jealous?" I teased back, staring at him.

"Yes, I am," Niranga said with such a force, the light flintiness we had between us abruptly vanished. His eyes got darker, and seriousness came over his face.

"Come with me." He grabbed my fingers, pulling me in a rush.

"Where?"

"Niranga, Thaththa wants you." He didn't get to respond as Aunty Nelum called out from across the room.

"I will find you!" Niranga dropped my hand with a promise in his voice.

"Hey," He stopped to turn around when I called after him. "You owe me a dance!" I smiled, hoping it was dazzling enough to hold his attraction.

"I do?" He blinked, eyes widening.

"Yes, for making me burn...... my hand." I paused, waiting for him to protest.

"I am cashing it tonight." I held my glare, showing him how determined I was. He stared back for a few seconds before his smile widened.

"You are clueless about how to make someone pay back!" Niranga said. *'Oh, I do. It is you who are not well versed! You will dance with a praying mantis.'* I shrug my shoulders with the secret knowledge.

"Be prepared to be dazzled." He walked away with a pledge, leaving me paralysed with his smile. *'Holy mother of Kali, he will give me into a cardiac arrest just with that look.'* I took a deep breath to calm myself, realising I was not strong enough for this seduction game I started.

I grabbed another glass of wine and joined Nadee and Janaka. I plunked down on the chair, feeling dizzy as if I had got off from a merry-go-round. My mind was spinning with anticipation of the night to come. Finally, I let myself calm down, joining the conversation going around the table.

"This is like a mini wedding; I am surprised they are not having this at the Grand Hotel."

Senaka was surveying the room, making the same observation I had made earlier. It was a lavish party with a lot of guests, food, and music. Today did not differ from their previous celebrations; the only fresh addition being the illuminated driveway and garden with colourful lights.

"If Niranga didn't interfere, they would have had it there," Janaka muttered. I was listening to their chatter with amusement and a bit of jealousy. They all knew Niranga, the way I used to, years ago, before we became strangers.

"Just imagine if their anniversary party is like this, how Niranga's wedding is going to be?"

"I think Aunty plans to have it this year. This is the practice run." The group laughed at Tharushi's response to Janaka.

"He has to find a woman first!" Nemantha sounded doubtful.

"That is why this place is full of gorgeous girls. I haven't seen so many in one room in ages. Last time must have been at my formal." The guy who joined the table commented, referring to his high school dance event back in Australia. It was true. There were a lot of beautiful girls in the room I thought had not seen in Nuwara Eliya before. I suspect Aunty and Uncle have invited all their acquaintances with beautiful daughters.

"I believe this is Aunty's plot to get Niranga to pick one." Nadee was sharing my exact thoughts. I noted a resentment building up inside me towards those unknown girls.

"Good luck with that! If he has his way, Niranga will sleep with all committing to none."

"Oh, you are jealous that you can't do that anymore, Ranga." Varuni, Senaka's wife, teased the guy who joined us earlier.

They were bantering on as close friends do, making fun of each other, giving no regard to me sitting silently listening to their conversation.

"It is not jealousy, sweetheart; it is a fact. Can you tell me the last time you have seen Niranga with the same girl for over three months? His longest affair was with that doctor he went out with. That lasted longer only because both their schedules didn't have an opening to break it off."

All at the table laughed at what Ranga said. I felt I was going through Niranga's diary without his permission, listening to his friend's chatter about his personal life. Niranga had aged, but he had changed little when it came to commitment. Even when we were in school, his love interests changed from month to month. Being one of the brightest students with his lovable persona, he got away with everything. He was so likeable; that others always made excuses for his behaviour.

"It wouldn't have lasted, anyway. Their interests were so different. Niranga needs someone to ground him. A woman who doesn't go smitten by his chiselled features and charming personality." *'Good luck with that!'* I wanted to say to Nadee. Luckily, no one heard what I muttered underneath my wine glass.

"I thought Yesha would be an excellent match," Nadee said, sounding a bit disappointed.

"Oh, I preferred the Irish girl from his office. She was so much in love with Niranga. I wonder how she coped when he broke it off with her."

"Do you know why he did that?" Janaka chirped in with a grin on his face; clearly, he was dying to share the story. "Because she didn't want to have any kids." Without waiting for any entice, he blurted.

"As if he is the settling kind!" Tharushi sneered with amusement. I recalled our conversation about kids in our commute to Kandy. I could understand his disappointment at having to be with a woman who wouldn't want children; it would be a deal-breaker for Niranga.

"Sometimes, I get the impression he is searching for something he has lost." Senaka changed the carefree tone around the table to a more serious note. "I know you ladies believe Niranga is a playboy, but he is genuinely a nice guy. He just hasn't met his soul mate yet." *'Someone has a man-crush.'* I hid my grin to disguise the admiration in Seneka's tone.

"Niranga doesn't do things lightly. I will never forget when he broke off with Nisha because she was mean to me." When Varuni spoke with sadness in her voice, everyone sitting at the table turned to her, expecting her to share the back story. "One day, Nisha saw me cleaning toilets when I was working as a part-time cleaner and mocked me, saying she didn't want me to touch anything on the table as I was not hygienic enough. Niranga was there, and from the next day, he stopped seeing her."

It was interesting to watch Senaka and Varuni both defending Niranga, being supportive of him. But, as they went on sharing memories of who Niranga had been with and how he had broken off with them, I didn't want to stay there any longer.

Listening to them made me uncomfortable, yet I chose not to leave the table to wander around in this house full of strangers. I hate idle chitchat, especially having to share personal details with strangers. I was shifting in my seat with discomfort when someone tapped me on my shoulder.

"Hey Saku, how about a dance?" I have never been so glad to lay eyes on Kasun. I ignored the contempt I would see on Akka's face when she caught me dancing with him or the little warning I heard inside me, reminding me I was encouraging his obsession. Just wanting to flee from the table, I eagerly followed him to the dance floor without waiting for any persuasion.

The big dining room was converted into a dancing floor by removing all the furniture. There were already a couple of dancers on the floor. Malli was in the middle dancing with Menaka, leading her on a quickstep, a dance routine I loved. I relaxed and followed Kasun's lead.

Kasun was a talented dancer. He was tall and personable, a genuinely nice guy. I would have enjoyed having him around in another lifetime and accepted him as a suitable life partner. Kasun's presence was comforting, not electrifying or exhilarating. I fell into a peaceful rhythm with him, enjoying the steps, staying in the moment, trying not to let my mind wonder about Niranga.

I was so focused on my steps that I didn't notice a change in shoes before I sensed the difference in the company. Niranga had stepped in to lead and was dancing next to me. I lost my footing and would have stepped on his shoe if he didn't swiftly steady me.

"Are you purposely falling to get me to hold you?" Niranga chuckled, pulling me closer to him.

"Are you complaining?" I asked offhandedly, following his steps comfortably. He looked surprised and pulled me closer to his chest.

"Not at all." This time, I knew he purposely brushed his lips on my ear when he whispered. The chemistry between us was so thick that I nearly lost my steps again. He quickly steadied me with a grin, enjoying my nervousness. I turned my neck to stare at his face and saw his gaze travel from my face to my exposed neck. I watched him inhaling deeply, knowing I had stirred him.

"You look gorgeous today," Niranga ran his eyes over me, eyeing the base of my neck resting on the neckline of the dress I was wearing. It was way too deep, giving a glimpse of my breasts. I felt a warmth spreading through my body as if eyes were caressing them.

"You don't look too bad yourself either!" I grinned, admiring his dignified appearance.

"Are you having a good time?" I asked, staring into his eyes.

"Now, I am." Niranga pulled me closer, purposely brushing his lips again on my ear as it has become a habit. I said nothing, as I couldn't trust my voice.

'So much for seducing him'. I heard the child mocking me when I couldn't even muster the courage to hold my end of the conversation.

We swayed to the music a bit longer in silence. I was glad the dance floor was getting filled with enthusiastic dancers. It gave us a perfect opportunity to dance closer to each other. I wanted to lay my head on his shoulder, put my arms around his waist and hug him tighter, but I didn't. I was hypersensitive to his presence: I could feel him, smell him, and hear him. And I was melting.

I felt the weight of his fingers on my waist and his hand where they touched, the tightening of his shoulder muscles where my fingers rested. I felt his arousal the same way I felt my nipples getting harder. I inhaled his aftershave, pinewood and mint mixed with his musk, noting the slight trace of scotch on his breath when he exhaled that barely graced my cheeks. I listened to his breathing, slowly calming down along with mine.

When we glanced at each other, we were conversing in a secret language. I was in an airtight container, ready to explode. I was falling into a bottomless chasm of desire. Unknowingly, I had pressed myself closer to Niranga when he slowly stepped back, giving me a curious glare.

"How much wine did you have, Cookie?"

"Not much. Why?"

"I hope it is not the wine!" His eyes were sparkling and his voice was muffled.

"It is for me to know and you to find out!" I felt reckless and brave.

'How about we get out of here?' When Niranga asked, all I wanted to do was leave. Go somewhere I can run my fingers through his hair, touch the softness of his lips, feel the warmth of his breath on me, and hear him purr my name with longing. Thinking about the possibility of it made me shiver with excitement, and heat engulfed my body.

'I have achieved my goal for the night!' Even after recognising the yearning in his eyes and the desire in his voice, I didn't want to walk away with him. I wanted five more minutes, freezing the moment. The queasy, tingling thoughts made me anticipate what could happen next. I tried to hold on to the rise of my heartbeat and the heat spreading through me.

"Niranga Aiya, I think Uncle Silva has a bit too much to drink." I was glad when Malli interrupted us, as I don't believe I could have gone on any longer keeping my hands to myself.

Uncle Silva was one of Senege's family friends, and he had a habit of getting drunk at any gathering. This meant a bit of negotiation about how to get him home without creating a big fuss.

Strangely, I felt a bit relieved when Niranga left the dance floor, leaving me with Malli. Before he left, he leaned across Malli and mumbled something in his ear, making Malli nod.

"What was that about?" I asked with curiosity, trying to ignore the hollow sensation and the sudden cold draft I felt around the places where Niranga's fingers lingered earlier.

"Oh, just boys' stuff." Malli dismissed my question with no intention of sharing. As probing would not get me anywhere, I ignored it. When we continued dancing, Malli seized the opportunity to show off his skills, making me work hard to keep up with his steps.

When Kasun came around wanting to dance with me again, Malli hoicked me off the dancing floor.

"Hey, let's have dinner before the food runs out. I am hungry."

"Malli, that was rude. Let me do this song with Kasun, and I'll join you." I tried to turn around, but Malli's grip was too tight.

"Don't worry about Kasun. He will be okay. I tell you, there wouldn't be much food left if we didn't eat now. Others have all eaten." I reluctantly followed Malli. Being intoxicated with excitement and anticipation, I was not hungry. Malli's intuition was correct as the buffet was nearly empty; most guests had already eaten.

"Sasoo, please make sure Niranga eats this." When Aunty Nelum came by our table to leave a plate full of rice and curries, it baffled Malli and me, as Niranga wasn't anywhere nearby.

"We haven't seen him around in a while, Aunty. Do you want us to find him?"

"No..no... I will send him here. Be a possum and make sure he finishes that. He hasn't eaten at all today." Aunty appeared worried. I would be, too, knowing Niranga's enormous appetite.

Malli and I continued to eat in silence, watching some guests leave. It was almost midnight, and only less than a quarter of the crowd was still lingering around. I played with the food, reliving the earlier moments, dreaming about my next encounter with Niranga when he came and stood next to me.

"Saku, Amma said you asked for me." Malli eyed me, grinning, realising what Aunty Nelum had done.

"Yes, you are going to sit with us and finish this plate." I pointed Niranga to the plate Aunty left for him.

"I want to. But I have to take Uncle Silva home. He is too drunk to drive."

"Can't he wait for ten minutes until you have something to eat?"

"Let me drop him and come back. I can't get him to stop drinking. The longer he stays here, the worse it is going to be." Niranga sounded tired.

"How about you give the car keys to Malli, and he drops him off?" As Malli had finished his dinner, I suggested. "Malli knows where Uncle Silva lives….. Um…. Malli, can you do that?" Without waiting for Niranga's response, I turned to Malli.

"Of course, I can. Give me the keys, Aiya." Malli was more than happy to be the errand boy and was up like a jack in a box.

"Are you sure, Manoj?"

"Yes, I can take him home."

"That would be a massive help." Niranga's shoulders relaxed, and the weariness on his face faded. "Here are the keys. Don't give it to anyone other than me." Niranga pulled out a chair and slouched next to me.

"How many more do you have to drop off?"

"Few others, actually. Most of Thaththa's old friends are too drunk. They have not thought about how to get back after dinner. There is no other way for them to get back home other than being dropped off."

"Malli, has Saman Aiya gone home?" I wanted to know if Saman Aiya could be the second driver, relieving Niranga from driving duties. I could have done it, but I knew there was no way Niranga would allow me to do it.

"He left earlier with Akka. I could ask Prasad; he is still here." Reading my thoughts, Malli suggested.

"Okay then, Niranga. Give the other car keys to Prasad. These two can drop off all the drunkards at home."

"Malli, remember you both need to be responsible, no speeding. It is misty out there, so be careful. When you finish the job, come straight home, no hanging around in town." Malli nodded his head like a muppet on a show. I could see he was already distracted by the opportunity to drive Niranga's new car. "I am sure Niranga wouldn't mind lending the car for a weekend when you want to go somewhere." Niranga nodded, making Malli grin even wider.

"The other car key is in my room, Manoj, in my desk drawer."

After Malli left, an awkward silence stretched between us. "Do you have these parties in Sydney?" I broke it because I was getting edgy sitting there watching Niranga eat.

"Not as much as Amma and Thaththa would have preferred to."

"Why not?"

"A couple of reasons; our house is small and doesn't have a large enough room for their dancing. Second, though we are loaded here (I noted the way he stretched loaded and the sarcasm on his face), we are ordinary people over there. We can't afford the same luxuries as maids, chauffeurs, and caretakers. Over there, it would cost us an arm and a leg."

"Oh, it is sad that they are missing their dancing."

"They go to plenty of Lankan dinner dances." He chuckled, showing his parents weren't missing much.

"Do you also go to those?" An image of a random girl in Niranga's arms popped into my head. Jealousy covered my heart.

"Not if I can help it. Dancing is not my thing."

"But you love dancing!" I exclaimed.

"Correction, you love dancing, and I enjoyed hanging out with you." I immediately got transferred to that magical moment we had on the dance floor earlier. Both of us gazed at each other, mesmerised by the memory.

"By the way, who are those gorgeous girls I saw on the dance floor? I didn't think we had so many beautiful girls in Nuwara Eliya town." I was exaggerating. Talking nervously, as I wanted to change the subject. Niranga eyed me as if I was speaking a foreign language.

"Come on, are you telling me you haven't noticed the array of beautiful girls parading around the house? Seriously, don't mock me."

"It would have been nice to check them out if I actually had some time. I still didn't have time to have a drink with any of my friends!" Niranga shrugged off with a bit of annoyance.

"How come you are so busy?"

"I have to monitor things as people are so disorganised. I have to remind them what to do and go after them like kids."

"In case you have forgotten, Aunty and Uncle were hosting these parties when you were in your nappies! I am sure they could manage it without you bossing them around." I mocked him, reminding him how well his parents managed these occasions for many years.

"I can't let them organise their own anniversary dinner, can I?" Niranga was cynical, reminding me of his duties.

"So, what else is there to be done tonight?"

"I have to pay the caterers and the band once they finish."

"I can pay them off if you give me the list and money." I offered.

"You are well experienced in how to organise things."

"It is called asking for help, Superman!"

"Yeah, I could have asked if someone didn't go out of her way avoiding me." Niranga glanced away, pretending he wasn't making fun of me.

"Oh, don't give me that bullshit. When you came crawling with a bag of velvet tamarinds, you didn't want to ask?" He got me annoyed, and I tried to punch him. He was too quick to get hold of my fist before it hit his arm.

When his fingers intervened with mine, I felt a warm rush running through my entire body, engulfing me like a burning candle. I held my pose, panting. That electrifying sexual arousal we experienced at the dance floor was back, and it was covering both of us in a thick blanket. Niranga tugged my hand, pulling me closer to him as if he wanted to kiss me.

"Hey, did you try the cutlet? This is great." He abruptly let go of my hand and pointed to the cutlet he started eating. Meera came to our table to leave two glasses of water for us, causing a sudden change in his mood.

"No, I didn't. You love anything, deep-fried." I laughed, masking the disappointment that bubbled in my heart.

"No, I am serious. This is superb. Try for yourself." Before I could say anything, Niranga forced half of the remaining cutlet into my mouth. As I didn't expect him to feed me, I ended up biting one of his fingers.

"You bit me. " Niranga pulled his hand away, complaining.

"Serves you right!" We both laughed, feeling relaxed and happy in our corner, oblivious to our surroundings. We both were just 'us', being here, enjoying each other's company. If I had a remote control to pause the time, I wouldn't mind staying here. It was such a peaceful and content moment.

"Now, unless you want to have some dessert, join your friends. I will pay off the crew. Where are the list and money?" I pushed my chair back, breaking the hold we had on each other.

"Gosh, you are so bossy!"

"Here, the key to my almari. Money is in the second drawer to the right." He handed me a folded paper and a key.

"Okay, got it. Now go and have some fun."

I left Niranga and headed towards his room to get the money. The last time when I stepped through his bedroom door, I didn't want to come to his house, let alone be near him. Today, I wanted to linger there, sitting on his bed, running my fingers across his pillow, imagining his head lying there that morning, tracing the imprint of the mark his head has left on the pillow, breathing the traces of his smell. The urge to lay my head on his pillow and stare at the ceiling, imagining if he would have thought about me while lying there, was intoxicating.

I forced myself to get up and collect the money from the almari. Niranga still seemed to be very organised and tidy. Everything had its proper place. We are polar opposite as mine was so disorganised, as if a cyclone had gone through it.

I dragged myself away from his room and got busy sorting out the payments to the crew. They were ready to pack up, as it was way past midnight. Only a couple of Niranga's friends were left in the house by the time I paid all. I could not locate Amma or Thaththa. Malli was still out, dropping off the drunken guests.

The house was almost deserted. The floor was unclean, as if crows had scattered discarded garbage with spilt food, empty beer and soft drink bottles, and paper plates and cups all over it. I sent Meera to sleep earlier, seeing how tired and sleep-deprived she was. It will not be easy for her to clean up the place in the morning.

Niranga was with his friends, enjoying a drink at the far corner. He could not see me preparing to leave as his back was turned to me. I nearly took a step to walk towards him, but changed my mind at the last second. More than the notion of not wanting to disturb him, I was concerned about the awkwardness it would bring up. I hadn't rehearsed how to say goodbye to him as I was leaving tomorrow. It worried me; if he hugged me, I wouldn't be able to let go.

I left the house quietly and stopped when Thaththa invited me to sit with them, pulling a chair for me. He was with Uncle Sarath on the veranda, enjoying a quiet drink.

"Hey, kiddo, come and sit with us."

I didn't have it in me to say no. So, I sat down and removed my shoes. As I was not used to wearing pointy end heels, my toes were in agony. I began massaging them to ease the pain.

"How about a drink?" Uncle pointed to what they were drinking. I automatically eyeballed Thaththa. It would be nice to end the day with a drink; however, I didn't want to cross any invisible boundaries. Thaththa typically gave me a sip or two from his glass when he drank alone and when Amma was not around. We had a secret code between us; I never drink with him in front of others.

"Go ahead. Have one. Amma isn't here." Thaththa searched the room and smiled, not seeing her nearby.

"Where is she?"

"They have already retired for the night." Uncle Sarath grinned.

"Do you have any wine?"

"I can get you one. What do you prefer, red or white?" Uncle Sarath was ready to head back inside. I stopped him, pushing him back in his chair.

"What are you two having?"

"Single malt."

"I'll have the same."

"Neat or with ice?"

"With plenty of ice, please." Uncle poured some scotch into a glass, added a few cubes of ice, and then handed the glass over to me.

"Cheers, happy anniversary, Uncle, stay blessed."

The three of us sat there quietly, sipping our drinks. There was not much sound around except the occasional bickering of crickets and traces of laughter from Niranga's group. I assumed they were staying over tonight. The drink made me sleepy. I wanted to curl up and go to bed. It was a full-on day, and tiredness was catching up with me.

"Okay, it is time for me to head home gents, I am leaving." I got up and nearly fell over because my foot had gone to sleep.

"Steady, are you all right, little one?" Thaththa reached out, sounding worried.

"Are you alright to go on your own, Sasoo? Let me get Niranga to drop you home." Uncle Sarah was also concerned, speculating I was drunk.

"What nonsense, Uncle. I can cross that hedge blindfold."

"I am not drunk. My feet have gone to sleep. Goodnight." I muttered with a bit of annoyance.

"Tell Niranga and Malli I went home." I turned, remembering I hadn't bid goodbye to Niranga.

"Niranga? No more Aiya?" Uncle teased.

"Yes, his vanity is bigger than his head. So worried he will look old if I call him Aiya."

"Is that what he said?" Uncle didn't believe me and laughed.

I slipped on my shoes and slowly began the walk home, enjoying the chorus of crickets and skirting swarms of mosquitoes. It was dark outside. Someone had turned off the lights that illuminated the driveway. It was not a full moon day, and I could barely make out the pathway. *'So much for walking blindfolded.'* I muttered to myself as I stumbled on a loose rock, nearly falling flat. I steadied myself, taking a deep breath of the icy air. Maybe the glass of scotch I had was still active in keeping me warm, as I was not cold and was not shivering as I would have. I was on the last stone step and about to cross the veranda to my room when I heard footsteps behind me. Before I turned, I sensed it was Niranga.

"You left without telling me." He didn't sound happy. I waited for him to get closer before I spoke.

"I have to return before I tuned in to a pumpkin." Though it was way past midnight, I joked, hiding my nervousness.

"Do I have a chance to be the Prince Charming?" He grinned.

"Did you bring the glass slipper?"

"Would a cape do?"

It was dark, and there was not much light except the weak yellow beam that filtered through the windows of our living room that Akka had left on for us. Niranga was carrying the shawl I had left behind when I sat with Thaththa and Uncle Sarath.

"Why did you leave without this? You could catch a cold." He came closer and draped the shawl around my shoulders. I didn't want to tell him there was no point now, as he was here to keep me warm.

"Cape will turn me into Wonder Woman." I laughed, putting my hands on my waist, imitating the Wonder Woman pose.

"You are more Wonder Woman than Cinderella." He tugged the shawl, pulling me closer to him. I gazed into his eyes, trying to read them, and could only pick the glitter in his eyes, getting more prominent as his face got closer to mine.

In a second, he put his arms around me and claimed my lips. His lips were soft and wet. His breath was warm and smelled of scotch. When his fingers cupped my face, a warm rush ran down my spine. I put my hands around his neck, kissing him back.

Niranga slowly pulled away as if he didn't expect it. I kept my gaze on him, gently stroking his hair. He smiled, claiming my lips again. A warm lava-like rush ran through my body, warming me from head to toe. I stood on my toes, pulling him closer to me.

I was unsure how long we had been kissing, as I didn't have any sense of time. All I can remember was it felt natural and right to be in Niranga's arms and have his lips exploring mine. I saw fireworks in my head, sending multi-coloured sparkles around me.

When we stopped kissing, we both were out of breath, gazing at each other in marvel. I was floating high above the ground, taking an astral body walk. We slowly crossed the veranda, standing next to my bedroom window.

"I gather you still use this as your door." It was not a question, as he already knew the answer. Niranga pushed the window open, and we were about to go into my bedroom when we both heard footsteps coming up the stone staircase leading up to the veranda.

Niranga quickly put his arms around me, pulling me closer to him. I laid my head on his chest, listening to his breathing, which was heavy as mine. Someone opened the front door and went inside. It was Malli returning home from his driving duty.

It amazed me I didn't faint from the panic I felt. The gravity of what we were about to hit me like a sack of rice. I guess Niranga felt the same. He stepped back and pushed me through the window. "Get some sleep." With that, he turned around and left. I questioned if I should tell him I wouldn't be able to.

"Goodnight," I uttered silently to the air that he left behind.

18 LONGING

"Tell me everything."

I had only been home for few hours when Reshani barged through my front door demanding. She plopped down on the sofa in my living room, making me share the sweet and painful memories of the anniversary dinner, reliving each moment of that night.

"Damn, couldn't Manoj pick a different time to return home? Just imagine what would have happened if he didn't!" I didn't tell her I hadn't let myself run that scenario in my head for fear of the pain it would cause.

"It is what it is hon, I wanted to seduce him and that I did!" I uttered with a weak smile.

I silently observed Reshani, who was plucking imaginary threads from the dress she was wearing. A disappointment spread across her face. Reshani didn't fancy the end of the night any more than I did. I could tell she took the outcome of the night as a personal failure from her account. She doesn't respond well when her predictions don't come true.

"So, what are you going to do about it now?" She sat straight on the sofa, looking at me as I had a Plan B.

"Absolutely nothing." I shrugged it off, getting up to make us some tea.

"Seriously, Saku, are you going to let it go with no attempt? You are not one to give up that easily." She followed me to the kitchen, reminding me of my tenacious attitude toward life.

"There is nothing much I can do about it. I don't have any plans of going home until Akka goes into labour." No matter how badly I wanted to see Niranga, I was not planning to head back home to chase a fantasy.

"Now, if he comes looking for me, that is a different tale," I said confidently, as I didn't expect Niranga to seek me out as a gallant knight in a fairytale.

"It wouldn't take him long to come and find you." Reshani declared with a beaming smile. "That night, that kiss can't be the last line in your story.

Niranga wouldn't stop at that………. Um…. Not after all the chasing he had done!"

For a couple of days, I carried that great faith Reshani gave me with her resolute, keeping it close to my heart, letting myself dream until reality caught up with me. Then, I made room for insecurity and doubt.

***

"I can't afford to pay you back everything now, Saku. I don't have that much money." Nilush stopped drinking his milkshake, soliciting my sympathy. He was clever at using his adorable appearance to his advantage. Unfortunately for Nilush, I am not a person to fall for his type. *'No wonder Sula fell for this crap.'* I muttered under my breath.

"I am not asking you to pay the total now, Nilush. Just the weekly amount."

"You got this week's due, haven't you?" I was working not to project the anger I felt for Sula on Nilush. I finally found out what had happened to our tour agency's earnings. Sula had lent most of it to Nilush. I was struggling to tell myself it wasn't his fault. Sula had the responsibility. It wasn't just his cash to give.

"Why are you involved? I borrowed it from Sula. I will return the payment to him." When his attempt to distract me with his pleading demeanour didn't work, Nilush got defensive. *'Nice try, asshole.'* I wished I had the guts to tell him that.

"How many times do I have to explain this to you, Nilush? It was not only Sula's cash to lend you. The money belonged to the business. I, too, have a stake in it." It was tiring to explain the basics. I could not follow why he wasn't getting the message through.

"If we don't have the cash to pay our bills now, we are going to go bankrupt."

I watched his face to find any clue of remorse, desperately wishing for him to accept the gravity of the situation. His expressions were blank; if he felt any guilt, he nicely hid it.

"Why don't you get it? You are destroying Sula! He is about to lose his business, Nilush. Unlike you and me, he doesn't have any other means of income!"

I wanted to pull Nilush by his collar and shake him until he got some sense into that hollow head of his. He didn't show any emotions at all. I wondered if I was dealing with a psychopath as he was indifferent to my plea, checking his wristwatch and surveying the room as if he rather be somewhere else other than sitting opposite me.

"Either you pay back, or……………… I will tell your parents about your affair with the married teacher!"

I sighed, digging deeper into a place I didn't want to go. It was my last resort. Nilush straightened in his chair. I was unsure what surprised him the most, me not threatening to share his liaison with the school teacher with Sula or threatening to go to his parents. I have been carrying the weight of this information. Not being able to share it with anyone. I didn't prefer to tell Reshani or Ravidu, as they would have cut all ties with Nilush, devastating Sula.

Initially, I was not comfortable bringing up the horrible news; I backed out each time I planned on confiding in Sula. I refrained, not wanting to witness the light in his eyes fade away and be the one to break his heart. Now, after months of silence, I suspected Sula was purposely ignoring the signs. Maybe he already knows and believes if he doesn't face it, it doesn't exist. In the same way, he approaches our financial crisis.

"You wouldn't!" Nilush turned pale, sounding worried. He would not want me to go near his parents.

"Try me!" I used my mean voice, the one I use with Malli or Akka when I want to get my own way. He didn't need to know that I would dare not approach his parents. It was not because I cared about him, but because I could not do that to Sula's or Nilush's parents, as that would shatter them.

"You are a total bitch!" His cry sounded full of hatred.

"Duly noted!" I shrugged off his comment with indifference. They have called me worse.

"If you don't start paying from today, I can easily find time to visit your parents to tell them what a naughty boy you have been!"

I watched Nilush slouch down in his chair, realising we had reached an impasse. I let him struggle with his own thoughts as I continued to sip my milkshake. After a few minutes of silence, Nilush slowly lifted his head and straightened up. I guess he had accepted that I could act on my threat.

"Okay, I will return the amount I borrowed. You stay away from my Amma or Appachchi."

"Deal." I stare at his eyes to confirm. He briefly nodded, glancing away uncomfortably. He was surveying the room aimlessly, avoiding my gaze, when his eyes light up.

"Oh my god, why is that gorgeous man coming this way?" When Nilush cried with his usual dramatic flair, I turned my head to check out who he was referring to.

"Oh, shit!" I exclaimed aloud.

"Is that Niranga?" Seeing my unease, Nilush asked.

"Yes." I couldn't believe it. I did not expect to see Niranga when I was in the middle of an argument with Nilush. But it was too late; Niranga had already spotted us and was walking towards our table. He was wearing a tight-fitting t-shirt and Levis. The stubble on his face was making him seem aloof and mysterious. His hair was messy, as if he had been running his fingers through it a lot.

"He is so gorgeous in the flesh."

"Oh, you pervert. Stop undressing him." I kicked Nilush under the table with annoyance. Before Nilush could say anything, Niranga came and stood next to me.

"Hey, Saku, good to see you." Niranga leaned over and planted a kiss on my cheek, casually touching my shoulder, brushing my neck with his thumb ever so lightly. I felt the slight scratch of his stubble on my cheek. He kept his lips on me longer than necessary, as if he was trying to make a point, reminding me I was attracted to him. *'Guess what? I don't need you to remind me. Since you kissed me. Correction, from the night you walked through our front door, I felt like an old motherboard, about to crash.'* I hissed silently.

I felt a rush of heat building inside of me, similar to a room filled with LP gas, waiting for a flicker of a switch to ignite. I adjusted my shoulder away to calm myself as a molten rush was going down my spine, fluttering my stomach. When I turned to greet him, Niranga appeared furious. Without waiting for my response, he casually turned to Nilush, extending his hand.

"Hello mate, you must be Sulakkana. I am Niranga." I had an internal chuckle, realising why Niranga seemed annoyed; he had assumed I was out with Sula.

"Oh, hellooo…… Niranga. Nice to finally meet you in person. I am not Sulakkana, I am Nilush." Nilush greeted Niranga with coyness, stretching every syllable, purposely lowering his voice. He was behaving in the same way he would treat one of his love interests. I wanted to vomit with disgust.

"Um…, I am sorry, mate." Niranga looked at me with disapproval. I couldn't stop the grin spreading across my face, watching him shuffling his feet in embarrassment.

"No biggy, everyone assumes I am her fake boyfriend because I am the handsome one." *'Holy mother of Kali, in what universe do you think you are better looking than Sula?'* I was angry, more at the comparison he made than about the information he shared with Niranga.

I leaned forward, desperately wanting to burst his bubble and ask him, *'Have you seen yourself in the mirror?'* instead, I kicked his leg hard under the table. He pretended he was oblivious to what he was doing. Niranga turned to me with laughing eyes. The anger I saw in his eyes earlier had vanished.

"I'm sorry, mate, I had my wires crossed!" He said with a bounce in his speech.

"You don't mind me joining you two, do you, Nilush?" It was not a question, and he was not seeking approval. He sounded authoritative and demanding. It did not bother him he was disrupting our conversation when he grabbed a chair and sat between us.

"All yours, mate. I had enough of an earful for a week." Nilush pleasantly smiled at Niranga and turned to me with disgust. His annoyance was obvious and nothing short of what I expected from Nilush.

"Okay, I am heading off." Nilush threw the napkin off his lap onto the table, grabbed his file and got up.

"Hey, hang on for a second. What's the rush? I haven't finished my milkshake." It felt strange being left alone with Niranga. I was trying to prolong Nilush's departure.

"Despite what you believe, I have an actual job Saku that pays many people's salaries."

'Pity it doesn't allow you to pay some of your debt.' I muttered, not surprise me when Nilush behaved like a proud peacock in front of a sophisticated guy. However, it surprised me when he chose to leave. He usually wouldn't dare to move if there was an attractive man in the vicinity. Niranga turned to me with concern, not following our exchange.

"Have you forgotten something?" I blocked Nilush's dramatic exit by stretching my hand across his path. I was asking for this week's instalment. It was the only way to work on the recovery of our tour agency. Sula didn't have it in him to collect.

"You are a total bitch!" If looks could kill, I would draw my last breath by now. Nilush was sullen, and his hate was apparent when he handed over the envelope I was after.

I saw Niranga uncoiling his back, curling his fits from the corner of my eye. His face muscles tightened in response to Nilush's outburst. I quickly laid my hand on his to stop his instinct to protect me; I could manage my fights. When I saw him staring at me with alarm, I smiled with reassurance. In return, he intertwined his fingers with mine. A warmth began running through my body, making me tingle. To pretend I was not distracted, I turned to Nilush with a smile.

"We already established that earlier, Nilush. Now go and imitate you are somewhat important; try not to trip over your ego on the way out." Nilush gave me another disgusting glance and walked away in a rage. I freed my fingers from Niranga's grip to tuck away the envelope with cash safely inside my bag.

"So, what brings you here?" I picked the half-empty glass of milkshake, masquerading a coolness that I didn't possess.

I left home on Sunday morning, earlier than usual, as I didn't want to face anyone, especially Niranga. Ever since then, I have secretly been hoping we would meet again. When days stretched beyond a week, I hid those emotions, letting my mundane life take over.

The way the anniversary dinner night ended left a bitter taste in my mouth, teleporting me back to a moment in my childhood, making me relive the anguish I felt when the wafer style ice cream cone filled with chocolate chip ice cream was knocked before I could finish it. It was the only memory I have of Appachchi taking us to Maligawa on a sultry afternoon. On the way back, he stopped near the boathouse to buy Akka and me ice cream. I still recall the way my mouth watered watching the street vendor scraping the bottom of the Styrofoam box to dish out the last bit of chocolate chip ice cream I wanted so much. When a passerby knocked it off my hand and made me drop it with a splash after my first taste of it, I could not stop crying no matter what Appachchi promised me. He gathered me in his arms and offered to get me another strawberry or vanilla ice cream. I wasn't keen on either, as I continued to wail, burying my head in the hollow of his neck, grieving about not having the chocolate chip ice cream. Strangely, I experienced the same unfulfilled emotions when I thought about my encounter with Niranga. The kiss we shared was the first taste of that ice cream cone I didn't get to finish on that warm day.

Whenever the phone rang at the tour agency, I expected to hear his voice at the other end of the line. Every time someone opened the door and walked in, I wanted that person to be Niranga. When nothing happened for over a week, my hope switched sides with despair. Now that he was finally here, sitting opposite me, I pretended I was indifferent to his presence, while deep inside, my heart was ready to fly away with wings.

"You."

"So, here I am." I laughed, hoping he wouldn't pick up the nervous anticipation in my voice.

"Can we go somewhere private?"

"For what?" Now that he has made the first move, I had the upper hand. I would not make it easy for him. *'Think carefully, Niranga';* I wanted to warn him as I did not want to hear him say, *'Let's talk.'* I didn't want to talk; I needed no more words. All I wanted was to be with him. I am not waiting for romantic reassurance. I didn't need any soft enticement; my body was burning with the thirst to be with him, touch him, smell, and taste him.

Outside the café, it was raining. Raindrops splashed around, washing away the dust on the window shields, making random brown patterns with the residue. I stared through the windows, not wanting to look at Niranga. I didn't want him to sense the hunger in my eyes.

"Come, let us go." Niranga pushed back his chair and pulled me with him. 'Where?' I didn't have to ask, as he could already read me.

"To continue from where we left."

19 EUPHORIA

I felt a tremor in my heartbeat, not being able to keep up with the nervous anticipation that gripped me. The huskiness in Niranga's voice made my legs go weak. I knew I should not be holding hands in the middle of a café in Kandy. But I was glad he was clutching mine, or else I would have tumbled to the floor. As I had already paid for my milkshake earlier, we didn't have to line up at the cashier. When we crossed the road to where Niranga's car was parked, Niranga tightened his grip on my hand, eyeing me with longing.

When we hurried across the road to the car, it was not to escape the rain, but eager to get to where Niranga was taking me. My legs were still wobbly. I tightened my grasp on Niranga's hand for support. Niranga opened the car door, pushed me to the passenger seat, and ran across to the other side to start the engine.

Throughout the drive, we didn't talk. I could sense the same fear running through Niranga's mind; we could change our minds if we spoke. I sat there, making no movement. Niranga was driving faster than usual. I barely noticed the rush-hour commuters and the darkness spreading with the evening shower. Though I sensed the car moving, my mind didn't register where we were going. I was in a daze, excited, giddy, and scared at the same time. I was replaying the kiss we shared the other night, drowning in that warm fussy sensation with no attempt to stop it.

I desperately wanted to reach out and kiss him, run my fingers through his hair. I craved to inhale his perfume on his skin that kept me up. Over the last few days, the sadness of not being able to do any of that weighed me down. Now the possibility of doing all of that made me float. I dug my feet to the floor of the car to ground myself.

When Niranga pulled the car in front of an old Victorian-style house and turned off the engine, the rain had stopped. Dusk was settling in; yellow-coloured street lights were on.

"Come." Niranga got out of the car; before he came across to open my door, I was already out. I never had the patience or the practice of waiting around for a man to open any door for me. Maybe it is the culture. Although I have seen men opening the doors for women in Western movies, I haven't witnessed that practice around me. Not that many of my family or friends have cars to begin with.

Even though Thaththa loves Amma very much, I can't recall him doing that when he had a car. Neither have I come across Saman Aiya opening the car door for Akka, although she is pregnant. Ravidu jokes, there are only two reasons a man opens a car door for a woman; either it is a new car, or the woman is incapable of such a simple act. I suspect he has twisted an old joke to annoy Reshani.

I followed Niranga, who took a few quick steps and opened the front door to the house with a key he had in his pocket. Niranga leaned across and switched on the hallway light as if he owned the place. Then he turned around and grabbed my hand, pulling me through the front door before closing it.

I didn't have time to survey the place before Niranga roughly pulled me into his arms and kissed me. I had my back to the door; I leaned on it for support, as I could not trust my legs anymore. I was lost and was slipping in my desire. I couldn't fathom how we ended up in the room or when we got there.

I could feel the heaviness of our breathing and the sound of our clothes hitting the bedroom floor one by one. I barely noticed the street lights in Kandy town and its shadows peeping through the bedroom window. Niranga eases me into the big double bed in the centre of the room.

There was no need for conversation. Niranga heard my inner thoughts. I didn't need to be persuaded. We were aligned in our lust, consumed by the desire to become one.

We released the hunger that was trapped in us, impatient and rough, wanting to melt into each other's bodies. Not allowing time for anything else. We both were scared someone would snatch this moment away if we did not hold on to it.

As the night stretched, we settled into a slower pace, exploring each other. I was running my fingers across Niranga, savouring the softness of his lips, tightness of his chest, the warmth of his breath, the same way his fingers sought me. We let us discover each other in the dark, letting the overwhelming euphoria be our guide.

It felt so natural to lie there beside him, using his shoulder as a pillow for my head, his arm around me, drawing me tighter to his body. It was there that I drifted off into a blissful sleep.

***

I woke up thirsty. It took me a while to realise where I was. Niranga was sleeping next to me, his arm possessively across my waist, holding me closer to him. I slowly moved his hand and eased out of bed. I was not familiar with this place to locate the light switch and look for my discarded clothes. I picked the first thing I could find in the dark - Niranga's t-shirt. I put it on and left the room, searching for some water and something to eat; I was starving.

The house felt intimate, like a distant memory. I found the kitchen and drank some water. I couldn't find anything to eat other than a tub of ice cream in the fridge. *'Well, this has to do.'* I told myself.

With a spoon from one of the kitchen drawers and the ice cream tub, I went to the living room and sat on the sofa facing the windows. The small clock on the wall showed it was after midnight. If you look closely, you can see the rooftop of the Maligawa through the glass, which meant we were in a house on the hill close to Lake Kandy.

As the ice cream melted in my mouth, I wondered what flavour ice cream Jeevani would call me now? I chuckled at the thought that I was no longer 'vanilla.'

I was in a stranger's house, half-naked, wearing a man's t-shirt. My lips and breasts were soft, bruised by Niranga's passionate kissing. My body had hidden marks of prolonged lovemaking. I was eating chocolate chip ice cream in the middle of the night. I felt unbound, unburden, and unleashed.

'It can't be chocolate chip. It is too ordinary. Maybe we have to create a new flavour.' My monologue got interrupted when Niranga called out my name, sounding worried. As I was sitting in the dark, he wouldn't have seen me when he came out of the room.

"Here."

Niranga, wearing only boxer shorts, rushed to my side and switched on a nearby table lamp. When he plunged next to me, I blushed, noticing his half-naked body. Luckily, he didn't see my discomfort.

"That could be expired. It will make you sick, don't eat it."

"Too late, I was hungry, and I almost finished it."

"Oh, well then, I will have some and become sick with you." He smirked, grabbing a spoon full of ice cream from me.

"What is the point of that?"

"Why?" Niranga frowned, moving his eyebrows closer.

"Shouldn't you stay healthy to look after me if I am unwell?"

"Do you always have to be so practical? Don't you have any romance in you?" Niranga didn't appreciate the teasing, sounding disappointed.

"Do you?" I wondered if he was a romantic guy. Reshani always teased me I am the kind who would walk past 'romance' with no acknowledgement because of my ignorance.

"Didn't your mother teach you not to answer a question with a question?"

"Amma taught me to challenge everything."

"Hmm… talking about Amma, mine was right." He murmured as he let his fingers started stroking my thigh under my t-shirt. "You are damn cute in my t-shirt."

He looked at me with a raised eyebrow. "So, was it as good as a chapter from Mills and Boom?" Instead of responding, I rested the ice cream tub on the floor. Then, putting my arms around his neck, I pulled him towards me as I lay down on the sofa and kissed him. I wanted to say 'Better.' But he was distracted already.

"Hmm…. ice cream taste so nice when it's on you," Niranga smiled as he lifted his lips from mine.

"Don't be cheesy." He was too busy fondling with my t-shirt to hear me mock him.

Later, Niranga woke me up to have some warm tea with biscuits. It was the first time a man had made me something to eat or drink, and I gulped the tea. When we emptied our mugs, Niranga carried me to the bedroom.

"Aren't you glad I am light?" I murmured into Niranga's ear. As he squinted his eyes puzzled, I mumbled again, "You can carry me around with little fuss." and laughed.

He kissed me and laid me on the bed as if he agreed with me. I can't recall falling asleep as I worked up the next day when Niranga shook my shoulder and whispered in my ear.

"Cookie, wake up."

"Why?" I didn't prefer to open my eyes.

"Don't you have to leave for work?" Niranga was stroking my hair, cajoling me into opening my eyes.

"What time is it?"

"It is after eight o'clock in the morning."

"I am sleepy." I whimpered. All I wanted to do was to curl up and drift back to sleep.

"Don't you have classes to teach?"

"What day is it today?" My brain was in a jumble. I couldn't recall what day it was. I thought I was in a dream and not actually with Niranga in a house in Kandy.

"Wednesday."

"The lectures are at one."

I buried my head in the pillow, drifting back to sleep, letting Niranga stroke my hair. When I work up later, the sun shone through the window, and it was late morning. Niranga was not there. I got up from the bed and realised I was in a large room, and there was not much furniture except an enormous bed and an almari.

Niranga's side of the bed was empty. Rumbled and discarded bedsheets reminded me of our passionate lovemaking last night. A warm rush spread across my body, bringing back those beautiful moments.

I couldn't bring myself to face Niranga. I was not accustomed to the etiquettes of spending a night with a man. My previous encounters haven't made me stay over at a man's place or have one spending a night with me. This was my first waking up in a strange bed. I crawled off the bed and walked to the adjoining bathroom. Niranga had placed all my discarded clothes, a towel, and a new toothbrush in a neat pile. I took my time in the bathroom to shower and change from Niranga's t-shirt to my clothes yesterday. When I came out, I heard the distant sound of a kettle boiling. I went back to the room and stood facing the window, watching the sun rays making random patterns on the young mango tree leaves, trying to gather my anxious thoughts and the nerve to face Niranga.

I was not sure how long I was planning to hide in the room, shy to see Niranga in daylight. For the first time in my adult life, I had no plans. In the last few years, I have been living with a carefully drawn blueprint for my life with multiple backup plans. As when our agency's financials collapsed, today I am disoriented.

I am a different person from who I was last night. I was no longer the woman in control who knew what she wanted in bed and dared to demand it. That woman evaporated at dawn, like a dewdrop that vaporises as the day matures. Having let my passion take over my rational thinking, I didn't think beyond my yearning to sleep with Niranga. I did not possess any inkling of how I should go about with the rest of today. I was grappling with awkward emotions foreign to my mundane life.

Lost in my thoughts, I didn't notice until Niranga came and wrapped his arms around my waist, pulling me closer to his chest. He planted a kiss on the corner of my right eye. I could feel his heartbeat and smell his aftershave.

"How long are you planning on avoiding me?"

"I haven't figured that out yet," I whimpered.

"Babe, look at me." I didn't have time to enjoy the warm, comforting sensation that wrapped around me when he called me 'babe.' before Niranga turned me towards him with an urgency in his voice. I kept my eyes fixed on the buttons of his shirt.

"Do you regret being with me?" The pain in his voice made me glance at him.

"No!" I did not have any misgivings about a single second I spent with him. Last night, everything that took place was what I desired and wanted. The passion we shared was ten years in the making, something I have carried from my youth to adulthood.

"Then why are you feeling awkward?" Niranga gazed into my eyes, his fingers caressing my face.

"I don't know... I feel different now than last night." When I told him the truth, the worry in his eyes got replaced by satisfaction.

"Let us change it then." Niranga pulled me for a slow, passionate kiss. I sighed with pure delight. It felt so natural to be there, standing on my bare feet, kissing him back, having my fingers run through his wet hair from the morning shower.

"You have shaved." I stroked one of his cheeks and grinned. He nuzzled his cheek against mine, showing me how smooth it was.

"I did. You complained I was bruising you last night." Niranga smiled with a glitter in his eyes. I looked at the unmade bed over his shoulder with longing to crawl back there with him. As if he sensed my distraction, Niranga spoke softly.

"Would you like to continue or eat?"

"Eat." I smiled as I was famished.

"Come." Niranga weaved his fingers through mine, leading me away from the room.

"Did you go out?" There was food on the dining table.

"Yes, I couldn't let you starve. Unfortunately, there was no more leftover ice cream." Niranga grinned, pulling a chair for me to sit. He sat opposite me, and we started eating in silence.

"Niranga, this house…. It feels familiar. Whose house, is it?" I had the same sensation last night -that I have walked these grounds before. Niranga stopped eating, surveying the room.

"You don't remember?" Niranga was expecting me to recognise the place.

"No, should I?"

"Yes, this is my cuz Upul's house. We used to come and stay here for the holidays." I have been to this house with Niranga and his family growing up. I had even stayed a couple of nights here when we visited Kandy during the Kandy Esela Perahara season. Some days, we watched the Tooth Festival from Dalada Street and came back to Upul's house to watch the tail end of the perahara from the garden. There was a wooden bench in the garden that I loved so much that I used to stand on and watch fireball acrobats blowing their lanterns into the air. Occasionally, Uncle Sarath or Upul's father used to lift me up and have me sit on their shoulder to give me a better view of the acrobats and elegantly decorated elephants.

"Oh… That makes sense… Where is your cousin these days?"

"He lives in London. We use this house when we are on holiday. I am so glad I have this house." He reached across, taking my hand to kiss it. Sensing he was referring to last night, I smiled.

Memories trickled in. I recalled asking Niranga if we could live here when we grew up. I must have been eleven and Niranga about fourteen. He said something to the extent of *'Of course we can. This is my cuz's house'* that recollection made me cast my eyes over him, and I caught him watching me. Maybe he recalled the same conversation. *'It can't be.'* I told myself. We couldn't be living our childhood fantasies.

Neither one of us said anything. We ate in silence until we both were full.

"Would you like to check out your favourite bench in the whole wide world?" Niranga asked, teasing me about how I claimed the wooden bench in the garden that gave Lake Kandy an unobscured view.

"You remember?"

"I do. You were obsessed with benches when you were a kid." He grinned.

"It was annoying to go anywhere because you wanted to sit on every bench you came across… If my memory is correct, this was your favourite out of all."

An enormous lump formed inside me, making me emotional. I stood up and put my arms around Niranga's waist, hugging him tightly, wanting to transfer all the warmth in my heart to his.

The garden was beautifully landscaped. The bench I adored was still there, but was no longer a wooden one. They had replaced it with a marble bench. It sat majestically in white on the green backdrop.

It was closer to midday; the sun's rays were seeping through the canopy of trees and were not too harsh. I stretched my neck, turning my face towards the light peeping through a branch of a mango tree. I loved the feeling of the morning sun spreading warmth across my face. Today, it reminded me of Niranga's gentle lovemaking.

"Don't do that." Niranga put his hands around my waist and kissed my neck. His voice strained.

"What?"

"That thing you do with your neck." He kissed me again before he spoke.

"Holy mother of Kali, does it turn you on?" I laughed and stretched my neck again, purposefully. Niranga drew a deep breath before he claimed my lips roughly.

"You little tease." When I pulled myself away, he bit my lip.

We sat there on the bench, admiring the gorgeous view in front of us. We could hear the faint noise of passing vehicles that were rushing somewhere tooting impatiently. When you stare longer, you could catch an occasional sparkle of Lake Kandy's waves glittering in the morning sun.

"Why did you lead me to believe you were with Sulakkana?" Niranga broke the silence, watching my face.

"That's on you. You can't blame me. You jumped to your own conclusion."

"You didn't stop me?" He wasn't happy.

"Does it matter now?"

"Yes, we would have been together way before yesterday."

"That is bullshit." I thought Niranga was overconfident.

"If I knew he wasn't your boyfriend, I would not have let you go that night." Niranga tugged me closer to him as if he was worried, I would drift away.

"When I couldn't find you the next day, I thought you left feeling guilty." He said with a voice filled with sadness.

"Did you really think I am that kind of girl to cheat on my boyfriend?" I pulled my head away to stare at Niranga. It bothered me he thought I could be unfaithful. Niranga could sense the hurt in my voice, pulling me closer to his body, stroking my back with tenderness.

"All I can think about was losing you again."

"Losing me again?" I blinked, staring at his face, searching for clarity.

"What are you talking about? We have never been together!" I asked, not able to contain my curiosity.

"We would have if things didn't turn out the way they did before I left ten years ago." Niranga smiled in his usual confidence.

"I was going to ask you to be my girlfriend before you hooked up with Channaka." Niranga's voice was filled with remorse. Though he was stroking my arm, I had an uneasy feeling that he was actually rubbing his own heart.

"Couldn't you tell how much I was pinning after you?" He stopped caressing my arm and peered into my eyes.

"I thought you were with Akka when I saw you two near the stream. I was so hurt believing you chose Akka over me. That is why I left when I did."

"Amali was never one of my girlfriends... we have always been friends... I admit, she attracted me when she first came home. That was entirely your fault."

"How on earth was it my fault that you couldn't control yourself?" I was angry, sensing the change in my tone; he grabbed my hands with a pleading look.

"When you didn't have any time for me, I should have known your focus was on the exam. Hell, I was the one who taught you that. I was a dick.... I knew Amali had a crush on me and used it, trying to make you jealous."

"So, if you two were not together, why was she there with you that day? I am sure I saw you both there at my stream." Niranga smiled, noting that I have gone back to claiming the steam as my private property.

"I went there to be alone....... I was nervous and excited......... I had this whole thing planned. I was going to take you on a boat ride and declare my intentions in the middle of the lake. I was hoping to visit Maligawa the next day. That stream was our place. I was there to think............ to enjoy the anticipation. Amali followed me, wanting to know why I was so distanced. I told her my plans."

"You mean you told Akka you were going to ask me?" I uncoiled my back with concern. 'Did Akka know all this time?' An uneasy feeling travelled through me, burning my stomach with anxiety.

"No, I didn't tell her it was you. She was a bit upset. She had a crush on me; I don't think she was in love with me or anything like that. What you saw was me consoling her."

"How come you didn't remember this the other day?" I may be spellbound by his exceptional lovemaking; however, I was not turning into a naïve believer.

"You were going on about a girlfriend, and she was never in that category. I was not lying. I was a dick; I am sorry." I knew at that moment, just as I was, he, too, mourned our lost youth, missing the opportunity to grow together.

"So, why do you go with this charade, letting your family believe Sulakkana is your boyfriend?"

"It is not my fault, they made their own conclusion, and I just didn't bother to correct it." Niranga kept on staring; his eyebrows raised and arched, puzzled and bothered by my response.

"It isn't like you to lie......." His eyes were challenging me. "You are direct and transparent, not one to keep secrets.... So what is the real deal?"

I look over to the lake, wondering if I would breach the trust if I opened up. But I knew Niranga would understand. He has been living in the West for a while, plus he had always been a progressive thinker. I took a deep breath and turned to him, watching his face.

"Because Sula is gay," I shared a truth known to very few in Sula's world. I told him how it started as an innocent prank to get back at Malli, who couldn't stop teasing me about Sula, implying he was my boyfriend. Soon we realised it was not a terrible travesty to deceive. It helped both Sula and me.

Niranga's eyes widened at first, as he didn't expect such news. His face and body relaxed with comfort as if he had just realised the other man in my life was no longer a competition to him.

"And Nilush is his partner….." Niranga smiled, remembering yesterday's encounter. So I shared how we have maintained the ruse for years to support their relationship. Sula and Nilush were struggling with the backward social norms that didn't accept same-sex relationships. The best way to maintain Sula's reputation and allow him to be with Nilush was to pretend Sula was conforming to the custom and had a girlfriend. I didn't have any qualm about it. As long as the world believed Sula and I were a couple, they would not suspect Sula having an intimate attachment to a man.

Becoming Sula's girlfriend also gave me the protection I needed to work in a male dominant industry. Everyone in the sector highly regarded Sula and his family in the tourism field, which helped me keep away undue advantages from lustful men. Further, it kept away Amma's and Saman Aiya's constant attempts to pair me with an eligible bachelor. And Amma's frequent quibbling about my age to be married. On many levels, it was easy to hide behind a facade of lies.

20 SALACIOUSNESS

When Niranga dropped me off at my annexe, I purposely didn't invite him in. I told him I was already late for my lecture, but the real reason was I was not sure if I could let him go. Though I felt tight and heavy in my heart, I had little time to muse. I was risking running late for my afternoon lecture.

I reluctantly had a shower, not wanting to wash away the smell that lingered on my skin. Just before we left Niranga's place, we ended up making love again. I finally could understand why some get addicted to sex. I had never felt this excited and fulfilled before.

I haven't been greatly concerned about correctness, conforming to society's seemly expected behaviour from an unmarried woman. Though I didn't hit the same scale as Nilush, I too treated sex as another need, such as clothes and food. I have had those so-called one-night stands (though I never spent an entire night with a man), the casual safe sex, more in response to a biological need rather than anything else.

Never before felt the desire to be with the same person; the pull I have for Niranga, the satisfaction I got being there lying next to him, differed from my other limited experiences. I was reminiscing about our early encounter and didn't hear the pounding on the door. It took me a while to realise someone was knocking on my front door. I sprint across the living room to open it, expecting my landlady to stand there with her silly grin to collect the monthly rent, when Niranga barged in and closed the door with a bang.

I didn't have time to speak or breathe before he pulled me into his arms and started kissing me. He was rough as if he was trying to punish me, urgent in a way he feared someone would pull us apart, concerned like we could lose each other.

I tore myself away from him and pushed his shoulders with both my hands to gaze into his eyes. My eyes were blurry, and hot wetness was sliding down my cheeks; I was crying. Beyond the haziness of my vision, I noted the moisture in his eyes.

"I don't want to leave!" He drew me back, hugging me tightly, and whispered. He sounded worn out, as if he already had a battle and was defeated. I gathered at some point on his way to Nuwara Eliya; he must have turned around, giving in to the urge of wanting to be with me again.

I understood it. I put my hands around Niranga's waist, hugging him back, drawing myself closer to him, embracing the warmth and tightness of his body.

"I don't want you to leave either." When I murmured, I realised why I felt heavy and sad earlier.

'Holy mother of Kali, is this what they call lust?' I could sense my anxiety.

"I can stay." This time it was Niranga who pushed me away to peer into my eyes.

"You can't, you have work to do, and I will be busy most of the time."

I didn't see a solution. We both held tight to each other, kissing with hunger and eagerness, expecting it would give us an answer we couldn't comprehend.

I was falling into a bottomless abyss, fearing not seeing any light ever again if I couldn't be with Niranga: I wanted to touch him, taste him, inhale him, feel the weight of his body crushing me. I no longer gave any second thought about being late for my class.

★★★

"I am late," I told Niranga's reflection in the mirror. He was sitting on the bed, leaning back on his elbows, watching me getting dressed. He had a guilty grin on his face.

"I can't say I am sorry...." Our eyes met in the mirror; both of us had satisfaction written all over.

"I will drop you off." He offered as a consolation prize. I couldn't refuse it as there was no other way for me to stop running late to the lecture. I nodded, accepting his offer.

"Can't you pretend you are sick and skip the lecture?" Niranga pulled the fold of the saree I was wearing with seductiveness.

"Wait outside so I can get ready." I pointed to the door, pulling the fold back.

I didn't want Niranga to watch me getting dressed or have myself distracted by watching him looking at me through the mirror. Niranga left with no argument, with a pouting face reminding me how he looked when he didn't get his own way as a kid.

Niranga was standing near the bookcase when I entered the living room. He appeared happy, holding on to the picture frame of his photo I placed there last week before going to his parent's anniversary dinner.

I only had pictures of those who are significant in my heart on the bookstand. I had given him a place in my life way before last night, and Niranga was sharp enough to grasp it. He came across to hug me, pulling my head to kiss my forehead. I laid my cheek on his neck and breath in his musk.

"Just when I think I know you, you throw me off balance. You are an enigma," Niranga said.

"Well, you are the mathematician." I joked on my way out.

"Challenge accepted. When can we meet again?" I felt a secret happiness building in me when Niranga asked. Earlier, as we rushed to get here, we didn't make any plans about the future. Maybe because we both were in a daze with the way things unfolded. Though we both were pining for each other, I don't believe either of us expected our union to be this powerful and exhilarating. It surprised me beyond my wildest imagination.

"When are you going to be back in Kandy?"

"I am at your command, my precious." He gave me a wicked grin, opening up the possibility of being with him again soon, extending our union beyond a one-night stand. I ignored his imitation of Kanmali, the fortune-teller Gypsy in Sigiriya. But her words, *'your stubbornness is going to harm your love,'* echoed in my head. I shook off the thought and got into the car with him.

"I have nothing lined up for the weekend." I was unsure if he would head back to Kandy in two days.

"I can pick you up Friday evening, and we can go to my place. Are you okay with spending the weekend with me?" His voice was full of energy and hope. I nodded. I was glad he couldn't notice I was ready to ride to hell if that meant I got to spend time with him.

"Will you be able to take the next few weekends off?" Niranga peeled his eyes off the road to peer at me.

"Easy there……. Let's take one weekend at a time and reassess how we go. I may get tired of you after a week or two." I didn't want to tell him it was not the right time to take time off from work when we were financially struggling to keep the business afloat. Niranga appeared hurt; however, he didn't challenge me; instead, he grabbed my hand and kissed it.

"I find your lack of faith disturbing." When he quoted Han Solo from Star Wars, I turned my head to watch the other side of the car suppress the laugher building inside me. Before I could respond, Niranga spoke again.

"Well, my precious, you better not make any plans for the next three months. I intend to spend every weekend with you."

"My, aren't you confident?" I mocked him while holding on to excitement bubbling inside me.

"What we had was a teaser. You wait and see." He smiled with faith. A warm rush ran through my entire body, making me tingle with anticipation. I didn't have any reservations about his capabilities, but I didn't possess the confidence to hold his interest.

***

"You look iridescent!" Reshani peered into my face with her usual gorgeous smile. I felt a bit embarrassed. Instinct made me pull the fold of my saree to cover the hickey Niranga had left on the base of my neck. Maybe I shouldn't have fidgeted as my action drew Reshani's attention to my neck.

"Is that a hickey?" Reshani reached out, moving my hand to scrutinise my neck. As she was inspecting the mark caused by Niranga's kissing, her eyes widened with a joyous smile that spread across her face.

"Oh my god, Saku, did you sleep with Niranga?" She perched on the plastic chair opposite me, bubbling with excitement. I avoided her eyes and nodded my head, trying to hide my grin, feeling shy.

"Oh my god, it finally happened!"

"Ten years of agony is over! Didn't I tell you this was going to happen?" She screeched with delight, making me scan around the canteen to check if anyone could hear our talk.

"I guess all the effort I put into anniversary dinner paid off," I muttered victoriously.

"Oh, don't you take any credit for that! Sula was right, Niranga was on to you, and with or with no attempt from you, he would have come after you." The conversation Reshani referred to took place on the morning of the anniversary dinner when Reshani and Sula dropped by my annexe before I left for Nuwara Eliya. They were there to give me the photos Sula helped to collect from the studio and to calm me down as they both had observed my anxiousness on our Thursday night dinner catch up.

"What if Niranga doesn't feel the same?" I recall sharing the nervous worry swirling in my stomach with Reshani and Sula with helplessness I was not used to.

"Are you kidding me?" Sulla uncoiled his back with annoyance, giving me a *'Don't be melodramatic'* stare.

"Do you think he would waste his time seeking you out bringing all those books?" He hesitated to check himself before he continued. "By the way, it was such a cliché thing to do. I bet he has secretly been reading a few Mills and Boons." Sula sounded vindictive, showing off his jealousy freely, as Nilush wasn't around. Though we will never be each other life partners, both Sula and I had a jealous possessiveness about each other that peeks its head out occasionally.

"Oh, oh, don't forget the velvet tamarind bag, brought all the way from...... Where was it?............. Galle? Being very attentive when you burned your hand......... Come on, who are you trying to fool here? Why would he do all that if he wasn't into you?" Reshani chirped.

"Why, can't that all be just to salvage the friendship?"

"Oh, for heaven's sake Saku, stop being naïve. He is into you! Why would he be chasing you like a *praying mantis* ?" I didn't lose the irony when Reshani referred to *praying mantis* . The male praying mantis risks being eaten by the female when they get attracted to the female pheromones and sometimes get their heads bitten off before they get to mate. Both Reshani and Sula always refer me to a female praying mantis as I scare guys off with my demeanour.

"For the love of god, woman, you have always been the mistress of your own destiny! Why don't you just take control, see where it leads. The reality is, after a few rounds of dancing and maybe a bit of cuddling around, he will head back to Sydney. Consider this to be one of those holiday romances; pretend he is one of your clients here for a brief holiday." Reshani pointed out calmly and squeezed my hand encouragingly.

"I can bet you anything; whether or not you wear Reshani's dress, he is going to come after you." I surrendered to my best friends' assurance than my doubts when I attended the anniversary dinner, drawing courage from that conversation. Now that it has come true, Reshani was basking in self-glorification.

"Oh my god, didn't I predict it?" She bounced in the chair as a kid who received a bowl of candy.

"So, tell me about it. Was it worth the ten-year wait?" Unable to contain her excitement, Reshani asked.

We were at the university canteen for our afternoon tea. The hall had seen its better days with its run-down wooden benches and plastic chairs scattered around. The rusted ceiling fans were humming away, trying to circulate the already warm, stale air in the room. I watched the way Reshani was sipping black tea. The cup's handle was no longer there, so she held it with both hands with an allure of a privileged lady from the Victorian era.

She took a deep sip, ready to take in every little detail. I glanced around the canteen to make sure no one was around to overhear our conversation. I shared our encounter from the moment Niranga caught up with me yesterday at the cafe until he dropped me off at the annexe earlier today. However, I didn't tell her what happened afterwards. I was still savouring that, and I didn't want to share it with anyone yet, not even with Reshani.

"How did he find you yesterday?" Reshani dragged me back to the canteen with her question.

"He had called the agency, and Sula had told him where we were."

"Sula knew I was catching up with Nilush yesterday to collect some money from him."

"You mean Sula willingly sent Niranga over to where you were?" Reshani puled up her neck like a peacock and dropped the empty teacup on the table, surprised as I was yesterday.

"Yes, and not only that, he has told Niranga I was out with my boyfriend." I grinned, remembering Niranga's angry face when he walked over to where I was sitting with Nilush.

"Seriously, he did that?" Reshani blinked, eyeing me with disbelief.

Being my friend, business partner, and fake boyfriend for years, Sula was not overly pleased with my attraction to Niranga. Our relationship was exceptional. There were times I had wished Sula was heterosexual, so we could have become a genuine couple. Reshani believes I am still struggling to accept Nilush, Sula's secret partner, for over five years. And that is why I understood when Sula didn't take the news about Niranga with open arms. Although, as did Reshani, he was confident Niranga was into me; he was still critical and doubtful, cautioning me to be careful of Niranga. We both have that possessive and protective stake about each other.

"Yes, Niranga came all worked up thinking I was with Sula." I laughed, remembering how his facial expressions softened when he realised he was chasing a ruse.

"Maybe it was a good thing that he thought that way….. Um… Giving him an incentive to chase you."

"Oh my god, you should have seen Nilush when he saw Niranga. He was drooling all over."

"Don't mention that to Sula," Reshani warned me.

"No, I won't."

"So, what are you two kids planning to do now?" Reshani had a mischievous smile playing on her lips.

"Niranga wants to spend the next few weekends with me," I murmured, trying to contain the happiness bubbling inside.

"Does he now?" Reshani mocked, grinning happily.

"I am not sure if I can take time off from work. It isn't the right time for rendezvous."

"You deserve this break Saku." Reshani leaned across the table and squeezed my fingers with a tight smile.

"We are nearly bankrupt, Resh."

"Saku, sometimes in life when you have to park everyone else's problems and pick up your own shit…… Let Sula work out the finances. We all have offered him help, and you have done more than your fair share." Reshani straightened in her chair and spoke with a sternness in her voice that reminded me of a preschool teacher disciplining a kid. "Reality is, even if you work all weekends, it won't make any difference. So don't become a Wonder Woman and mess this up. Go and be with Niranga. You deserve it." She reached across and squeezed my hand as if she wanted to pass on some of the strength and confidence I lacked.

"I don't know what this will turn into." After some silence, I shared the concern that was going inside my head. I felt as if I was in the middle of a river flowing fast, trying to keep myself afloat without getting drowned in desire. "I am lost. I only wanted a one-night stand, and now I have more than that. I was not expecting to see him again. I am perplexed." I admitted with reluctance.

"Why are you worried?"

"Because I am not clear where this is going."

"Where do you want this to go?"

"If I knew I wouldn't be this distressed, I would make sure I get there," I was not sure who I was annoyed with, Reshani or myself.

"Be like that old man in one of those Zen stories the Dean always rattles on about, the one that falls into the massive waterfall.......... Remember?........ Just let the current carry you, don't fight it, let it be." Reshani watched the wheels of my thoughts turning. I haven't been one to sit back and let destiny take control. Not having a plan would undo me.

"Don't overthink. I know you have your life plans and a big checklist you want to tick off... Just live in the moment and give it a chance........ Um....... Take things one at a time. Remember, he is not here to stay." Reshani leaned forward to pinch my cheek and giggled as if she knew something that I did not.

21 SENSUALITY

It was a beautiful day to visit the Udawattakele Forest reserve in Kandy. I gaze across the group, catching Niranga's eyes staring at me, shimmering. I glanced away, focusing my attention on another visitor to calm down my rising heartbeat.

Niranga has been pining to visit the forest reserve and has been pestering me to arrange it. Although this was not exactly what he had in mind, I watched him easing into the outing, engaging in conversations with others in the group and Sula.

Kandy is one of the ancient cities of Sri Lanka and was ruled by the last monarch, King Sri Wickrama Rajasinghe, before the country fell into the hands of British invaders and became another one of its colonies in 1815. Situated close to Kandy town's heart, Udawattakele does not welcome unmarried couples. They considered the park ground a sacred place - not because it was part of the palace grounds, but because the old royal palace houses the Tooth Relic of Buddha. There was no other way for Niranga and me to visit the park, so I persuaded Sula to include us on the tour we organised for foreigners. As it rained a couple of days ago, there were few visitors, and our group was small. There were only two married couples, three young British guys, Sula, Niranga and I, to share the forest with noisy monkeys and colourful birds.

We were on the shady lovers' walk that runs parallel to the banks of the small lake in the middle of the rain forest. It was peaceful to stroll under the green canopy, taking pictures of the lush green habitat, orchids, absorbing the serenity, being amazed by the unique collection of flora and fauna, and stopping when we spotted rear birds or any orchids.

As the tour progressed, Niranga was not pleased he couldn't hold my hand or pull me in for a quick hug when he wanted. I already warned him to keep his distance from me. As far as the other guests were concerned, he was another visitor who had joined the morning tour.

I have been seeing Niranga for over eight weeks now. Even after so many weeks of being together, we find our desire to be with each other still intense. This was the first time we were outside in the company of others. We have behaved like mastermind criminals plotting the next heist, secluding our existence to Niranga's cousin's place.

I dragged my feet as it was getting harder to walk near him. It was challenging to share the same space and keep my hands off him. I was trying to block the provocative thoughts manifesting in my mind, wanting to feel the softness of his lips, the smoothness of his skin brushing mine when I was near him. A sense of urgency was brewing inside me, craving to take Niranga's hand and steal a kiss behind a giant tree trunk. I reluctantly acknowledged my arousal. Catching Niranga's eyes, I took solace in knowing it was the same for him.

"What the hell? Why can't I hold your hand?" Niranga whispered for the tenth time with frustration, catching up to me by closing the gap. He purposely stood beside me, letting his fingers caress mine, making my body shiver.

"Because others know me as Sula's girlfriend."

"How long you are going to carry that on?" There was bitterness in Niranga's voice that I didn't appreciate. Our affair had to be private, no public appearance as a couple: Niranga was clearly aware it was one of the ground rules I stipulated when we started our relationship. Those who knew Sula and me in the industry believed us to be a couple. I had no intention of discrediting that for something temporary.

"We already talked about this before…."

"Why do I always get the second-class treatment? What do I have to do to be on top?" Niranga was in a whiny mood, and the physical distance we were maintaining was aggravating it.

"Please…… don't be such a cry, baby. It doesn't suit you." I voiced my disappointment and annoyance that shut him up for a while. After some silence, Niranga turned to me with so much yearning in his eyes.

"Let's go home, babe."

"Not yet. We haven't seen all the caves or the Emerald Dove." I reminded him of some of the unique features in the reserve that he should aim to visit.

"This is ridiculous." Niranga moaned like a frustrated kid. I could relate to his agitations. I was battling them too.

"Screw the cave and the dove. Let us leave." His voice sounded rough and urgent.

Noting our distraction and lagging the group, Sula strolled back to us, demanding our attention, pointing us to the top of the giant tree where a bunch of brightly coloured pigeons were resting.

"Hey, you two, get those binoculars. There is a pair of Emerald Doves up there."

When we finally ended the tour, Niranga was impatient, making me jog along with him to the car we had parked near the entrance to Tapovanaya, the Buddhist temple at the outer boundary of Udawattakele Forest Reserve. Our initial plan was for Niranga to drop me off at the university after our excursion. I was behind grading assignments, so we agreed I would work on those until late evening and join him for dinner. But, as the need to be with Niranga was overpowering my logistical thinking, I quickly gave into his seductive persuasion.

Heading back to Niranga's reminded me of the first time I went with him to his cousin's place. I felt giddy with excitement. I could sense Niranga was experiencing the same. He grabbed my hand, kissing it with eyes filled with longing.

"You arranged this purposely, didn't you?" His eyes were steamy, glistening and inviting. The burning arousal lay between us as thick as the fog that engulfs Nuwara Eliya town at dusk.

"Don't blame me. Blame yourself. You are the one who doesn't have any control." I pretended I was indifferent to the raw urge consuming me, demanding my full attention.

"Are you telling me it was okay for you there, not being able to at least hold hands?"

"It wouldn't be the first time," I reminisced about how I wanted to be with Niranga when we were descending from Sigiriya. That was the first time I felt an ardent desire for him. Niranga arched his eyebrows, eager to find out what I hadn't told him.

"Remember Sigiriya? That was where I first wanted to kiss you so badly." I watched him going through his memories of the day. I am sure he also could recall the moments we shared similar yearnings. Niranga turned to me in scepticism.

"You are joking! I was trying to get through to you, but you were like an ice queen." I laughed at Niranga's disbelief.

"That day was hard, but walking in the rain with you was definitely harder." I dug into the past, conjuring my memories of how I shrugged Niranga's arm away when he tried to keep me warm in the rain. I chuckled to myself, reflecting on the internal struggle I suffered.

"Oh gosh, how many days we have wasted in vain," I uttered with disappointment. Niranga gave me a sympathetic look, understanding my frustration.

"What about you?" I turned to Niranga in anticipation.

"I have already told you."

"Remind me." I pleaded. I want to hear again, feeling the warm glow spreading through my chest, "When did you feel that first uncontrollable pull?"

We were already home and walking towards the house when Niranga stopped in his tracks. He pulled me into his arms, kissing me before he responded.

"I wanted to do that on the day you burned your hand." The flashback of that day came to me clearly. I could touch the electrical shock I felt going down my spine, being so near to him.

"I wonder what would have happened if you had?" Niranga laughed at my outburst and nudged me inside the house.

"You would have slapped me."

"You were going to push me to that stream." He teased, reminding me of the early days.

"Yes, I would have slapped you; still, I never intended to let go of your hand, babe. It was just a fit of millisecond anger."

"Well, you have a lifetime to make it up to me." Niranga teased me with a sparkle in his eyes. I happily wrap my arms around his neck, pulling him for a kiss. The passion we have for each other was an uncontrollable wildfire consuming us.

When we are together, we go into a bubble of our own. Every second, I collect each moment with Niranga, similar to a woman collecting dewdrops of water in a drought-stricken area. I live on those memories nervously, waiting until the next time I see him.

And then, when the weekend ends and Niranga gets ready to leave, I hold my breath and wait for him to tell me when he will pick me up again. Deep down in my mind, the hourglass was running out of sand. My biggest worry had been the anticipation of Niranga losing his interest in me before his holiday ended. Maybe that must be why I have not made my other work a priority. I am no longer a planet revolving around Niranga. Instead, I have turned into an asteroid on an exhilarated burning path, heading for a crash landing.

***

"Hey babe, I wouldn't be able to see you for a couple of weeks," Niranga said, making me stop breathing for a second. I didn't want him to pick up the disappointment in my voice. Before I could choke, I put on my brave face.

"We lasted a while. It must be a mini record for you."

"What do you mean?" Niranga pulled his brows, peeling his eyes off the road to rest them on me.

"Exactly what I said earlier. You are known for your brief affairs, and we have lasted a few months!" I smirked.

"Aha…." Niranga nodded his head, connecting the dots.

"I am taking Amma and Thaththa to Colombo to visit some of their friends. Then I have some urgent business matters to attend to. I wish I could take you with me." He turned his attention to the traffic in a wishful tone. "Can't you come to Colombo and pretend you are there for work and bump into us? We could hang out."

Niranga's voice was laced with hope and mischief, oblivious to the internal battle I had a few seconds earlier. I inhaled softly with relief and called up my rational persona. It was easy to be practical and understanding when I knew I would see him again.

"No, spend some time with Aunty and Uncle. You have been with me every weekend."

"What, are you tired of me already?" Niranga sounded disappointed.

"What would you prefer me to say? Please don't go, babe. I will be so lonely without you?"

"Can't you at least pretend you will miss me?"

"I don't need to pretend. I am going to miss you, more than you think!" I leaned across to kiss his cheek. Niranga spun his face to steal a quick one on lips.

***

The impatient pounding on the door got my attention, making me sprint to the front of the house. I wondered if it was Niranga; although he said he wouldn't visit me, it wouldn't be the first time Niranga came blasting through the door like a storm claiming he couldn't stop thinking about me.

Though we meet on weekends, I haven't been able to predict Niranga's impromptu visits. I was still getting used to his spur-of-the-moment drop-ins in the middle of the week or turning up at the hotel unannounced when I was on tour.

I unlocked the front door with apprehension and excitement. Underneath the pleasure of being in Niranga's arms again, I was mindful that a visit from him would put me behind my coursework. There were so many assignment markings I had to get through the week that I couldn't afford to be late with another assignment. I was secretly waiting to have some time of my own.

"What, did you expect the loverboy to walk through?" When Reshani shoved me aside and walked in, I felt relieved and disappointed at the same time. I forgot it was Thursday and my night to host our usual weekly dinner. I was playing catch up, always a few steps behind with my life outside of Niranga.

"Watch out. She is in one of her pissy moods!" I didn't see Ravidu was with her until he stepped through the door and hugged me.

"Is Niranga going to join us?" Ravidu asked, as a way of making a polite conversation.

"How many times do I have to tell you?" Reshani barked in a condescending voice.

"The only reason we get to see her today is that Niranga is not available this weekend." Reshani's sour tone was sharp as a knife, though not clear if her irritation was with Ravidu or me. Ravidu shrugged his shoulders, keeping quiet to avoid further lash backs from his disgruntled wife.

"Let us try to see if we can fill that giant void, he had left inside her!" When Reshani declared full of self-confidence, I didn't argue. I was not ready to cross this woman who picked up my emotional cues way before I did. She knew I was in physical pain, wanting to be with Niranga, not knowing how I would bear the vacuum he left. I would not pretend otherwise.

"Saku is like a female lion in heat these days, ready to get nonstop action!" She winked at her husband, making me blush and turn away in embarrassment.

"Oh, when did the roles reverse? Wasn't it Niranga who was chasing Saku like a *praying mantis* ?" I glared at Ravidu with displeasure, noting he was trying to crawl back to Reshani's good books.

"Did you two come all the way here to talk about my sex life?" I turned to Reshani with irritation.

"Yes, we came to remind you sex isn't the whole shebang. The only reason you go at it like rabbit now is that it is new." Reshani plunked next to Ravidu on the sofa.

"You watch too much of Animal Planet." I mocked, noticing how Reshani's reference changed from a lioness to a doe within a few minutes. As her discontented glare didn't change, I challenged her.

"What makes you assume it is the only thing we have going?" I wanted to tell her sex wasn't the only thing that bounded Niranga and me together, but I would be lying. We did nothing that didn't end in bed or gasping for air in an orgasm.

I couldn't tell her we shared a passion for cooking because Niranga cooked while I sat there and watched him. He enjoyed it and said it was one of his stress relievers after a long day at work. There was something sexy about watching a man cook, mastering pots and pans in the kitchen. Maybe that was why most of the cooking sessions end up in the bedroom, having to scrape away the burned pots or go out to buy food to eat afterwards.

Maybe sitting outside in the evening watching the sun setting over Maligawa was something we could build on. I prefer the twilight; quietly sitting there and talking. Niranga's head resting on my belly, stretched out on the bench, observing that golden glow appearing behind the Maligawa rooftop. It was like the glow I have inside when Niranga was around me.

Perhaps our inkling towards exploring the country when we go for a leisurely drive in the mornings could be our thing. I love it when Niranga brings the Jaguar and lets me take it for a spin on winding roads leading up and down the citadel.

"If there had been anything more than sex, you wouldn't be so stressed out right now!" I realised how much I hated Reshani for not wasting time with her straight to the point approach.

Distracted by salaciousness, I have lost focus on my life goals; struggled to balance my conflicting priorities. I am the first to admit that I need to take a step back and realign myself, but I didn't want to give Reshani the satisfaction of agreeing with her.

"Hey, you are the one who gave me that damn Zen talk! All that bullshit about take in the moment, don't think about the past or the future...." I mimicked Reshani, mocking her wisdom speech.

"When I asked you to embrace the occasion and live in the present, I didn't expect your brain to stop functioning!" Ravidu was right. Reshani was in a foul mood.

"You are way behind on your coursework. That leeway you have with the head of the faculty and your students will not last long!" Reshani spattered. "You are allowing your infatuation with Niranga to consume your entire life!"

"Listen, Reshani is right." As predicted, Ravidu leaned across to peer into my face before glancing at his wife, seeking approval to continue who was still burning like a fire acrobat. Knowing great love and affection were hidden underneath Reshani's anger and Ravidu's concern, I let them get on with their planned, choreographed conversation. I could visualise their debate along the way to my place, Reshani demanding Ravidu give me a stern lecture while he was saying he didn't want to interfere. I have been the third wheel on most of such conversations before, around their family and Sula. I was pretty good at dissecting the pattern.

"If I go all science on you, all that you are experiencing right now is a mere chemical reaction in your body. You are sweating a bit more, feeling excited and happy because of the dopamine rush... that sexual desire, arousal you are sensing around Niranga is because of testosterone. Dopamine enhances the release of testosterone; that is why you feel as if you are in a constant high. Eventually, those chemicals are going to wear off if you don't find something else to ground you." I felt uncomfortable, subconsciously accepting all of it to be the truth. I was drowning in that rush, yet I didn't want to tell them I had never been so happy to be suffocated by the presence of the formidable man.

"Thank you, Doctor Ravidu, for that science lesson. I will remember it is the dopamine that makes my heart go faster next time I am with Niranga."

"This is serious, Saku."

"I know Ravidu, and I appreciate it." I nodded my head to show my agreement. "Yes, I may have been distracted lately. But I promise you, I haven't lost my focus."

"It is not only about you being focused, Saku. You need to share your life goals and challenges with Niranga. So, he can understand your priorities. Then, he might help you in ways that you can't even imagine." Ravidu spoke to me as if he was addressing one of his patients, very concerned and with clarity. I fidgeted with my nails, avoiding his eyes.

"You need something solid other than sex as the base for your relationship," Reshani interject, and she and Ravidu share a look, appreciating each other. "Sex is going to wear off. Not every day is going to be like a page out of a Mills & Boon. When that happens, you need something strong to….."

"Hold on a second," I put my hand up to stop Reshani. "Aren't you all forgetting this is just a holiday romance? It is not like I am planning to spend the rest of my life with him." I spattered with annoyance and ignored the amusing look Reshani shared with her husband.

"Is the intervention over now?" I was so relieved when Sula poked his head through the front door with a comical look on his face. Those three have planned the evening. I am not new to such meddling as I created that playbook when we formed our friendship group.

"Did you bring the food? I am starving. " I got up to greet Sula and take the dinner packets he had in his hand.

"Where is Nilush? Isn't he joining us?" Ravidu was curious about Nilush's absence. I haven't shared details about the recent disagreements between us. Nilush is avoiding me, not because of the debt he still owes, but because of his infidelity, which was no longer a secret to me.

"He can't make it tonight. Too much work to do." Though Sula dismissed it with a carefree attitude, I picked up the longing in his voice.

Sula had always been a very private person, never sharing the struggles he endured. He had been doing a great job masking his distress and pain with a smile or a joke. When he suspects no one was paying attention, he let the mask slip, and then you see the tears at the base of his eyes and hear the sob stuck deep in his throat. However, if you are not quick enough, it vanishes in a flash. Seeing this, my heart contracted with agony. I wanted to put my arms around him to comfort and reassure him he was not alone.

When I first got the winds of Nilush's adultery, I told myself I was misreading the clues. I scolded myself for suspecting a friend, saying that Nilush would not hurt Sula. But when Nilush continued with the affair, I carried the secret for months. I told myself I had missed the opportunity to share. Sula wouldn't forgive me for holding onto the secret for too long. He would not trust me again. Underneath that facade was my genuine concern. I was too scared to admit Sula was already aware of the treachery. I feared, if I voiced it, I would stop seeing Sula the way I see him. I didn't want him to be someone who accepts unfaithfulness in the name of love.

I have not figured out how I could look into his eyes afterwards, whether I could respect him the way I do now. It made me question all I believed in Sula. *'Do I actually know him at all?'*

I was projecting this on myself, self-doubting my own choices. If Sula was not the person, I made him be, would that turn him into nothing? Didn't I learn anything from the fallout I had with Niranga? We are not just a sum of our failures; we are much more than that. Can we exist in the grey? Or do we always have to be in black or white?

My monkey mind wouldn't stop twirling. For this same reason, I was mindful not to share any of my burdens with Reshani. I have been holding on to this secret like the guardians of the Pharaohs, protecting the pyramids.

22 AFFECTION

"Hey Sasoo, do you have a few minutes?" I pulled my eyes away from the book I was reading, wondering what Malli was up to now. I am home after nearly three months to meet the recent addition to our family. Akka gave birth to an adorable little baby boy a couple of weeks ago.

As lovely as having a baby in the house, I needed some time to get used to his frequent wailing. So I came outside, seeking silence I desperately craved. I was out on my favourite bench under the pear tree when Malli slid next to me.

"Sure, what is it?"

"I wish to enrol in the University of Technology in Sydney." For a split second, I thought a giant jackfruit fell on me from nowhere, making my head wobble. I stared blankly, not being able to comprehend what I heard.

"I prefer to enrol in computer studies and become a software engineer specialising in computer gaming." Picking up my numbness, Malli continued like an express bus on Kandy Colombo road.

"I have been doing my research and have also spoken to Niranga Aiya. He suggested I should attend the University in Sydney." While Malli explained the details of the universities he had shortlisted and the process, I watched his eyes shimmered with excitement, secretly deliberating how Thaththa was going to finance Malli's dream.

It was easy for Niranga, an only child from an upper-class family with a large inheritance from his parents. We are a middle-class household and both our parents are retirees. Thaththa is only a few months into his new job as a financial controller in Uncle Sarath's factory. It was an average job that didn't come with a big pay pack. We don't have any savings, nor do we have the potential to apply for any loans.

I couldn't imagine how he would fund Malli's overseas studies when struggling with day-to-day expenses. As if he could sense my unease, Malli inquired about financial support.

"Is there a way we can look at a loan against our house? I can pay once I pick up a job there. Niranga Aiya said he could help me find a job. I can also stay with him in his apartment until I find a place."

"Are you able to work and study to support yourself and send money home for the loan payments?" I voiced my concern carefully. I didn't wish to dampen Malli's dream, neither did I want him to run before he could walk. There were so many basic things Malli needed to factor in before he embarked on this seemingly complex journey.

"Yes, Niranga Aiya said he would help me. A lot of his friends have done it. The university I wanted to enrol in is actually where he had done his master's degree. He highly recommends it."

I was unsure. There seemed to be a lot pivoting around Niranga, and I was not comfortable with that dependency. I was curious why Niranga didn't mention any of this to me. Niranga shared news about Devan's visa application and how Thaththa was settling into his new role in the factory. He shared his encounters with Saman Aiya, offhand remarks about Renuka, yet never anything about Malli's plan. I realised Malli was waiting for my response.

"Did you speak to Amma and Thaththa about it?" I wondered how Amma felt about having to let her baby boy leave the nest sooner than she expected.

"That is where I need your help."

"What do you mean?" My stomach sank with fear. If Malli thinks I can assist him financially, I will disappoint him. I lost all my savings to the agency.

"Last time I mentioned this, Saman Aiya got pretty pissed."

"Why was that?"

"Saman Aiya said it was a stupid and expensive idea! He said I should focus on doing a local degree, even after telling him we don't have the specialisation I am interested in Colombo or Moratuwa universities. He suggested I should do part-time study and start working soon as I finish the exam." Malli was gripping his hands, twisting and turning as he spoke. "I thought because he worked in Singapore and all, he would understand what I was saying. Why doesn't he prefer me to study abroad? It is not as if I am going to use his money?"

"What did Akka say?" I asked, controlling my tone, not wanting Malli to notice the anger swirling in my mind at hearing about Saman Aiya's negativity.

"Akka doesn't have a say with Saman Aiya! His word is the last one."

"Did you speak to Amma or Thaththa?"

"No." Malli shook his head with glazed eyes. "I am worried Amma would listen to Saman Aiya."

"I was wondering if you could speak to them about this….. Please?" Malli's voice was shaky, and his eyes filled with tears. His powerless demeanour was foreign to me; Malli was our dreamer, the superhero. I wish I could hug him and reassure him everything would be all right. However, I didn't. I couldn't give him that assurance.

"Is this what you really want to do, Malli?"

"Yes."

"I did a lot of research. I also discussed this with Niranga Aiya. And with Senaka Aiya when he was here for the anniversary dinner. Senaka Aiya is doing the exact job I want to do one day. He told me what that involves and what subjects I need to take. I want to do this, Sasoo." Malli was rocking his body, clutching his hands, unable to stay still.

I recall having a similar chat with Thaththa when I wanted to go to Kandy for my AL studies. Though my decision was based on a knee-jerk reaction to seeing Niranga and Akka together and my attraction to Channaka, I still built up a pretty good argument to justify my move to Kandy. But, of course, I was younger than Malli when I decided.

I wondered if he was making the right decision. From the day Malli came across a computer at the science exhibition at the University of Peradeniya years ago, the machines have fascinated him. When it turned into an obsession, everyone blamed me for taking him to the science exhibition in the first place.

We couldn't enrol Malli in a prominent school in Kandy after he got through his O-level exam because we couldn't afford it. So maybe, this time around, we owe it to Malli to follow his dream. Rightly or wrongly, the decision I made when I was sixteen made me achieve my goal and paved my path to a better one. Now it is Malli's turn, and he wants me to argue his case. I want to help him build his courage to have that tough conversation.

"Let me talk to Niranga first." I pattered his hand and smiled. "I need to make sure he had not polluted your mind. And you are not going there to go after girls!" I pushed Malli's shoulder with mine and teased to lighten the atmosphere that felt heavy around us. Malli smiled and shoved me back.

"Maybe I can find a cougar with a nice inheritance."

"Hey, be respectful to women!" I stare him down.

***

Jeevani was nearly six months pregnant now and was proudly showing off her baby bump. I got the usual scolding plus additional teasing as she could straight away pick out the difference in me. Before I could say anything, she already knew about Niranga and me.

I was not surprised; in so many ways, both Jeevani and Reshani held my affection the same way, accommodating a significant part of my heart. Jeevani and I are light years apart in our dreams and aspirations. Still, we were sisters who did not share the same womb, a consciousness that I couldn't hide from.

"What gave it away?" I asked, wanting to be super careful around Amma and Akka.

Jeevani laughed. It was cheerful, similar to the one she has when she finds one of her kids being mischievous. "Your face lights up when his name comes up, and your eyes look dreamy. So, no more vanilla?" she smirked.

"Nope, more like fruit and nut." I smiled, not being able to disagree with Jeevani. Niranga had bought a lightness that didn't exist in me before.

"Tell me, why are you keeping this a secret? Your parents would love it."

"Because there is no point in sharing something that will not last after he leaves."

"If you are not sure about the future, why do you take the risk and sleep with him?" Jeevani voiced her disappointment.

"Because I enjoy sex, woman, and I am kind of getting good at it." Sometimes I love to shock Jeevani, and that is precisely what I did. Jeevani is a conformist. The only controversial action against her name was eloping with Devon.

Until I slept with Niranga, sex had only been another natural need. Perhaps it is my upbringing, where the culture taught me that sex was an act to populate, not a pleasurable one. It could also be the education as I can't recall enjoying the act of intimacy before Niranga. But it was different when I was with Niranga. I devour the process, before, during and after, when we made love. He had helped me dig out this person buried underneath the tough exterior, who was sensual, giving, and caring. I love the person I was becoming.

I didn't share any of this with Jeevani, as she wouldn't comprehend my disposition. Along with birth control, abortion, gay relationships, sex before marriage was something that did not sit well with her. Sometimes I wonder how we are still friends with each other; when we are polar opposite.

"Don't talk like street trash; it doesn't suit you." Jeevani was annoyed. She stood up and went to add some firewood to the hearth to make us some tea. That was her way of indicating, this conversation is over.'

"You have changed!" After a long stretch of silence, Jeevani turned to me with a sharp glare.

"What do you mean?" I swung to Jeevani, seeking clues in her face.

"Your priorities have shifted!"

"Because I am enjoying sex?" I laughed, as it was funny.

"No, that's not it. You always have been someone pushing boundaries!" She stopped fiddling with her jasmine clad hair, staring outside the window.

"Then what?"

"Before Niranga sir, you would have rushed home to see the baby. " Jeevani's voice was heavy with disappointment, sounding the same way all of my family was when I didn't return home to see the baby when he was born weeks ago.

"I was busy." I shrugged my shoulders. "It wasn't as if the baby was going to disappear if I didn't hurry home." I mocked Jeevani, being very careful about guarding my real reason. On the other hand, Niranga leaves in few weeks; I am savouring my time with him. As I have committed to spend weekends with Niranga, I waited for a time when he was away to return home.

"All I know is that you have changed."

"What is this? You tell me I lead a vanilla life when I conform to expectations, and now you complain when I don't? Give me a break, woman! It isn't like I have abandoned my family; I am just a few weeks late seeing the little man. Do you think he is going to remember his Aunty not turning up on the first day he drew a breath outside his mother's womb?"

"You can dress it any way you choose...... I think you are too smitten by Niranga sir!"

I felt heavy and uneasy. My friends believe I have changed or derailed. Reshani and Ravidu have been in my ear with their stern warnings, and now Jeevani was on to my case. I didn't want to get into an argument, so I just smiled.

***

When I returned home after visiting Jeevani, Aunty Nelum and Uncle Sarath were in our living room with Amma and Thaththa.

"There she is." Uncle Sarath turned to me with a wide grin on his face.

"What did I do this time?" I was apprehensive, not knowing what Niranga had done this time to annoy Uncle.

"Oh, no need to worry possum, just wanted to thank you. We had a fabulous time in Colombo. Niranga took us to most of those lovely restaurants you had recommended. Some places were top notch." Uncle sounded thrilled, and Aunty was nodding her head in agreement. I breathe in with relief.

"Oh, Sasoo darling, I didn't get a chance to thank you for the gorgeous present you gave us. Niranga said that was one of your own photos?" It was good to hear Seneges appreciated their anniversary gift. I remember Niranga mentioning how impressed his parents were with my sentimental gift and how much his mother adored the picture frame I gave her of Niranga, the one I have on my book rack.

"I love Niranga's photo. He is such a handsome boy, isn't he?" Aunty was grinning with pride. I nodded my head in agreement.

"Where is this lovely boy now?" I haven't seen Niranga since coming home, as he had been away on business. I felt the dopamine rushing through my brain, making me sweat and my heart slamming against my ribcage, excited by the anticipation of seeing him.

"He is with Amali and the baby."

"I am surprised how much Niranga adores babies." Amma was making conversation with Aunty.

"Yes, he would love a big family. Niranga hadn't stopped nagging us about being an only child."

"Haven't you been able to find a nice girl for him yet?" Amma inquired with interest.

"No, he refuses to go on visits these days." I was holding my breath, waiting for Aunty's response. I was unsure how I would have felt if Niranga had been visiting girls while he was with me. *'Am I jealous?'* I was not ready to discover an answer for it yet, so I pushed that thought aside.

"How is he going to start a family if he doesn't find a suitable girl?" Amma sounded disheartened.

"I keep asking him the same question. He used to say that if he didn't find the right girl before turning thirty, he would adopt a child." I hid my amusement, seeing Amma's horrified expression. Her traditional mind couldn't comprehend Niranga's desire to become a single parent.

"Something is different with Niranga these days." Aunty Nelum lowered her voice and glanced over to check if anyone else was in the room before she continued. "He is more grounded and happier. I can't place my finger on it. He is up to something; maybe you can find out for us?" Aunty turned to me with a quizzical eye, making me all edgy.

"Ha?" I blinked and quickly closed my mouth.

"Why are you looking so surprised! Aren't you Niranga's trusted confidant? Maybe you can catch up with him next time when he is in Kandy and find out for us?"

"Are you asking me to spy on him?" I asked Aunty in disbelief.

"Not exactly, spy. Try to find out if he has met someone. He goes to Kandy quite a lot these days! It has to be a girl. Most days, he is behaving like a teen in love!" Aunty Nelum said with assurance in her voice. My heart pounded hard when she didn't take her eyes off me.

"Don't bother Nelum. Sasoo will share nothing; those two always have been thick as thieves. She might already know what is going on." I didn't expect Uncle Sarath to listen to our conversation when he gave me a piercing stare. He was challenging me to prove him wrong. I tried to look innocent and grinned all the while, wondering how I could leave the room without drawing much attention to myself.

"My little one, can you make us some ginger tea?" When Amma asked me, I didn't need a second invitation. I got up and left the room, heading to the kitchen with a sigh of relief. I have dodged a bullet.

Despite having the hearth burning throughout the day, the kitchen was cold. I forgot to bring my jumper with me. I tried to warm my hands, holding them closer to the burning coals while waiting for the water to boil.

"Keep away from the kettle; I don't want you to burn your hand." I swirled around when I heard Niranga's husky voice. He had come into the kitchen, and he had my jumper in his hand.

We were like magnets, gravitating towards each other. I rushed into Niranga's arms to be greeted by a tight hug. I laid my head on his shoulder, filling my lungs with his musk. When Niranga turned his head, claiming my lips for a warm, passionate kiss, it felt comforting.

"Here, put this on. I know you are cold." Niranga held the jumper over my head, allowing me to put my head and arms through it. He pulled the hem down to cover my upper body. I watch him recognising it and eyeing me with surprise.

"This is mine." Niranga ran his fingers over the faded symbol of Ralph Lauren trademark the Polo horse, making my nipples go harder.

"Was yours!" I corrected him. It belonged to him years ago, and it has been mine for so many years now.

"I remember you stole this from me."

"I did no such thing!" I denied his accusation.

"Yes, you did." He pulled me into his arms and kissed me again, this time for much longer.

"Can you tell me how you got it then?" Niranga challenged. "You can't. Can you?" When I didn't respond, Niranga laughed and pushed me away to peer into my face.

"You stole this because you were angry with me for going away on holiday without you to London." He smiled; I could tell he recalled the afternoon I boldly declared I wanted to become a Senege to travel with him. "This was my favourite jumper." He pulled me to him, tugging the hemline, his smile widening. "I wonder I couldn't find it." Niranga laughed, reminding me how I became the owner of this dated garment I love so much. I felt embarrassed, and I hid my face in the crook of his neck.

"I can't believe you have kept it." He turned and kissed my forehead with a chuckle in his voice. "You, crazy girl."

I stretched my arms, pulling his head down for another kiss. Have been without him for so many days, I was trying to fill the void I felt. What started as a slow, passionate embrace soon turned into a fervent, demanding one. I heard myself moaning with pleasure, wanting more. My fingers were unbuttoning Niranga's shirt with an urgency I couldn't control.

"We can't, not here, not now." Niranga got hold of my hand and whispered in my ear, bringing me back to the moment. I buried my face in the crook of his neck again, surrendering to disappointment and embarrassment. *'So much for being in control!'* I ignored the sarcastic voice, reflecting on one of the internal conversations I had in the last few days during Niranga's absence, promising myself to be in control of carnal urges.

"Later, I promise." Niranga pulled my chin and planted a quick kiss. "Let's get this tea ready before Aunty regrets sending me into the kitchen."

He slowly turned away to button his shirt, giving me time to compose myself. I walked away from Niranga and got busy with the tea preparation. Niranga sat in the corner, watching me work. Except for the crackle of burning firewood in the hearth, the only sound in the kitchen was the rattling noise my spoon made when I mixed sugar into the tea jug.

It reminded me of the last time we were here. Although there is no difference in my heart rate, today, I am excited and happy. I couldn't stop thinking about the dopamine rush Ravidu talked about a few weeks ago.

"What are you grinning about?"

"Nothing, just happy you are back," I admitted.

"Happy enough to keep your window unlocked?"

I froze with excitement. It wouldn't be the first time Niranga sneaked into my room through my window. He had done that so often when we were kids, though it would be the first time I would be in his arms. For a second, the mere possibility of being in Niranga's arms made me breathless.

"No, please don't. Saman Aiya comes out for smokes at night." Niranga straightened like a meerkat, his face darkening with annoyance.

"How do you know? Do you hang out with him?"

"No, silly," I dismissed the sourness in his voice with a chuckle. "The smoke sweep through the window." I went back to preparing tea, ignoring the niggle feeling..... *'Is he jealous?'*

"Hmm… it will kill me tonight knowing you are a few yards away." I leaned across and kissed his lips lightly to reassure him he wasn't the only one going to have a sleepless night.

"I want to talk to you about Malli." I redirected my nervous energy and changed the subject.

"So, Manoj finally talked to you." Niranga sounded relieved.

"Yes, he did. And I am disappointed you mentioned nothing about it." It hurt me he didn't share this information with me.

"Sorry, babe. Manoj wanted to tell you first. I had to honour his wish."

"I thought we share everything?" I asked. *'Hypocrite.'* The adult whispered. The relationship I have with Niranga is more physical than emotional. I can indeed talk to him about anything because he listens without judging and isn't condescending, although sometimes we disagree. Yet, I haven't opened myself to him, and I was not planning to either.

I had fenced my life only to share the good bits with him. I kept the ugly and complicated behind a curtain tucked away, not allowing it to be seen. I didn't reveal to him we were about to lose our tour agency. Despite all our efforts, we hadn't recovered from our debts. So, inevitably, sooner, my role in the business will change from entrepreneurs to employees. Nor have I shared Sula and Nilush are on the verge of breaking up, waiting for torrential rain to swamp the sandcastles they had built. We all can sense the tremors, anticipating an inevitable earth slip after copious rain; it is just a matter of time. Or that I have been indecisive about my PhD studies. The university grant I was eligible for would not remain open until I decide where to direct my energy and efforts in life.

'Did we begin our relationship with the premise of being truthful with each other? What does it even mean?' Then, as if he was responding to my question, Niranga gave me his answer.

"Not with someone else's life. It has nothing to do with us." He was firm, as if he was expecting me to disagree.

"Can we talk about it? I have a lot of questions. Do you have time tomorrow? Maybe I can come in the afternoon to your office?" I doubt my ability to handle myself and be focused if I was not around other people in Niranga's presence. I needed a boundary to remain fixated on discussing Malli's plan.

"Sounds good." Niranga quickly recognised my intention and smiled.

***

Thaththa, Saman Aiya, and Malli were chatting with Aunty, Uncle and Amma when we returned to the living room. When Uncle Sarath asked me if Niranga behaved himself and did not burn my hand again, I didn't want to tell him the burn was much more severe this time as it was internal, not an external mishap. I only need to stand next to Niranga to have my entire body on fire.

"Sasoo, would you mind going to Hatton and buy some baby stuff I need for the bath mix tomorrow?"

"Yah, I can do that, Amma. I have little except catching up with Niranga to go through some computer stuff." I was glad we made plans earlier. It was easy to share our program without having to do much explaining.

"How are you going there?" Niranga was concerned.

"By bus, of course."

"Why don't you take my car." Niranga ignored my snide and offered.

"Oh, that's okay; I can take the bus." I shrugged his offer, not paying much attention to his constant need to make things comfortable for me.

"Why get squashed on a bus when you can take the car? I don't use it during the day."

"You trust your Jaguar with Sakunthala?" Saman Aiya blinked in surprise. When he travels for business, he leaves the car in the garage locked up. He let his pregnant wife take the bus because he couldn't trust anyone with his beat-up car.

"Yes, why wouldn't I?"

"You will regret it when you have to spend hours in a garage having to get the car fixed. Spare parts of such luxury car would cost you an arm and a leg." Saman Aiya shook his head and smirked.

"Have you seen her driving?" Niranga sat straight, becoming all defensive. "Saku is an excellent driver. I wouldn't blame her if there was an accident!" The pride in his voice made me glow. "The probability of escaping an accident is very low here when there are drivers not even qualified to take a billy cart out on the roads." I watch Saman Aiya's lips turn down with resentment in response to Niranga's sarcasm. I controlled my urge wanting to slide across and hug Niranga.

"Ah, yes, you did the driving last time when you two went to Kandy, didn't you?" Aunty Nelum placed the team cup on the saucer and turned to me with a smile.

"Yes, he was sleep-deprived and grumpy as a wounded elephant, Aunty. I cannot believe you asked him to go to Kandy that day." I laughed, reminiscing about how we began our journey.

"So, she rightly told me off and took over the wheel." Niranga joined my laughter.

"Okay then, since you are insisting, I will take the car, though it will be a bit later when I return it."

"That's okay, you can drop by on your way back. We will need about an hour or two to go through your questions, and then we can come home."

Saman Aiya watched our exchange in silence. Although I sensed he was agitated and was not pleased about how his comment was received by the group. He joined Thaththa and Uncle, who dominated the conversation with their two bits on economy and politics. I could see Aunty Nelum was getting bored when she tried to suppress a couple of yawns that tried to escape.

"When are you heading back to Kandy Sasoo?" Running out of patience, having to listen to the men who thought they could resolve world issues by participating in a healthy round of a debate, Aunty turned to me, wanting to break the chatter.

"Day after tomorrow, Aunty."

"I am going in the morning; you can ride with me," Niranga said.

"You are?" Both Aunty and I asked, surprised. Niranga's routine was from Friday afternoon to Monday. I didn't expect him to travel to Kandy on a Wednesday.

"Yes, but you have to get ready in the morning." Niranga had a wicked grin on his face. On the weekends, when I am with him, I usually get up when he emerges from a shower after exercising. Few times he tried to coax me into getting up early and gave up, realising that I was in a better mood when left to my schedule.

"Oh, no... no, thanks, I will take the afternoon bus." I ignored Niranga's annoyed look, as I was not planning to leave home in the morning.

"No, you will go with Niranga." Amma addressed me with a stern voice, indicating she expected no argument from me.

"Aney, Amma, it is too cold in the morning. I will freeze before I reach Kandy."

"What do you do when you have early morning tours or classes?" Thaththa sounded as if he was telling me not to be silly, accept the free ride.

"Oh, she sleeps......." I gave Niranga a warning look, stopping him in the middle of his sentence. I didn't want Amma or Aunty to speculate how Niranga knows I sleep in until my alarm goes off a couple of times or until he had to cajole me on odd occasions to be up early. Niranga grinned and lifted his shoulders. My heart started pounding heavily when I realised Aunty had noticed our exchange.

"Think of it as one of your tours. Go with Niranga. You can always catch up with your sleep later in the afternoon if you want to." Oblivious to all, Thaththa continued to talk.

"Okay, that is settled. I will pick you up around eight in the morning."

"Aiyo Ran, make it nine; eight is too early." I pleaded, not wanting to be up so early.

"Ran?" It was too late to correct myself, as Aunty had already picked up the affectionate way I addressed Niranga. The term of endearment adorned him, showing my fondness, which I also sometimes used to manipulate Niranga, slipped through my tongue.

"Don't be a princess. You won't feel the cold, just layer up and wear a beanie." Noticing the horror shoot through my body, paralysing me with jitters, Niranga jumped in. "What is this? I am giving you a free ride, and you are whining like a kid? On second thoughts, take the bus. I can drive in peace and don't have to stop over to buy those unclean vegetables and wildflowers." Niranga projected annoyance to distract his mother.

"Okay, okay, no need to get so annoyed. I appreciate your kindness, and I will be ready at eight." I played along, breathing in with calmness.

"What's the point of you rushing back mid-week? Why not stay over the weekend?" Saman Aiya interjected, surprising me. "I have a couple of friends coming to see the baby. You can catch a ride with one of them on Sunday afternoon." I saw Niranga fidgeting with agitation on the other side of the room. I hope Amma and Thaththa wouldn't get caught on to the idea. Though I was on a break from work, I was leaving early to prepare for the semester exams.

"I have lectures on Thursday and Friday." I was getting good at deceiving. I had lied to Amma and Thaththa when they asked me to return home on weekends, because I preferred to spend those days with Niranga. I also lied to Akka when she wanted to know if Niranga and I had become best friends again. I even lied to Reshani the other day, saying I would be alright when Niranga left.

"Is that the real reason?" When Saman Aiya confronted me, I froze, thinking that he was on to us. I felt perspiration forming around my temples and armpits. I was short of breath, and I could feel the palpitation.

"What do you mean?" I cleared my throat and asked, projecting a calmness masking the agitation.

"Is it really the work, or is it Sulakkana that takes you back to Kandy?" I exhaled slowly and relaxed. I was unsure why he was trying to get me to talk about Sula in front of my parents and the Seneges. I saw Niranga giving me a sarcastic smile, insinuating, *'You dug the hole. You better crawl out.'*

"Both. " I smiled, purposely lowering my voice. I avoided looking at the others and toyed with my hands, exhibiting a shyness I didn't possess. My response generated an uncomfortable silence amongst the group. Niranga got up from where he was sitting to head home, with Aunty and Uncle towing behind him.

23 DISCONTENT

When I walked into the living room, Saman Aiya stood up, tying his loose sarong in a knot. Then he stopped me, waving his hand in anger.

"Where have you been?" It seemed like he had waited for me, which meant he could have seen Niranga dropping me off at the bottom of the stone steps. '*Did he see us kissing?*' I felt my heart plunging with fear.

It was already dark outside. I quickly peeked down to where the car was parked a few seconds ago. I breathed in with relief; with the thick fog spreading around, only the vehicles' tail lights would have been visible from where I stood.

"What is wrong?" I assumed the worse that something was not right with Akka or the baby.

"What? I should ask you that? What are you doing roaming around with a guy late into the night?" He picked up the folds of his sarong and tied it in a second knot, challenging me. He looked repulsive in the way he was behaving, resembling an unskilled labourer on road works.

"What? First, it is not even seven o'clock yet. Second, I did no such thing. I went to Hatton to buy stuff for your baby!"

His comment baffled me. I had already told Amma when I took off in the morning that I would be late, stopping over at Niranga's office on my way back. Thaththa also knew where I was when I saw him before he left the office to return home with Uncle. It was draining to be an independent twenty-six-year-old woman and still have to inform everyone under the roof of my whereabouts.

"Don't play with words Sakunthala, you should know better!"

"You are behaving like street trash and disgracing this family." I did not appreciate the way Saman Aiya was addressing me or the comments he was making. I was aware he suspected something going on with Niranga and me.

Yesterday, after everyone left, Saman Aiya came and stood next to me on the veranda, away from Amma and Thaththa, where no one was listening to our conversation. He lowered his voice to ask inquisitively. "So what's with you and Niranga? Is he trying to get into your pants?"

"What? Are you insane?" I widened my eyes and pretending I was shocked.

"Why would he go all lovey-dovey and lend his expensive car for you to drive around?"

Did you think your wife was also returning favours when Niranga chauffeured her around when you were away?' The inner child wanted to ask, but the adult stopped. I love Akka more than I hate Saman Aiya.

"The car is only a staple for Niranga, not a symbol of his status."

When I shared this exchange with Niranga earlier, he asked me to ignore the comment, as Saman Aiya could be feeling left out. Saman Aiya had always been an outsider. Even after five years, he is not entirely woven into the fabric of our family. We have accepted him as Akka's husband. However, outside of that, nothing binds him to our family.

In the beginning, we all tried to make him an integral part of our family. But he is someone no matter how hard you try, you cannot generate affection for. I still cannot understand what made Akka fall in love with him. There is something evil underneath the masquerade of an affectionate husband he tries to project. I feel there is undercurrent viciousness inside him lurking to be unleashed.

In the years we have known Saman Aiya, he had not volunteered to help our family. He had been a freeloader most of the time, riding on the love we have for Akka. It didn't matter how tough it was for Amma and Thaththa to support Akka while he was abroad; he still did not contribute to the household expenses. I detested his self-centeredness.

He had never fitted into our way of life. Where the Seneges have always been part and parcel of our life from our early days. Niranga claimed it was logical for Saman Aiya to feel jealous and threatened because he must subconsciously compare his status with Seneges.

The Seneges blended into our daily routine even after a ten-year gap. We are back to being each other's extended family members. It is so ordinary for Uncle Sarath to come to our house expecting a meal or to bring food for everyone when he prefers dinner at our home. The friendship between Amma and Aunty Nelum was free of jealousy and competition, which allowed them to call across the hedge to have afternoon tea at each other's verandas or swap their cooked meals. If anything had changed, it was the distance Niranga and I pretended to maintain these days. We don't go barging into each other's rooms the way we used to. Because I was cold to Niranga last time I was home, I carried the same facade to camouflage my true feelings from both our families.

"The baby must be stressing him, Saku. Cut him some slack." Niranga said with a tight smile.

"Stressed? Why? Was it he who suffered the ten hours of labour?" I was not sympathetic as Niranga was.

"New fathers find it difficult to adjust."

"How do you know about new fathers?" I ignored the flash of doubt that skipped through my mind. *'Do you have a kid that I don't know about?'*

"I have seen it with my friends and colleagues. Having a baby is a challenging time. Your entire life changes, and to top it all up, you get a little sleep." Niranga chose not to answer my question and went on stressing his point. Despite what Niranga said, I was not in a mood to tolerate Saman Aiya's disrespectfulness. So, I turned to him with all the anger boiling inside me.

"You don't have any right to talk to me like that, so back off!" My outburst shook Saman Aiya, who had only seen my placid demeanour around him. I don't think he ever expected me to be that candour. If he figured he could throw his weight and act as an older sibling, he had gravely misjudged me.

Thaththa must have overheard us as he came out of his room with a concerned expression.

"Is something the matter?"

I stood there in my Wonder Woman pose, challenging Saman Aiya to speak up. I doubted he was bold enough to say what he said in front of Thaththa. If looks could kill, I would have been struck to death by his eyes. Saman Aiya walked out to sit on one of the veranda chairs, saying nothing.

"Did Niranga help you with your computer problem?" Thaththa asked.

"Yes, Thaththa, it took a bit of time. I don't have the same understanding of computers and the internet as Niranga. Poor Niranga, he must have felt as if he was teaching a dummy." I babbled with a smile and went inside, searching for Amma. I found her and Akka in the kitchen preparing dinner.

"Did you get everything on the list, Sasoo?" Amma stopped stirring the curry she was cooking on the hearth to glance my way.

"Yes, Amma, I got extra as well, so it should last for a few weeks."

"Thanks a lot, Nangi. Saman will get the next batch." Akka looked tired and sleep-deprived. The baby had been keeping her up through the nights.

"Anything for the little one," I replied, feeling contented that I could help.

"It was good of Niranga to give you his car," Amma said. Her voice oozing gratefulness.

"Yes, it made things easy."

"Did you two come together?" Akka asked.

"Yes, He dropped me off."

"Sula must burn with jealously these days." Akka grinned.

"I'll mind, Sula. You look after your bulldog, either keep him on a tight leash or tell him to stop freeloading before he acts as the head of the house." Akka didn't deserve my rage, yet I couldn't help it. Without staying for her response, I stormed out.

"Hey, Saman Aiya had Renuka waiting for you. That is why he is pissed with you." Malli said as soon as I entered my room. He knew I was catching up with Niranga on his study plans and must have been waiting for my return.

"What? How does he know Renuka?" I couldn't connect the dots. Renuka was one of Malli's dancing buddies.

"He is trying to set you up with Renuka so he can go into business with Renuka's father." He said, lowering his voice as Saman Aiya was still in the veranda sulking. I wanted to ask Malli, *'Isn't that what you did when you wanted me to come to your dance class, to get favours from Renuka?'* Being intuitive to pick my thoughts, he smiled sheepishly.

"It is not the same; he is actually trying to set you up."

"What? How do you know?"

"I caught him telling Amma and Akka that you are better off with someone like Renuka who has a lot of money than with Sulakkana Aiya. He was going on about how lucrative Renuka's family business is and how they are interested in expanding it to Singapore."

I was furious and wanted to smash something. I fought the urge to run out and put a brick through Saman Aiya's car or punch him into a pulp. In the same breath, I realised I was the person who would worry about the mess I would make or the logistics of getting Saman Aiya to the nearest medical centre.

"And what did Amma say?" I sat next to Malli on my bed and asked.

"Amma said she didn't interfere with Akka when she fell in love with him, so she did not intend to meddle with your life either."

"How nice of her." I was surprised, as Amma never approved of Sula.

"Saman Aiya noticed how Renuka was dancing with you at the dinner and had figured out Renuka has a crush on you. I swear I said nothing to him. Not after Niranga Aiya warned me." Malli glanced away, shifting his feet nervously.

"Niranga did what?"

"He asked me to keep Renuka away from you at the anniversary dinner. I don't want to cross him. He is going to give me free lodging when I get to Sydney." Though Malli's laughed, I heard the flicker of fear in his voice, making me recall the intimidating man hidden underneath Niranga's calm facade.

"Just so you know, neither Saman Aiya nor Niranga has any say in who I want to see," I warned Malli, reminding him that no one could decide on my behalf.

"I will work on your plan and talk to Thaththa next time I am back. You continue to focus on your exam, don't get distracted. We have plenty of days to work out a strategy." I said with a confidence I didn't possess. The earlier chat with Niranga only added to my concerns, not foresight on financing Malli's dream. Although it would be harder for me to honour the personal commitment, I was not ready to yield to hopelessness *'Sleep now. A better idea will present itself in the morning.'* Suddenly one of the overused phrases in Russian fork stories I read as a kid appeared to be insightful.

***

"Do you think something is going on between Niranga and Sasoo?" Amma's voice made me stop in my tracks. Amma was having a conversation with Thaththa in the living room, assuming I was asleep. If I pay attention and listen in, I could faintly hear the discussions taking place there. It had been a secret I kept from everyone for years.

"What do you mean?" I visualised Thaththa removing his reading glasses while closing the book to give his full attention to Amma.

"They seem to be very cosy these days." I panicked. *'Did she notice us flirting?'*

"They have always been like Siamese twins. Last time Sasoo was shy around Niranga. Now they have become friends again. It is good to see them getting along." Thaththa uttered, disregarding Amma's comment.

"Nelum asked me how serious Sasoo is about that boy in Kandy."

"Sulakkana?"

"Yes."

"Why is Nelum interested in him?"

"She is saying if those two are not too serious, we should talk to Niranga and Sasoo."

I slid into the love seat beside the window as my knees got wobbly.

"No," Thaththa said.

"Why?" I caught the surprise in Amma's tone. *'Yes, why?'* I was wondering the same thing.

"We shouldn't intrude, Thanuja. If they are destined to be together, they will. Remember what happened to Amali? If we didn't interfere in the first place, maybe she would not have got involved with Saman." Picking up the regret in Thaththa's voice made me feel dejected.

'Why does he blame himself for Akka's decision?' ' I wandered. I vaguely remember Akka having an affair with someone Amma thought was beneath the family's expectations when Akka was in her first year of university. I never got the complete picture of the drama as I was away from home. From what I pieced together, Akka had become stubborn, resorting to avoiding coming home and continued with her relationship despite every reasoning Amma had attempted.

When she failed her first-year exam at the university, and the affair broke off, she returned, reclaiming her place at home. She smoothly went back to being who she was as if nothing had happened. After that incident, Amma didn't meddle in Akka's affairs when she got involved with Saman Aiya, although no one could withstand him.

Our love for Akka did not fuel our aversion to Saman Aiya. (If I am honest with myself, we all would be happier knowing Akka is comfortable than having her living with us. Something about Akka's presence put all of us on edge). Our relationship with Akka was complex.

Akka is one of those people with dual personalities; you can't keep up if you are getting Dr Jekyll or Mr Hyde. Fortunately, or unfortunately, I often saw the selfish and utterly uncaring girl I grew up with. In that sense, Saman Aiya is the perfect man for her. He doesn't have two sides to him, only a black hole of a personality that drained your energy and left you lifeless with his self-centred, egotistic sociopathic tendencies. Yes, I loathe him.

I wondered if the guy Akka was first involved with was a better match for her. Without our parent's interference, would her relationship have lasted?

Would she have married him? Did he have a dark personality that led Akka to seek Saman Aiya as an improvement? Or is Akka similar to a few of those unfortunate girls I have come across who get attracted to the wrong guy? Thoughts in my mind were turning like a swirling river.

It made me reflect on Niranga and myself. I am yet to understand what I expect from him, let alone from myself. I had succumbed to my desires, the gravitational pull he has on me. I have been evading contemplating the meaning of our relationship if it has any purpose beyond the intense sexual attraction I have for him.

I never believed sex and love should go hand in hand. I remember the utter disbelief spread across Sula's face when I said they can exist in vacuums. For him, love, sex and marriage came as the Three Wise Men. Sometimes I found it funny seeing how a non-conventional man held such firm beliefs when I had the polar opposite. Nor am I a believer in marriage. For me, it was an unnecessary bureaucratic burden. However, I was open to follow the tradition as long as it didn't derail my plans; help Malli with his higher studies build my career. Then, if I am lucky, let the right man sweep me off my feet. Despite my outlook on life, I haven't closed the door on a dream of a romantic happily ever.

"She will be thirty soon. I am worried she wouldn't think about marriage until the little one graduate from university. Then it would be late for a girl." I rolled my eyes hearing this, as they expected me to be married with two kids at a certain age. If I didn't, society would not only frown upon me but on my parents too, wondering what's wrong.

I had always wanted to support Malli with his studies before I settled down. My dream was for Malli to follow his, enjoy the last few years of uncomplicated freedom he will ever have in his life.

When I was young, I couldn't wait to grow up, earn a living and be independent. Now I am an adult, my life isn't a bed of as I expected it to be. I failed to factor in the responsibilities that shadowed adulthood. Until it struck me on my face, I didn't grasp the accountability that came attached with the freedom of making one's own decisions.

How many times I have woken up in the morning wishing I was not a twenty-six-year-old woman! Countless times I have wished I could turn the clock and become a ten-year-old, where I didn't have to fret about what to wear or eat; worry about going to work, meeting deadlines, and balancing life from one payday to another. I wish someone had advised me that adulthood came with a liability; I would have spent more time being a child rather than clutching onto an impatience to become an adult, wishing my childhood away.

I want Malli to have more of his childhood, focusing on his studies rather than worrying about home finances. Now that he wants to study abroad, I have to figure out a way to support his dream. If not for Malli, we owe Thaththa for taking us in when he did and giving us security and love.

"I worry about that too. I wish we don't have to take money from Sasoo. Putha's studies are getting very expensive. I was wondering if we should ask him to stop his computer classes. They are costly."

"Sasoo will get angry. She is like a mother hen with putha, very protective."

It was strange to stand there and realise how well my parents understood me when I always assumed they didn't get me! I wished I could reassure them: I will be all right, have a plan, and have no regrets. Life isn't all about marriage; it has more facets.

"So what should I tell Nelum? She is so adamant that we should try to get them together."

"We expected them to fall for each other when they were kids. Now, I am not convinced it is good for either of them. If Sasoo is serious about Sulakkana, we should not interfere." Thaththa sounded philosophical, as if he had pondered about our union way more than he should have.

"Niranga clearly adores Sasoo, but those two live in two different worlds. Niranga is too sophisticated. Sasoo is a rebel, too headstrong……." I smirked, nodding my head, agreeing with Thaththa.

"If we try to force them together and if they are not ready for it, we would not only hurt them, it could destroy all of us and damage our friendship with Sarath and Nelum."

There was a quiet sternness in Thaththa's voice, as if he was warning Amma not to press the matter any further. Thaththa made the right call. Niranga and I will not last beyond his holiday.

"Let us leave things for Sasoo to sort out, Thanuja. So far, she has done nothing to concern us. She is sensible. She will make the right choices." Though the confidence Thaththa had in me made my heart pump with euphoric joy, I also felt the heaviness of the responsibility grounding my feet.

24 HESITATION

As soon as we left our driveway and reached the corner, Niranga stopped the car.

"Did you forget something?" I turned to him, wondering why.

"Yes." Niranga removed his seat belt and unclipped mine swiftly. He leaned in, wrapped his arms around me, started kissing me.

"I forgot to say good morning."

The hollow space of the car was filled with Niranga's unique aroma, reminding me of the freshness of a forest after the rain. I no longer noticed the cold I felt when we left the house. His cheesy, romantic embrace warmed me from head to toe.

"Behave. We are on a public road." I squeezed Niranga's fingers, fondling inside my shirt.

"I can't control myself when I am with you." Niranga smiled.

"More reasons for you to get us home quickly." I marvelled at how easily I have adopted Niranga's cousin's house as 'home.' It seemed natural to call it ours, where we were free to be ourselves enjoying each other's company.

"Not so soon, my precious. I am taking you on a date." Niranga's eyes were glittering, and his face was bright with a beaming smile.

"You are?"

I felt light and happy when I left the house in the morning. I looked forward to our trip down the citadel together, to hold his hand, steal a quick kiss when we stop at a traffic light, mock each other's song choices, talk about random things that mattered little. I was already expecting an exciting day ahead. Now he made me wish for more.

"Yes, and for that, I need you blindfolded." Niranga opened up into the glove compartment, pulling out one of Aunty Nelum's scarves.

"Do you always blindfold girls when you take them on a date?" I teased. I watched him having a monologue as he shook his head and smiled.

"Just the extra special ones."

"So, I am that?"

"Aren't you a liberated woman who doesn't need reassurance from any man?" He mocked me. Before I could respond, he wrapped the scarf around my eyes and fastened my seat belt for me. Next, we were on the move. I was trying to guess where we were going, being mindful of the movements of the car. I knew Nuwara Eliya - Kandy road like the back of my fist, so much so, I knew when we passed Jeevani's house and took a right turn onto a gravel lane. Though I have seen the road leading up the hill, I had paid no attention to it before.

"You okay?" Niranga squeezed my hand, and I could sense him making a sideways glance to check on me. I nodded. I was going through the area's geography, trying to guess where Niranga was taking me and what he had planned. After a few more minutes of driving up the hill, Niranga stopped the car.

"Are we there?"

"Yes, you need to stay in for a couple more minutes before I bring you out."

Leaving me in the car, Niranga got out. I picked up the sound of him opening and closing the boot door. After some time, he came to fetch me from the car.

"Now, I am going to remove your blindfold, but you have to keep your eyes closed until I say so." I obeyed reluctantly, keeping them shut while Niranga removed the seat belt and the scarf. He put a beanie over my head, covering my ears.

"What is that for?"

"It is cold outside. I don't want you to complain. So, put these on." He took hold of my hands to slide woollen gloves on them. He has observed how sensitive I am to the temperature and had planned for everything.

"Why do I need those when I have you?" I teased, trying to pull him for a quick kiss.

"I will remember that next time you complain about being cold." He brushed my lips, and I could tell he was smiling.

"Come now, slowly," he guided me to get out of the car.

"What? No carrying? Where is the romance if I have to walk with my eyes shut?"

"Now that you have dressed me up, shouldn't you carry me as they do in the movies?" I teased while keeping a tight grip on his arm. I couldn't see his expressions, how his eyes were checking me, or how his lips were curling when he was contemplating a response. All I felt was his arm going around me, and when he lifted me up, I instinctively draped my hands around his neck.

I was glad Niranga put a beanie and gloves on me as I felt the coldness on top of my nose when I contacted the warmness of the skin on his neck. I pushed myself closer to him, trying to warm my face, burying it in the crook of his neck, breathing in his scent.

"Gosh, you are getting heavy." I heard the chuckle in Niranga's voice.

"Whose fault is that? You are the one who makes me overeat."

"Eating isn't the problem. You don't exercise at all." He reminded my lack of interest in exercising. Niranga has a strict exercise regime that he follows. On days I am with him, I wake up to him sweaty coming back from a jog or finishing his sit-ups. No matter how persuasive he had been, I have refused, preferring to gorging on his sweat dripping shimmering body than join him.

"I think I am burning more than enough calories when I am with you."

"Not enough, one make-out session will burn about 70 calories… so 70 into….."

"I am not interested in the math. If I am too heavy for you, why don't you find someone skinnier who is interested in exercising?" Though I am fully aware it was not my beauty that got Niranga attracted to me, I still didn't want him to remind me. I cut him off with annoyance.

"Hey, hold on, no need to bring your claws out." He gradually put me on the ground.

"Now, open your eyes."

I could not believe what was in front of us. We were standing there, watching the sunrise. Up ahead, Mount Pedro stood like a massive green giant with its lush green top covered in thick fog. The sun's rays from the east spread across the top, creating God's fingers across the valley. Standing behind me, Niranga pulled me closer to his chest. "Breathtaking," I whispered in amazement.

"It is still misty over there, but by the time we leave, it will be clearer."

"It is still gorgeous with the blue, green mountain top and clouds." I glance across the scenery, stunned.

"How did you find this place? I have never been here before." It impressed me Niranga brought me to a location I hadn't been to before.

"You think you know every inch of the town, don't you?" Then, reading my mind, He teased.

"Well, technically, I should. It is my job to know."

"Now you know a new location."

We were two dwarfs standing there between the fading mist around us. The morning sun was making shadows on the mountain peak illuminate brightly. Sunlight on the clouds made so many shades of white. The scenery upon us was a photographer's nightmare. There were many shades and angles that one would feel inadequate no matter how well you tried to capture it. Beauty that captures the naked eyes was far better than a good set of lenses.

"I wish I had my camera." I signed, regretting the missed opportunity.

"And have you not give me any attention? Let's sit down." Niranga clutched my hand and led me to a blanket spread on the ground. He had prepared a picnic. A thick, old blanket was on the floor with two cushions to sit on and a plastic container, a flask, paper plates, and two cups.

'This must be how he treats his girls back in Sydney.' I ignored my resentment towards unknown women in his life. Niranga appeared happy, unaware of the jealously floating underneath my smile. He snatched another blanket from the ground and draped it around my shoulders to keep me warm.

"Come, let us sit."

Beneath the happiness Niranga created for me, there was a subtle sadness that reminded me I hadn't been on a date before. Channaka was the only boyfriend I had, but we did nothing romantic, except me listening to Channaka recite his poems (it must be a memory thing, as I can't recall any of them being heart-fluttering romantic). I haven't been on a picnic, gone to a movie or a party with a boy. Nor have I ever held hands and strolled in a park or received a greeting card telling me how special I was. I have never got a gift to celebrate an important date or a moment. I had missed none of that before because I never craved to have someone in my life. I was happy in my skin with friends who fulfilled my world.

I grew up accepting I was not that attractive to catch a boy's attention beyond asking what my friend's name was or could I pass a message to one of them. When I was at university, my personality became a magnet to those after a challenge, yet I didn't have the time or the interest to entertain such whims. Then I started the con with Sula, playing happily in love, devoted girlfriend. Amid the busy life, I didn't encounter anyone intriguing enough to take an 'unfaithful' step, even in my dreams, until Niranga walked into our living room.

Dating was a new concept for me, and I guess what they say is true; you don't know what you have missed until you encounter it. I have missed existing in a warm cocoon, this floating sensation that was coating me like a second skin, a rainbow of emotions filling my consciousness.

Niranga and I have done none of the conventional activities a couple does when they are together. Our union differed from day one. Being with him just happened. Like a giant star, he pulled me into his orbit; I was a lonely asteroid floating on my own when he changed my trajectory.

We have skipped so many steps in the traditional mating ritual. It worked perfectly well until now. After all the efforts Niranga had made, preparing this outing, the happiness I saw in his eyes made me realise I could enjoy more of this.

I sat down on the blanket next to Niranga. He put his arms around me and pulled me close to his heart. We sat there for a long time, not saying a word, each lost in our own thoughts. I had my head on his chest, watching the sun warming up the mountain top. The fog was slowly dissolving, opening the view to layers of clouds.

Seeing the array of clouds spread across Mount Pedro reminded me of the cloud river they say that goes over the Amazon. I recalled one of my professors saying it would be the longest river on earth if measured. I wondered if we, too, have a cloud river going over the mountains that float across the Sri Lankan island.

My heart was as light as those clouds. I was happy and content to be there. I didn't want to be in any other place than in Niranga's arms, feeling the gentle rise and fall of his breath. We were far away from the main road, and the village below was just waking up. There was not much sound around us except the slight hum of the breeze that carried cold air.

I wanted to bottle the happiness I was experiencing at this moment. Maybe when Niranga leaves in a few weeks, I can open the lid to bring this moment back to life to escape the return to my mundane life. I could live this moment forever, feasting on the sensations as a tape that got stuck in a cassette player playing the same melody repeatedly.

"Thank you, my darling, this is beautiful." I lay my palm across Niranga's heart, wishing there was a way for me to transfer the happiness in mine to his before I burst.

"I thought you might like it here."

"This will now become my favourite place in Nuwara Eliya." Niranga tightened his grip on me, pulling me closer. I leaned back a bit more and felt his arousal along with mine. I wanted more: I wanted to feel him in me, feel his skin brushing against mine, filling me, and making me whole.

I wondered how I would exist without him, how would I fill the giant void he would leave behind. As if Niranga could sense the disturbance in my utopia, he spoke.

"Why don't you come with me to Europe?"

It took me a few seconds to realise what he was suggesting. He just invited me to join his tour around Europe that he had planned to do with two of his friends as part of his self-discovery journey.

"Nice idea, but I can't."

"Why not? I thought it was a kind of offseason for you. Wouldn't there be fewer tours? Isn't there going to be a semester break in the university in a week or two?" I realised it was not a spur-of-the-moment request. Niranga had thought it through.

"Isn't it a boy only trip to test the boundary of your freedom?"

"I am sure Jason and Matt wouldn't mind and would love to meet you." He bent his head and kissed my lips, trying to convince me. It was really tempting; he was visiting most of the places on my wish list. If I had money, I would have loved to see those locations with Niranga.

I remembered the photos of Reshani and Ravidu's Europe holiday; both of them standing in front of the famous locations in Europe: Colosseum and Pantheon in Rome, St. Peter at the Vatican, the Acropolis and the Temple of Olympian Zeus in Athens and Mont-Saint-Michel and Eiffel Tower in France, Ravidu's arms were around Reshani, both of them smiling happily at the camera, making lasting Kodak moments.

I had a mental image running through my thoughts replacing Reshani and Ravidu in those photos with us; Niranga and I standing together, his arms around me, we both happily smiling at the camera.

I have never dreamt of visiting any of these places with anyone before. The urge I felt to see them with Niranga was overwhelming. I cleared my throat

THE LABYRINTH OF MY LIFE   259

to get rid of the lump forming inside me. I didn't want Niranga to know how badly I wished I could join his trip or how financially drained I was.

I knew I only had to say yes, and Niranga would take care of all expenses. My financial worries would no longer be a burden; Niranga would sweep in and make them go away.

In many ways, Niranga harboured traditional values that were inbuilt in him. He takes care of his women; he doesn't allow them to spend money on anything. Niranga finds it appealing when girls are dressed up in beautiful clothes and jewellery (I have not been blind to his admiration of girls in lovely outfits, I pretend I don't notice); he is born to be a knight in shining armour who rescues the damsel in distress.

"You boys have been planning that trip for ages, and you deserve some quality time together. Why not play the tour guide to me some other time, so I don't have to share you with your friends?"

I was careful with my response, not wanting him to be my knight. I didn't need rescuing.

"Fair enough, so tell me, what are your dream destinations?"

"Hmmm… My dream destinations. Let me see, the top three are Rome, Greece and Egypt."

"I bet they are all work-related. Tell me, if you can choose any location, where would you like to go?" He stopped for a moment as if he was trying to be careful with his choice of words. "Let's say for your honeymoon?"

"Then it would be the French Riviera or Venice."

"Interesting choices. Why those?"

"Are you aware of how the tradition honeymoon started?"

"Nope," Niranga shook his head. "Whoever did it, I love the idea."

"The term honeymoon dates back to the 5th century. Historians believe newly wedded couples used to drink a honey-based alcoholic drink to arouse sexual desires in the first month of their marriage."

"Hmmm… Not all need such." Niranga had forgotten we were in a public place, as his fingers were trying to undo my shirt buttons. To distract him, I got hold of his hand and continued talking.

"Travelling during the honeymoon period only started in early 19th-century in England."

"So, it is a POME tradition."

"POME?" I was not sure who he was referring to.

"It is Australian slang for English immigrants."

"What does POME mean?"

"Prisoner of Mother England."

"Oh, that is interesting. The tradition started as newlywed couples visited relatives and friends who couldn't attend the wedding. Then it spread to Europe."

"French Riviera, Italy and Venice became popular destinations."

"So that is why you want to go to French Riviera or Venice?"

"Guilty", I smiled.

Niranga got distracted by the sound of a car coming up the gravel road. Another young couple had discovered this hidden oasis.

"As much as I love to stay here with you, we have to head back. Let us eat something." Niranga opened up the plastic box sitting on the blanket to reveal toasted sandwiches. I wish not to eat or drink anything, knowing the consequences I had to suffer later. Yet, I didn't have the heart to say no to Niranga after all the trouble he had gone through to prepare the picnic.

I grabbed a toasty, and a cup filled with coffee, saying nothing. Niranga was eagerly waiting for me to devour. I did not care what would happen later; there was no way I would hurt his feelings. I took a small bite of the sandwich and watched Niranga's face, filling with satisfaction and pride.

"Who made all this stuff?" I asked, with the fear of remembering my parents' conversation last night, not wanting Aunty Nelum to find out about the picnic basket.

"The chef at the Grand Hotel is one of my schoolmate's fathers. I arranged it through Harsha." He took a sip of coffee, eyeing me curiously. I let my shoulders relax and drank a small sip of the coffee, allowing the warm liquid to slide down my throat.

"You look relieved. Were you worried that my Amma would find out I got all this made for you?" Sometimes I am amazed at how accurately he reads me. I grinned and nodded my head in response.

"Eventually, we have to tell our parents about us." He bit into the sandwich in his hand and spoke while munching away.

"Why?"

I was not ready to share the intimacy we had with my parents, let alone his. I didn't expect Niranga to talk about anything remotely related to the future anytime soon. He caught me off guard with his comment.

"Amma already suspects I am seeing someone. She made a few suggestive comments about my visits to Kandy." My mind instantly went to the conversation Aunty Nelum had with me the other day. I decided not to share this with Niranga. I didn't want to give him any encouragement.

"As long as she doesn't know it is me, we are okay."

"She suspects you." There was laughter in Niranga's voice, his eyes glistering with joy.

"Why does she suspect me?" I already guessed the reasons, yet was keen to find out Niranga's thoughts on it.

"She had noted us flirting the other day." He grinned.

"Also, I may have slipped a couple of times." Niranga had a goofy smile, saying, *'I am sorry, I couldn't help it.'*

I didn't see the point of sharing our affair with our parents. Naturally, our parents will automatically expect us to get married, but neither one of us has spoken of a life to come beyond a week, let alone a marriage. Niranga was not a settling type or one to have a long-term relationship. It suited me well. I was not interested in a commitment, either.

"They all believe I am with Sula. So, there is no need to tell them."

"If we tell them, you can come and visit me in Sydney."

"I can come and visit you in Sydney even if we share nothing." I challenged him.

"Why don't you want to tell them?" I was not keen on answering Niranga's question but gave up to avoid his intense glare.

"What is the point of telling them anything now? You are leaving in a couple of weeks. It will devastate them if they find out we have been lying to them for months."

"Let's say we only hooked up this week." Niranga was grinning.

"And what do you want to tell them after you leave?"

"What do you mean?"

"You haven't thought this through, have you?" I straightened myself to look into Niranga's brown eyes and saw something similar to irritation clouding its brightness.

"Can you imagine what it will do to our parents when we stop seeing each other? They are best friends, and they love both of us equally. Why do you wish to put them in an awkward position by sharing this?"

Niranga continued to eat his sandwich in silence. I waited in silence, not wanting to repeat myself. When he finished eating, he stared at my face, trying to read my thoughts.

"What do you think will happen to us after I leave Saku?" He asked very slowly; each word came out of his mouth, weighed like a sack of rice, all the while watching my face.

"Do you know?"

"Yes, I do." Niranga gave me a daring look, challenging me to confront him. He already knew I was not going to.

'At least one of us does,' I muttered under my breath, and luckily Niranga didn't hear me.

"Tell me, what do you expect this to become?"

"I don't have any expectations."

"Nothing? Are you kidding me? All this time, you were just sleeping with me?" He sounded hurt, more than surprised.

"Isn't that the first rule when you are with a Casanova?" I grinned, reminding him I was fully aware of his nature.

"Guess I have to change that perception then!" I watched Niranga leaning forward, wanting to kiss but changing his mind as we were not the only two on the lookout.

"Shall we go out for dinner this Friday?"

'What is this? Change the ground rules marathon?' I was bickering inside with annoyance. We agreed on a couple of rules of engagement when we started our liaison, as I wanted *'us'* to remain a secret and had no intention of changing them at the eleventh hour.

"You mean another date? Are you going to blindfold me again?" I played along and joked.

"Yes, another date. I can blindfold you if that's what you want." He winked.

"Are you going to come back this weekend?"

"Yes, I will be back."

"Oh, I thought you were going to Kandy today because you can't make it this weekend."

"I made it up because I want to bring you here." Niranga glanced over my shoulders and planted a quick kiss on my lips, grinning.

"I don't have any plans for today except to be with you. I am coming back in the evening."

"Oh…" I felt my heart plunged, sensing the coldness of my bed without having him beside me tonight. I was expecting to spend the night with him.

"Don't be so sad, babe. I will be back on Friday, and we can go on a second date."

"So, where will we be going?"

"Are we allowed to go out to dinner in Kandy?"

"I wanted to say yes, but someone could see us, and I don't want that."

"Then let's go to Colombo. We can leave on Friday and return on Sunday. What do you say?" Niranga faced me pleadingly. I could sense that he wanted more than we had agreed on.

"Do you really want to go?"

"I would love to go out than be stuck in the house."

"Are you already tired of us? Is that why you are after a change?" I was reacting to the word *'stuck'*, as I didn't like what it implied. I watch his pupils enlarge with surprise. His lips twitched because he was trying to masquerade his annoyance.

"I didn't mean it that way babe; I am not tired of us. I only want to take you out to dinner, to a movie, be normal like other couples."

"Don't they do all that to keep the novelty and things interesting? You just said you are not tired of us." I didn't know why I was looking for a fight, but something inside me was brewing.

"There is more to a relationship than sex. I feel we only exist behind bedroom doors!" Niranga sounded annoyed and frustrated. He was trying to understand me. I baffled him as I have myself. I love this new experience of being here with him, but I did not want it to spiral out of control and no longer be a secret.

"You must be the first man to complain about too much sex!" I mocked, pretending I was blind to his need. Niranga was edging to take an alternative route that I wasn't prepared to travel.

Niranga continued to sip his coffee in silence, staring at Mount Pedro. The green giant was becoming more visible as the clouds were drifting away along with a light mist it had on its cap. It felt as if we were in a similar stage. The dissolving fog was like the sensual attraction that bound us together, and I was not ready to look into the core to face what else could be there to bind us.

25 DISDAIN

I felt sick. My stomach was turning like a food processor making grinding noises. I was feeling nauseous, excessive saliva was building up in my mouth, I wanted to vomit. I tried to suppress it, hoping we could make it to the restaurant where Raju works to use the washroom quietly. We were about half an hour away from the restaurant.

My poor condition was worrying me, but I was more nervous about Niranga finding out about it. Luckily, since we packed up our picnic and recommenced our journey, there had been little to no conversation between us. Niranga was brooding, which was unusual, as he loved a good chat when he drives. As I was also dealing with a headache developing behind my temples, it suited me well. I kept my eyes closed, pretending to be asleep, concentrating on my breathing to distract myself. Unfortunately, that strategy didn't work; I knew if I didn't make the stop now, I would end up vomiting in the car.

"Ran, can you pull over?" Niranga peeled his eyes from the road, question in his eyes.

"I don't feel good; I need some fresh air." I opened the window preparing for the worst. The gusty icy wind hit me hard, making my teeth chatter. It was still cold outside.

"Are you alright, Cookie?" Niranga reached across to squeeze my fingers. I gave him a weak smile, as I didn't want to speak. I just wanted to get out of the car.

Nuwara Eliya-Kandy road is not one of the widest roads in the country. I bit my lip, waiting for Niranga to drive further down to find a broader section to stop the car. Before the motor came to a halt, I undid the seat belt and leapt out. I sprint down to the tea plantation to conceal myself from Niranga. I didn't want him to witness one of my weakest moments.

The next moment, I was throwing up. It felt as if my stomach would come out of my throat. I was making unpleasant sounds like a wounded animal. I bent across to keep the vomit away from my body and shoes.

I hated having to throw up and disliked being near anyone who was vomiting. Even though no one enjoys the feeling of nausea, mine was more of a phobia. It had arisen from childhood exposure to being around people with motion disorders. We used to take the bus quite a lot to Kandy and back, and the journey had not always been comfortable. Next to Kandy Mahiyanganaya road, Nuwara Eliya- Kandy road is one of the windiest in the country. It is inevitable not to come across at least a single person going through motion sickness. That agonising animal-like noise one makes when throwing up used to haunt me as a child.

Because of this, I avoid travelling in the mornings and keep off food if my journey starts before noon. I am more susceptible to nausea when I have a full stomach. Today I didn't follow that practice, and now I was paying for it. My throat was hurting from gagging, and my head was pounding. I was feeling low. It got worse when Niranga came and started rubbing my back.

I didn't want him near me. It was hard enough having to throw up beside the road on someone else's property; and even harder to accept Niranga beside me, stroking my back, witnessing my vulnerability.

"Here, rinse your mouth with this." Niranga gave me a bottle of water. I grabbed it in silence and rinsed my mouth. It didn't matter how many times you cleaned; I knew it would take hours to get rid of that stomach-turning smell. It was already around me like an invisible aura, choking me and aggravating my headache.

"Are you okay now?"

I emptied the water bottle, rinsing my mouth, face, and hands. Still, I didn't feel clean enough to face Niranga with eyes blurred with tears, tears of humiliation.

"Babe, are you better now? Do you want another bottle of water?" I could hear the worry in Niranga's voice. I nodded my head without turning around to face him.

"It is okay. We can see a doctor later." He stroked my back to reassure me. I crawled up the hill to where the car was parked in silence. I didn't want to talk; I was tired. Once I got in the car, Niranga put a blanket around me and wound the window up. I closed my eyes and let myself drift into sleep.

"Babe, do you want to freshen up?" I woke up with a jolt when Niranga stroked my arm. When I opened my eyes, we were parked in front of the Pussellawa Restaurant.

I nodded my head and got out of the car. Grabbing my backpack head straight into the restaurant. I ignored Raju, who came to greet us and ducked into the washroom, determined to wash away any traces of vomit I had on me. I cleaned my face and arms with icy cold water, which was a pleasant distraction as the heaviness I felt earlier was subsiding. I felt better after changing my trouser and the shirt I was wearing with the change of clothes I always carry with me.

When I joined Niranga, he and Raju were in a deep conversation with a familiarity I didn't expect. As soon as he saw me, Niranga got up from where he was sitting and pulled a chair for me.

"How are you feeling?" Niranga's voice was heavy with concern.

"Heaps better, thanks."

"Here, drink this. I got you a lime juice. Raju said it is the best for nausea." Niranga gave a grateful nod to Raju, who was still lingering around.

"Thanks, yes, this is good." I took a sip of the lime juice and let the sweet and sour taste linger in my mouth before gulping it down. I needed my brain to make fresh memories and override the earlier unpleasant taste and smell I had experienced.

To have my brain focus on something different, I turned my attention to Raju. "How is Nadan doing, Raju? Is he enjoying school?" He shifted his weight from one foot to another and smiled happily.

"Yes, miss, he loves his school and is really into his studies. He scored well on all his tests. Sir also helped a lot. Thank you, miss, for getting sir to help us. I put that money aside for Nadan's expenses." I glanced at Niranga, as I couldn't follow the conversation.

Lost in his own thoughts, Niranga appeared pale and distracted. I tried to catch his eyes, but he was miles away. Noticing my lack of awareness, Raju explained how Niranga had given him some money for Nadan's school expenses. It didn't surprise me that Niranga had mentioned none of this to me.

"So, you have become Raju's favourite person now." As Raju left to attend to another customer who walked into the restaurant, I turned to Niranga, expecting his sly grin and *'Why are you jealous?'* comeback. He still looked distracted and gave me a superficial smile that didn't reach his eyes.

I let it pass and finished my lime juice. I noticed how Niranga was checking me out from the corner of my eye when he thought I was not aware. He was playing with the empty glass, unable to keep still.

"Are you really feeling alright? How about we see a doctor? Raju said there is a private practice near the petrol station. We can stop there." Once we were in the car, he turned to me with concern.

"Stop worrying babe, I am okay. I don't need to see a doctor. If you want proof, I can drive." Despite my reassurance, Niranga remained uncertain and started the car.

It felt as if something distanced us. Unlike other days, we didn't have the usual banter going. Niranga kept sneaking in glances when he thought I wouldn't notice. His face was pale; his knuckles on the steering wheel had turned red as he gripped it way too tight.

'*I wonder what he is so concerned about? Surely it can't be because I vomited earlier. Is he thinking…. no, he can't be……*' When I caught him glancing at my stomach, the penny dropped.

"Ran, pull over." Niranga looked alarmed, the nerves ticking on his temple.

"Do you need to vomit again?" We were near Gampola road, which was on a broader stretch, making it easy for Niranga to bring the car to a halt.

"I'm fine, wait," I pulled his arm as he was trying to get out of the car to come around to help me. He turned around, puzzled.

"You don't want to get out?"

"No, I don't." I let go of his arm and smiled.

"Then why did you want me to stop the car?"

"What's the matter with you?" I inquired.

"What do you mean?"

"You look like you have seen Casper!" My attempt to get Niranga to relax with a joke didn't pan out.

"Casper? What do you mean?"

"Remember Casper, the Friendly Ghost?" I reminded him of the cartoon we watched religiously as kids about a young, friendly ghost.

"You have turned pale as if you have seen a ghost! What are you worried about?" I peered into his eyes that were avoiding mine.

"You, of course. I am concerned about you. I want to get you to a doctor."

"Aney, if every time a person goes to see a doctor for motion sickness when one is on the Nuwara Eliya - Kandy road, doctors will not have much time for other patients." It took a while for Niranga to register what I said. He continued to stare, not being convinced.

"You didn't vomit the other day we drove to Kandy." His voice had a hint of doubt.

"That is because I only get sick if I eat or drink in the morning."

"Are you sure?"

"Believe me, the only reason I threw up is that I suffer from motion sickness. Can you stop worrying? I am not pregnant!" I clutched his hands, gazing into his eyes. Niranga was panting, his chest going up and down like a printing press. He paused, bewildered, as if he didn't expect me to pick up the troubling thoughts he was grappling with. *'What? Did he seriously believe… I couldn't read his mind?'* I had a chuckle.

"Are you sure? There were a couple of times I didn't get to use any protection." Niranga sounded regretful and defeated.

"Don't worry, I did." We never talked about using protection before. I didn't need to because I have always been on birth control pills to regulate my irregular menstrual cycle and manage my stomach cramps.

"I am sorry, Saku, I should have been responsible." Niranga hugged me. I could hear the remorse in his voice.

"Stop worrying and drive. You will not be stuck with me because of an unwanted pregnancy." When I joked, Niranga pushed back my shoulders with irritation.

"Why do you say that?"

"You should have seen your face. I am surprised you didn't faint." I laughed, even though Niranga didn't appreciate it. Saying nothing, he started the car and eased it onto the road.

"I admit, I was worried." He turned his eyes from the road to start at me for few seconds. "It was not because I thought I was going to be stuck with you and a child."

"Then what made you worry so much."

"I wouldn't know how to face Aunty and Uncle. I can't believe what an idiot I have been. I should have known better." He rattled on more to him than to me.

"Why, only my parents? Wouldn't you be concerned about yours?"

"Let's just say that they are more surprised I have got no girl pregnant yet!" For the first time since I vomited, I saw a smile come on Niranga's face.

"I couldn't think how I would face Aunty and Uncle when they have so much trust in me. I have never been this scared about having a conversation……." Niranga's voice was strained. I could understand his worry, as I would rather die than have to share such news with my parents.

I couldn't stop wondering how Saman Aiya would react to such an account. He was expecting me to have a child out of wedlock. I could imagine the triumphant smile on his face if I ended up carrying one. He would eventually be right in saying I was destined to humiliate our family. Picturing the look on Saman Aiya's face made me grin. When Niranga heard my chuckle, I shared my thoughts. He gave me a blank stare, not seeing the irony.

"Are you sure we don't need to get a test done, Saku?" Niranga reached out and squeezed my hand with a trace of worry in his voice.

"I am positive. I told you already." Maybe I shouldn't have used the word *'positive,'* as Niranga's worry lines didn't leave his forehead. "Tell me, what do you need me to do to make you stop worrying?" Noting he wasn't convinced, I turned to Niranga. "I am happy to go for a check-up. But I know my body, and I have been responsible."

"I am glad that one of us had some brains to act responsibly. I clearly haven't." When I heard Niranga murmuring with frustration, I let him delve into his own thoughts.

"Promise me you will tell me if there are any signs to be concerned about?" Niranga pleaded, still struggling with concern.

"Sure," I said non committedly. Niranga doesn't need to know; he would be the last person I would consult for advice.

"What would you do if something comes up after I leave? I will not be contactable for months while I am travelling. I can check in with you every other day or so, but it will be challenging with both our schedules and time differences." Niranga's hands were holding the steering wheels too tight that his knuckles had turned red. Despite my reassurance, he was in agony.

"If something comes up, I will deal with it. Now, can you stop worrying?"

"What do you mean?" He peeled his eyes off the road to start at my face.

"Niranga, let me be honest. I will not bring a child into this world no matter what, unless I am ready! For any godforsaken reason, if I fall pregnant with or without you around, I will have an abortion. Can you please stop fretting about a thing that will not happen? I will not make you responsible for something neither one of us is ready for." I was frustrated and didn't want this talk about pregnancy to go on any longer.

"You mean you will decide without consulting me?" Niranga's jaw dropped, and his eyebrows went up.

"What is there to consult you about?"

"What do you mean? I will be the father; don't I get a say?" Niranga was behaving as if I had slapped him. If he was not driving the car, he would have shaken me by my shoulders.

"Not really. It is my body; I am the one who has to carry the baby to term, so it is my decision, despite who the father is!"

"Wow… Seriously? You would abort without consulting me?" I watched Niranga's eyebrows arching and how his jaw dropped. I noted the flicker of anger passed through his eyes, which was only there for few seconds.

"That's exactly what I said earlier."

"What about religion? Isn't it a sin?" For the life of me, I didn't expect Niranga to bring morality into the argument. I stared at him for a moment in contempt.

"I don't give a shit about what any religion says about abortion!" I felt the stiffening of Niranga's posture. "I am the one who has to live here and now. I will deal with the afterlife or next life whenever that happens…… Motherhood is a choice, and I will make it when I am ready." My voice was elevated. I was desperately trying not to scream to drive my point home.

Niranga glared at me as if he was crumbling to pieces in front of me. His lips were twitching with anger, and I was sure it wasn't any different from the frustration I was going through.

"I understand this may be difficult for you to comprehend, and I frankly don't get why we are even having this conversation because it is such a waste of time and energy……………. Um…. If you don't mind, I don't want to talk about it anymore. For the last time, I am not pregnant, and I am not planning to be unless I am ready." Now I was the one who was panting. I couldn't fathom the depth of my fury. I fixed my gaze outside the windscreen to compose my aggravated emotions.

"You are such a hypocrite." Niranga broke the long stretch of silence that separated us. "You have more compassion for fish in the water than an unborn baby." When he spattered with contempt, I pretended I didn't hear him. I felt the whole conversation have sucked the life out of me as I felt drained. So, I ignored how Niranga was sneaking glances from the corner of his eye. I could clearly see he was wondering how he missed seeing this side of me before.

Maybe it was because we never discussed these topics or because I guarded my innermost feelings. Our weekend escapes in Niranga's cousin's house pivoted around sex with little to no time to have a deep conversation. Between the bedsheets, Niranga saw only one part of me. Though my ugly side seemed to surprise and appalled him, I no longer cared about his perception of me. If he could expect me to sleep with him with no commitment, I guess he should also be willing to accept me making my own decisions for my convenience.

Perhaps I was hardening my feelings towards Niranga, stacking up reasons for him to leave me, so I could accept his departure amicably.

I changed the radio channel to my favourite one and turned up the volume as I preferred to listen to music than talk. We covered the rest of the journey in our own worlds, ignoring the disdain that sat between us.

I reflected on how easily our mood transformed from euphoria to disdain.

It amazed me how our body changed our chemical disposition from dopamine and serotonin rush to angry hormone adrenalin. It didn't take me much time to go from the woman who ate toasted sandwiches to bring joy to Niranga to a one who stormed out of the car without even saying goodbye when Niranga brought the vehicle to a halt at my annexe.

26 PERPLEX

I woke up gasping for air as if I was drowning. I inhaled greedily, filling my lungs with the stale air in the room and tasted the saltiness of my tears. My cheeks were wet; I had been crying in my dream.

The bedside clock showed it was just after five in the morning. Niranga was peacefully sleeping. I am glad that my sudden rise from the bed didn't disturb his sleep. I was in a state of distress. This dream had become a recurring event over the last few days; I was trapped in a maze, searching for someone.

Knowing I wouldn't be able to go back to sleep, I tiptoed into the bathroom, not wanting to disturb Niranga. I washed and dressed quickly and quietly left the house, seeking fresh air.

I had no preconceived idea where I wanted to go; I felt claustrophobic and just needed to get out. I didn't wish to take the car because I feared the start of the engine could awaken Niranga; I didn't want to face him, not yet.

Until last night, our last trip to Kandy was the most disastrous four hours we had. Though we began the journey like a page out of an old Mills and Bloom novel, romantic and sensual, that atmosphere didn't last long. By the time he dropped me off at my annexe, if Niranga had told me he ended our liaison, I would not have been surprised, and secretly I would have welcomed it. It was a miracle we wished to see each other again yesterday. Now I feel the emotions we went through that day were insignificant compared to last night.

Yesterday evening was the ugliest night we had since we got together. It could be because we both were on edge, dealing with what transpired unexpectedly between us. Cracks formed in the happy dome we had built for ourselves.

My mind was already on the verge of despair. I dealt with the unexpected, heavy emotions that have invaded my heart since our trip down from the citadel. Our relationship seemed to head on a path I was not ready to travel. I actively avoided the unwanted sensations bubbling inside me, pretending that they would eventually disappear if I did not confront them.

When Niranga arrived unusually late, I was hungry, tensed and irritated. I was like an overblown balloon, only needing one prick to blow into pieces.

He was very apologetic, explaining he had to finish up some work at the factory before heading to pick me up. The rush hour traffic in every town centre had compounded the delay. I can't recall how that ugly conversation began as we headed to Niranga's cousin's place. Yet I could remember the point when it leapt into a landslide.

"Why would you share such a private thing with Janaka?" I got annoyed when Niranga recounter his chat had with Janaka. Niranga eyed me, confused, not understanding why I was irritated.

"What is wrong with sharing how scared I got thinking you were pregnant? You share everything with Reshani!"

"Yes, I do. But she will never make them into dinner conversations when there is a stranger amongst us." Niranga didn't appreciate my snide remark. I still remember how Niranga's friends laughed, sharing stories about his array of girlfriends at the anniversary dinner.

"What do you mean?" I sense the anger trapped in his tone.

"I don't wish to be another funny story about your encounter with a woman. I may be your latest fling while you are holidaying in Sri Lanka, yet I don't want to be discussed by your friends over drinks!"

"What are you saying, Sakunthala?" It was the first time I heard him addressing me by my full name. It sounded so strange that I gawked at him with my mouth open. *'What is it with everyone wanting to call me Sakunthala when they are annoyed with me?'* Inner child sneered.

It was a short drive from my annexe to Niranga's place. We were already there, and he sharply pressed the breaks bringing the car to a hold. I jolted forward and nearly hit my head as if it was not for the seatbelt I was wearing. Usually, Niranga would have been concerned and checked if I had hurt myself. Without even a glance, he turned off the engine and undid the seatbelt.

"I can list all the women you had been with in the last three years and how you broke off with them." I challenged him silently, wanting him to make me say their names. Niranga didn't even try to respond to my qualm.

"I would appreciate it if you didn't share my details with your friends! I don't want a random stranger in Sydney knowing how I slept with you and how scared you got because you thought I got pregnant!"

"You have taken things out of context." Niranga eyed me with a sneer. "They are my closest friends. None of what they shared would have been news to any. The only reason you got invited to sit with them was that I asked them to keep an eye on you. I know how much you hate small talks with strangers. My friends already knew how I felt about you. If you were a random girl, they wouldn't have had you sitting with them. They trusted you because they know I trust you. Don't you ever question their loyalty!" I have never heard him talking with such venom in his voice.

"Right, got it. I will never question your friend's loyalty. I still would appreciate it if you could keep my personal details from them."

I was angry because Niranga thought it was alright for his friends to air his dirty laundry in public without considering the privacy of the women he had been with. None of my friends would be that disrespectful. *'What does he mean his friends knew how he felt about me?' We were not even sleeping with each other, then. Does it mean they will welcome any girl Niranga was interested in with open arms and share his life story?'* My mind was like a blender, random thoughts spinning around.

"Sure thing, your highness, duly noted." Niranga gave me a quizzical stare and got out of the car. He grabbed the duffle bag he always brought with him for the weekend and walked towards the house. I remained in the car, in shock. I couldn't understand how things got this ugly so quickly. I haven't seen this side of Niranga before. Just like that, the lovable man I was so used to had disappeared.

I sat there, trying to calm myself, not wanting to go inside. I didn't trust myself to be near Niranga because, at that moment, I hated him.

When I didn't follow him inside, Niranga came searching for me and shouted from the veranda.

"Aren't you coming in?"

I got out of the car and grabbed my bag from the back seat, planning to head back to my annexe. It didn't matter anymore; I was ready to leave the warmth I was pinning for all day. Without responding to Niranga, I slammed the car door and trampled down the driveway towards Lake Kandy.

"What the fuck are you doing, Sakunthala? Come inside. It is late." Niranga came running and grabbed my hand.

"Let go of me Niranga, I am heading home." I didn't want to go inside, fearing the enormous ball of anger inside me turning into a volcano, burning us beyond recognition. I attempted to shrug off his hand, but he tightened his grip.

"Oh, for heaven's sake, when are you going to grow up? Stop running away every time we have a disagreement." Niranga let go of my hand, grabbing my shoulder to turn me towards him. He was angry, his grip was tight, and it hurt me.

"Let go! You are hurting me." Niranga dropped his hands and stepped back. I watch the anger in his eyes turned to desperation.

"I am tired and hungry. I will not chase after you. If you really want to leave, do it in the morning." I stood there, not saying anything. I shifted my weight from one foot to the other, contemplating my next move.

I swayed between needing to hug him and lash out. One second, I wanted to put my arms around him and embrace him because my heart ached, wishing to be near him, wanting to take away the pain in his eyes and tiredness in his voice. And the next second, I wanted to scratch him till his cheeks bled with the resentment I felt.

"It is almost ten o'clock. It is not safe for you to walk on your own. If you really can't stay here tonight, take the damn car."

Niranga combed his hair with his fingers and offered me the car keys. He was right. It was not safe to walk on my own at that hour, and especially around the lake. I knew there were no buses, and I would not get into a trishaw on my own this late at night. Nor did I want to get behind the car. Given that there was no other option than to stay, I walked past Niranga to the room we shared.

Not bothering to switch on the light, I dumped my bag in a corner and collapsed on the bed. I shut my eyes, wanting to fall asleep, hoping when I open my eyes tomorrow, this would no longer be the worst evenings of my life.

Never in my wildest dreams did I expect us to argue over something so trivial. I replayed the conversation, trying to find the exact moment I made Niranga angry. *'Did I have any right to criticise his friends? Was Niranga right to defend his friends?'* I heard a doubtful voice questioning me.

I was dealing with layers of emotions. I lay on the bed, peeling off my anger one by one, trying to identify the cause behind the temper. On the surface, it was Niranga's friends' carefree outlook towards his array of sexual encounters. Below that was the expectation I had of Niranga to treat me differently from his other women. Underneath all that, it was the fear of being judged for being a non-conventional woman of my time.

I can't recall how long I had laid there or if I had fallen asleep. I came out of my daze when I felt the mattress on the bed giving into Niranga's body weight. He had finally come to bed. Earlier, he poked his head in to ask me to have dinner. I pretended I was asleep and didn't respond. After lurking beside the door for a couple of seconds, I felt his frustration in his heavy footstep when he left.

I knew I had to make amends; I no longer cared who was at fault. I didn't want to go to sleep with anger bottled up. I slowly turned to face Niranga and stretched my arm to say, I am sorry when Niranga did the same. Our fingers collide, and we intertwine them with force.

The room was dark, and we couldn't see the emotions on our faces. We mangled into each other's arms and kissed hungrily. It didn't take us long to get lost in our desire to be with one another. It could be because we knew our time together had already ended, or perhaps because it was the best way to show each the depth of our feelings. But whatever it was, what I felt last night was different. It was deep; it was sensual, and it was fervent.

The urgency we had when our hands touched turned into slow, passionate lovemaking. It felt as though we both had a secret desire to prolong the ecstasy. We were holding on to our climax, fearing the ending. Our union was exciting as it was the first time still heavy with the anticipated loss. Later, Niranga was clutching me tight closer to his chest when he whispered.

"I am so sorry, babe. I will never speak to you like that again. Please forgive me." I pretended I was asleep, as I didn't want to talk about what happened earlier. We both were at fault, letting our emotions run high.

"You are not a holiday fling I am having. You are much more than that to me!" He murmured as if he was reminding himself and kissed my forehead. When he didn't get a response from me, he assumed I was asleep. I felt the wetness of my tears sliding across my cheeks. I slowly turned away from Niranga, burying my face in the pillow to muffle my weeping.

★★★

I have walked to the Maligawa in autopilot mode and have joined the early morning worshipers lining up at the main entrance. It did not surprise me I was here. I always come to Maligawa when I want to calm myself, sit back and process things. If anything was out of the ordinary, it was coming here so early as I am not a morning person.

After worshipping the Buddha's Tooth Relic, I sat down near the entrance to Paththirippuwa, watching the worshipers. Maligawa is one of those unique places where all types and shapes of people come and go. From old to the young, worshipers bring their happiness, sorrow, dreams and hopes, taking refuge in the relic. Though I am not a person believing in any external power with the ability to mend my journey, I believe in the temple's power to calm myself and get me to reflect on my thoughts.

I let my mind wander about the nightmare I had earlier. Though I had the same one for a couple of nights, other days when I woke up, I couldn't recall all the details. Today I can.

I was dressed in a hideous white dress, in a style that I would dare not wear with a veil over my face. I was running around a maze asking everyone if they had seen *'me.'* It turned out; the random people I was talking to were no strangers, but Reshani, Jeevani, and Sula. The last one I spoke to was Niranga. He was dashing in his suit as he was at the anniversary dinner (strangely, he was wearing the same). Niranga had a beautiful red rose tucked into his suit jacket. He was happy, and his eyes lit up when he saw me.

Niranga lifted my veil and cheerfully declared, 'There you are' and kissed my lips while others around us clapped. When I didn't believe him, he got a hand mirror from behind his back and held it in front of me. When I peered into the mirror, all I could see was a faceless white shape glaring at me that was not me. That was when I woke up scared.

I was not sure what the dream meant. I wish Reshani or Sula were beside me, although I could already guess what Sula would say; the same thing he told me on Thursday during our weekly dinner catch up.

"You are your worst enemy."

I was still pondering the question when I walked back to Niranga's place. We had to talk. There was no way I could avoid the conversation we needed to have. I have to tell him. Things were getting too complicated for me, and I wanted my vanilla life back. I stopped over at Bakehouse to buy some short eats Niranga loved to eat as my peace offering for him.

Soon as I got to the top of the road, my heart sank. Niranga's car was not there. *'Did he leave without telling me goodbye? No, he was not bitter when we fell asleep last night. Maybe he has left to get some food.'* My mind was lacing tales.

The front door was open as if Niranga had left in a hurry. *'Maybe he has gone after me?'* When I left in the morning, I didn't leave him a note, leaving quietly and quickly. He must have thought I had left because I was still furious over last night.

My heart was pounding fast with anxiety. I was on the verge of tears when I heard a car coming up the driveway. I tuned in hope and anticipation. When Niranga brought the vehicle to a sudden stop, I ran to him, wanting to be in his arms, surround myself with his warmth. He leapt out of the car and hugged me so tight.

"Ran, I can't breathe." I wiggled, turning my face away from his chest and laid it on his shoulder, kissing his neck with my arms around him, clasping him. I could feel he was shaking and unstable. His heart was beating so fast, and he was breathing so heavily as if he had run a marathon.

I laid my palm on his heart, gazing into eyes filled with tears. Sighting his devastation made me want to cry. Before I could say anything, he leaned forward and laid his forehead on mine and whispered. "I thought you had left me." He was breathless; his voice fluttered as if I had sucked the life out of him, and he had lost everything. Recognising the impact, I had on him made my legs go weaker. I put my arms around him and tightened my grip on him.

"I am here," I murmured, my voice shaking with pain.

"You scared me Saku, you never get up so early. We fought last night." Niranga was still struggling with his breathing, as if he had a panic attack. I took his hand and guided him to the bench, and pushed him to sit down. Standing there, I cradled his head on my stomach and stroked his back, allowing his breathlessness to subside.

"I am sorry, I didn't think," I admitted. When I left in the morning, my focus was on my pain and anxiety. I wondered if I had ever thought about Niranga in the last few months or in any decisions I have made. I didn't stop to think if he was tired of driving back and forth on weekends or how it was for Niranga to be stuck in the house with me, isolating him from the rest of the world. I have never stopped to ask.

"I am sorry, Ran!"

"I am sorry about last night and this morning. I couldn't sleep, so I went to Maligawa to clear my head." I cupped his face, peered into his eyes. They were filled with the hurt I hadn't witnessed before. It devastated me. Not being able to bear his pain, I knelt in front of him and hugged him tightly.

We stayed there for a long time, without speaking, just listening to our breathing. When Niranga's heartbeat became regular, his grip on me changed from tight to a soft, comforting one.

He told me he had gone to my annexe, and realising I was not there, had returned without knowing what he would do next. He said he had never felt that lost before. I could not relate to that status of mind. I have been fighting my whole life to avoid such a predicament, giving the power of my happiness to another human being.

I didn't want to address those feelings. I have been avoiding it all my life.

"I brought your favourite short eats. Let's have breakfast." I rose from where I was kneeling, pulling Niranga to his feet. He stood up; put his arm around my shoulder, drawing me closer to him.

"Don't you dare do that to me again!" He warned me, I said nothing.

27 SURPRISE

"Hey, sleeping beauty, stop leaving marks on me like this." I woke up to the sound of Niranga's voice. He was standing beside the bed with a silly grin on his face, still looking sensational. Niranga had just come out of the shower with traces of water dripping from his torso and hair. He was pointing to a hickey I had left on his chest after our night together.

He smelled of fresh shampoo and soap mixed with his aftershave. He saw me admiring him and smiled seductively.

"Um... I was marking my territory." I murmured, pulling him by the towel he was wearing. He effortlessly fell on top of me, claiming my lips with a warm kiss.

"Hmm.... You smell so good." I tugged him closer, filling my lungs with his scent.

"There is a better way to mark your territory." Niranga leaned back on one elbow, running his hand under the t-shirt I had on. Since the first night, I have formed a habit of wearing his t-shirts to sleep. I love falling asleep, breathing in the traces of his smell that lingered on them.

"There is? Do share? I am all ears." I stretched my arm to run my figures across his wet hair. I can't believe the woman I have become.

I was waking up to warm memories of passionate lovemaking leading to another ardent embrace in the morning. I have become provocative, pulling this gorgeous man into the abyss of my lust. I have never been this happy. Beginning the day with Niranga, having him next to me, being able to touch him, feel his lips on mine, to be admired by eyes full of desire was something I didn't expect when I shared that fateful car journey with him.

'What about when you have your fights?' I pushed away the sarcastic voice in my head, reminding me of the few unpleasant moments I had. The promises I made, swearing I was not ready to take on the increasing weight of this relationship anymore. When I returned from Maligawa, I planned to talk to Niranga, tell him that his intensity scares me, and suggest we slow things

down. Yet each time I wanted to bring up the subject, I got distracted. I procrastinated, delaying it to the next hour, the next day and now to the following week.

The predicament I was in surprised me, as I was waiting for Niranga to leave. Never in a million years did I expect I would be the one to say I wanted to breathe freely; Niranga's affection was suffocating me.

Perhaps Niranga was right. I have a habit of running away when things get challenging. Maybe because I always said I don't want the issues to be more complicated than they already were. My life was hard enough. I didn't have the energy to deal with another layer of complexity.

Niranga wanted to break all rules; he wanted to tell our parents about us; he wanted to share us with the broader world; now he is talking about a future I haven't thought about. I wasn't ready to change the rules. I was comfortable with what we had. It gave me a framework, showed me where the boundaries were.

"Marry me and make me yours!" Niranga said with the same lazy smile he had earlier. His eyes were full of laughter.

"Didn't I tell you before? Archaeologists are only interested in dating." I smiled. I have never told Niranga that deep in my heart, I am an aspiring archaeologist biding my time until I discover the long-lost city, Alakamanda.

"If you say yes, you can keep excavating me." He was adorable, making an archaeological joke.

"There are other trophies I need to conquer before you!" I pushed him on his back and laughed. I didn't give him a chance to respond before claiming his lips with the urgency I felt.

★★★

"Tell me again, why can't we come out to our parents?" Niranga shifted his gaze off the road and probed.

"If you tell them now, we wouldn't be able to spend the next weekend here unless that's what you want."

"Why wouldn't we be able to be together?"

"Are you kidding me?" I turned to Niranga in disbelief. *'How can he be so naïve?'* The wise one questioned.

"In what universe would Sri Lankan parents tell their kids it is ok to sleep around when they are not married?" Niranga's endless questioning annoyed me.

"That is why I proposed!"

"What are you talking about?"

"I was not joking when I asked you to marry me." Niranga glared at me, disappointed, if not angry.

Earlier today, when Niranga proposed, I assumed he was joking. I guess I was in denial, as no man would make a joke out of a proposal. In my defence, it was not as if he declared his undying love, and he wanted to spend the rest of his life with me. I guess that explains the foul mood I found Niranga in since we started the short drive to my annexe.

I reined back my memories to the present, glancing at Niranga, who had his eyes fixed on me.

"I am sorry, babe; I thought we were fooling around." I should have recognised Niranga isn't the kind to joke on something significant. I have never told him I don't believe in marriage; it was for those scared of feeling lonely at old age or looking for social approval to be intimate.

"If I didn't make it clear in the morning, I am serious about marrying you." Niranga sounded irritated, as if he was running out of patience with me.

"Oh.... Um.... I need time to think. " Not having had any time to process this recent development, I stuttered.

"What is there to think? I thought you would want us to be together. Don't you want to be with me? Is that it?" Niranga asked, astonished.

"No, that is not what it is."

"Well, you have a bizarre way of showing it." Niranga's cheeks have turned light pink with anger that he was trying so hard to control. I glanced away with discomfort.

"Whatever your problem is, Saku, you need to figure it out soon. I plan to tell my parents, and I want to talk to your parents before I leave. We have to register our marriage so I can apply for your visa and work on a date for the wedding." Niranga stopped the car in front of my annexe, dictating a task list as if he was working on one of his new projects.

"How can you spring this on me now?" I felt perplexed. I was fighting the claustrophobic weight that was pressing down on me ever since Niranga started talking about wishing to tell our parents. He just made it worse by choosing to spend eternity with me.

"I am only giving you the highlights. We can fill in the details later."

"I am not one of your project managers Niranga for you to give me highlights to work on." I slammed the car door on my way out. My bewilderment quickly turned into a wave of irritation. Clearly, we are on two different routes.

I fumbled with my door key and opened and shut the door with a bang. Tears were rolling down my cheeks because I couldn't control my rage, although I couldn't tell why I was so irritated. Was my anger because Niranga proved I was wrong about him? I didn't expect him to be interested in me after the following weekend, let alone ask me to marry him. Or was I angry because I thought I had everything planned and Niranga had hijacked my best-laid plan?

"Babe, what on earth is wrong with you? We are not even married yet, and you are behaving like an old married woman. Slamming doors and walking out without even a kiss." Niranga had followed me and teased, sounding jovial, with no trace of the anger I saw in him earlier.

"Oh my god, what's wrong, babe?"

When he saw my tears, he dashed across the room, pulling me into a hug. He has assumed I was crying because I was hurt. I stretched my arms and hit his rock-hard chest; I didn't want to feel his warmth and become bewildered. I wanted to dwell on this anger and forget about the little excitement I felt brewing inside me.

I did not want to become distracted by a marriage proposal. Although it came out with no bells, whistles, or warning signs, it still was solid evidence of Niranga's commitment. But, I was not in a mood to rejoice or to celebrate: I had broken the *'Casanova.'* I was not ready to ignore everything else that was wrong because he assumed I would marry him.

Niranga ignored my rigidity, took hold of my hands to draw them around his waist. He pulled me closer to him, not leaving a gap, filling my nostrils with his perfume he knows that intoxicates me. Niranga is fully aware of how his touch melts me, letting my bony self, slide in between his arms. He was purposely weakening me.

We were miles apart, no longer a part of the jigsaw puzzle that seamlessly fit in. I sensed Niranga was feeling the coldness in me. He tightened his grip and stroked my back gently.

While I was fuming with anger, I still appreciated his ability to be calm and focus his attention on my emotional state. I am not sure how long we had been standing in silence when he guided me to the small sofa and got me to sit next to him.

"Is it because I didn't make a grand gesture? If that is what you want, I will propose to you again. I will get you a ring and kneel." Niranga whispered in my ear, brushing his lips ever so lightly on the sensitive part of my earlobes, bringing back memories of countless intimate moments we shared that began from the night at the anniversary dinner.

I heard a trace of laughter in his voice. I was not sure if he was hoping to lighten the mood or provoke a response. I sat there struggling to keep my attention on my breathing, trying to calm myself, suppressing my anger.

"Can we talk now?" After a long silence, Niranga lifted my face and peered into my eyes. He pulled out his handkerchief and wiped my tears. His action reminded me of how he cared for me when I burnt my hand with hot water. He had a similar worry in his eyes. I kept quiet; eyes focused on my hands in a tight knot on my lap.

"Can you tell me what is the matter, babe?" He grabbed hold of my hands and got them to open up from its tight fist. He started caressing my fingers softly, trying to stimulate a physical reaction from me.

"I am the first to admit, I am not the easiest person to live with. But I never assumed a mere thought of marrying me would send a woman into a hissy fit." If Niranga assumed the humour was the best way, he was wrong. All he did was get me more aggravated.

"Is this a joke to you, Niranga? Have you thought this through? This is not like when you date a girl back in Australia. Once we tell our families, there is going to be eight of us in this relationship." Niranga looked lost. As he said nothing, I continued.

"If this thing doesn't work out between us, we are not the only two going to get hurt. It will hurt the other six as well." Our families are too interconnected. It will not be just the two of us getting married. *'How come he doesn't see this?'* The adult was concerned.

"I know all that." Finally, when Niranga spoke, he sounded annoyed.

"So, then why are you rushing this?"

"Have you forgotten I am leaving in a week?"

"So, that is your solution? Because you are leaving, let's just rush in and close this off so you can tick off your *'to-do list'* while you are in Sri Lanka?" When I air quoted *'to-do-list,'* Niranga glance away with unease.

"Uncle's office set up - ticked."

"Found a woman to get married - ticked."

"Wedding date fixed - ticked." I simulated Niranga ticking off an imaginary checklist, going one by one, ensuring he had covered all his tasks.

"You have got it wrong, Saku." Niranga sounded let down. He combed his hair with his fingers.

"Have I? So, tell me, where are we going to live once we get married? Are you going to move here?"

"You know I can't do that." Niranga gave me a *'Don't be stupid'* stare.

"So, how do you propose we consummate our marriage if we get married?"

"You would come to Sydney, of course." He still had that *Don't be stupid* gaze, aggravating my anger.

"So, no regards to my life here?" I was so disappointed I got up from where I was sitting to build a distance between us. Niranga grabbed his head with both his hands, staring at his feet. Not only did he appear frustrated, but also a bit ashamed.

"Okay, I admit I didn't plan every step. We can work on those details later; however, wouldn't it be the most logical thing to do?" Niranga gave me a lopsided grin. Even amid my fury, I couldn't disregard how adorable he was.

"Really? So, you expect me to drop everything in my life and follow you? I didn't take you to be an arrogant prick, Niranga."

Niranga blinked, not expecting me to call him that. Neither did I, still that was precisely how I felt towards him.

"My god, Aunty was right. You have a foul mouth." When Niranga said this in a disapproving tone, the irony hit me. We were two people who were deeply attached to each other having this insane argument over a marriage. A belly full of laughter replaced my anger and animosity. I bent over and laughed until tears streamed down my cheeks. Niranga got on to his feet, staring at me, confused, wondering if I had gone crazy.

"What is so funny?" He inquired with irritation.

"You were right. Look at us, bickering like an old married couple." I stretched my neck, laughing. Niranga took a sharp breath and crossed over, pulling me into his arms.

"Don't do that," Niranga whispered in a slightly hoarse voice and kissed me.

"What are you doing?" After returning his kiss, I pushed him away.

"Making out!" Niranga laughed, and my heart rose, creating butterflies in my stomach.

"In the middle of an argument?"

"You changed the mood when you stretched your neck. You know that turns me on. So, we have to pause the fight now." He grinned, unbuttoning his shirt.

"Ran, what on earth are you doing?" I tried to suppress the laughter building inside me and pretended I was still angry with him.

"Removing my shirt." He swiftly removed it and draped it on the arm of the sofa, and started unbuckling his trouser belt.

"Why?" I put on a facade as I was oblivious to his plan when my entire body was tingling with excitement.

"I am running out of excuses to tell Meera why my shirts are missing their buttons. I can't tell her I am dating a very impatient woman, can I?" He gave me a mocking smile, making me glance away from his torso, feeling embarrassed.

"You are exaggerating. It was just one time." Once I was so impatient and tore one of his shirt buttons while unbuttoning it. "If you go by those standards, then how many of my tops have you damaged?" I reminded him which one of us was the more earnest of the two.

"Well, I have been replacing them two for one." Niranga gave me a cheeky smile.

"Oh, was that what you were doing? I thought it was because my fashion sense embarrassed you." I glared at Niranga, challenging. His love for finer things hadn't gone unnoticed. I have been ignoring how he preferred me to wear beautiful things I couldn't afford. He had been spoiling me with his weekly gifts that I have accepted, pretending I am blind to his intentions.

"Oh, I wouldn't argue about your fashion sense, but you will never embarrass me, babe." Niranga pulled me into his arms and kissed the base of my neck. I arched my back to look at him.

"You can't be seriously thinking of having sex now?" I was still stubborn and was denying the inevitable.

"Makeup sex is the best thing about arguments. Why do you think married people argue so much?" Niranga wasn't ready to give up, as he could read my body language. He was already working through my shirt buttons. It was hard to concentrate and fight the excitement of having his lips and fingers making random impressions on my skin.

"Sex isn't the answer to everything, Niranga," I said.

"It sure isn't the problem. Let us work on the elimination theory." Niranga gave me a nerdy look.

"What theory?"

"When there are a lot of variables determining in an outcome, you can work on systematically eliminating variables to identify the root cause." He was grinning, being in his element. I nodded my head, curious to find out where he was going with his theorem.

"Okay, let us start with the obvious; Sex, there is no disagreement on that part, is there?"

Niranga's eyes were beaming. He had me held in a way I had my upper body arched back, similar to a bow. My fingers were gripping his shoulders to keep my balance. Knowing he had the power to save me from falling backwards, Niranga smiled temptingly. We both knew he had won the battle; I gave that to him. What he didn't realise was that the war hadn't begun.

"Good, we agree." He nodded happily.

"Now, families, both our families are heavily invested in us. This conversation wouldn't happen if they were not, so it is another tick." I raised my eyebrows, not agreeing with his comment.

"What? You don't believe?"

"I still can't understand why your family would settle for me?"

"Oh my god, are you seriously looking for compliments?" Niranga asked in disbelief.

"Maybe… You guys are loaded, and you are good-looking. So why settle for a plain lower-middle-class Jane?"

Niranga immediately sensed my insecurity. He pulled me back and hugged me tight, closer to his chest. The electrifying sexual tension I felt earlier in Niranga's arms transferred into a protective comfort. Just like that, Niranga could gather me in his arms and make me feel cherished and protected.

"Babe, beauty lies in the eyes of the beholder. I will not say you are the most beautiful person on earth because that would be a lie." I kicked his leg. He sure had a funny way of reassuring a girl in one of her weakest moments. He grinned and planted a kiss on my lips.

"Your definition of beauty and mine are different. For me, you are my everything. You already know I am obsessed with you, don't you? You make me whole." Niranga gave me an earnest look. I put my arms around his neck and kissed him standing on my toes. He made me feel beautiful and cherished, which was so foreign to me.

"Amma and Thaththa already consider you to be my saviour."

"How come?" I interrupted Niranga with curiosity. Realising I was in the dark, he sat on the sofa, pulling me to sit next to him.

"You saved me from being a lonely, insecure, overweight boy." He sounded as if he was far off. For a moment, I lost him to his flashbacks. Though his eyes were fixed on me, his mind was elsewhere. I was bewildered, not understanding why he referred to himself like that, because I had never perceived him in that manner. In my memories, Niranga was a reliable, caring and confident boy that I always admired.

"Before I met you, I was always alone. I didn't have the confidence to make friends in school. That's why I was still playing on my own. The funny thing is I didn't realise any of that until a few years back. I only remembered my childhood in two phases, before meeting you and after meeting you. I can't remember anything significant before meeting you. Becoming your friend changed me, brought me out of my shell. Gave me the courage I lacked. That's why Amma and Thaththa say you are my saviour. They are ever so grateful for your presence in my life. When you marry me, I am pretty sure if Amma could, she is going to turn you into a saint." Niranga gave me a confident nod, reassuring me about the love and acceptance of his parents.

"But Ran, you are the one who actually rescued me. I wouldn't have survived moving to Nuwara Eliya if it was not for you." I have never thanked Niranga for being my hero.

"Is this how you thank me? By not accepting my proposal?" Niranga voiced his disappointment.

"I can't marry you, not now."

"Is it because of your stupid promise to Sulakkana?" A burst of anger oozed out of Niranga. His cheeks were flushed, and I could see the elevated heartbeat through the rise and fall of pulses on the side of his temples.

Weeks ago, I told Niranga how I promised Sulakkana some time back that I would marry him to offer him the cover he required to face our backward society. I was ready to act on it, knowing that Sula and I would always remain best friends and support each other's dreams. Part of the reason was that it would give both of us the freedom we desired to be who we are with no obligations. It was a perfect plan until Niranga walked into my life, and Nilush started demanding to migrate to a country where same-sex relationships were accepted.

"If that is holding you back, I will help Sulakkana get permanent residency in Australia. I can recommend a couple of good migrant lawyers that can work something out." When I didn't respond, Niranga reached out to grab my hand. He squeezed it tightly to convey his sincerity. *'Does he think migrating to Australia resolves everything?'* I shook my head to turn away from my inner voice.

"No, it is not because of that silly promise."

"Then what?"

"It is too soon," I uttered softly.

"What is too soon?" Niranga sounded confused.

"You are moving too fast, Niranga. I can't keep up." I spoke with frustration. Why couldn't he understand I need time to process and allow us to grow some roots.

"What are you saying? You don't want to get married?"

"I am not ready. I don't believe we are ready to get married." I told him the truth.

"What? How come you are not ready to get married?" Niranga sounded hurt. He stared at me in disbelief. His face looked as though someone had punched him and was out of breath.

"Marriage is a serious thing, Niranga. It is a lifetime commitment. It is not a joke."

"Who said it was a joke? Why do you think it took me all this time? If not, I would have proposed to you on our first night." Niranga gave me his signature smile that reached his eyes and made his face brighten up. I didn't smile, and he saw I didn't consider it to be true.

"I am serious Saku, why don't you want to marry me?"

"It is not you, Niranga. It is me. I am not ready for a commitment. I need time." I finally said it. The thing that I didn't want to admit to myself, I told Niranga. I watched his pain turning into anger. His face got darker, and he was huffing.

"Did Janaka put you up to this? Did he ask you to say those things?" Niranga got hold of my shoulders in a tight grip. His fingers digging into my shoulder were hurting me.

"What does Janaka have to do with this? Why would I even talk to him about marriage?"

"If you are joking, it is not funny." Niranga got up from the sofa and paced back and forth like a caged animal in frustration. After a long silence, Niranga laughed. It was a painful, beaten-up laugh, a self-mocking laugh.

"I guess this is payback for all the girls I have turned down!" He sounded defeated and hurt. I saw there were traces of tears in the depth of his eyes. My heart ached for him. The last thing I wanted to do was hurt him.

"Help me understand, Saku. What do you mean you are not ready for an engagement? You wouldn't have slept with me if you didn't love me and you didn't plan on marrying me?"

"I was not joking the other day. I expected nothing more than a holiday romance."

"You are kidding me, aren't you? Girls over here don't sleep around without expecting a commitment." I sensed Niranga regretted the moment he said that as his face darkened with embarrassment. But it wasn't anywhere near the dismay I felt.

"I thought you were better than that, Niranga. I didn't expect you to stereotype me."

"I am sorry, babe. I didn't mean it that way. We had so much history and love between us. After fighting for years, when we finally got together, I assumed you loved me and wanted me the same way I did. Don't you love me, Saku, is that it?" I heard the anguish in his voice. I felt defeated and hopeless, as I couldn't come up with a way to give him what he wanted without being honest with me.

"I am not sure Niranga. I wish I could tell you what I feel for you is love, not lust." I wiped away silent tears streaming down my cheeks. The pain in my heart was all-consuming. I wanted it to stop and go back to those intoxicating flirtatious moments we had.

"Why are you rushing this? We hardly know each other. Let's give us some time before we rush in." I pleaded in desperation.

Niranga stopped pacing to study me.

"Because I don't want to wait anymore. I know what I want. I want you! I want to get married and start a family with you."

There lay the problem! He had a coherent plan, clear comprehension of his needs. Yet, I didn't know what I wanted, other than marriage or a raising family were not my priorities at present.

Niranga came and knelt in front of me, taking my hands in his. He gave me his best smile. Even with despair and frustration, I felt a warm rush running through me. His smile was tugging the deep corners of my heart, filling it with warmth.

"What do you say, my love? Will you marry me?" Niranga held my face in both of his hands and kissed my lips passionately before he proposed again, hope shimmering in his eyes.

I felt heavy, as if I was wrapped in thick iron chains and got dumped into a river. The weight of Niranga's expectations was drowning me.

"Please….. I need a bit more time." I kissed him to avoid watching his eyes filling with anguish.

28 DISSOLUTION

"You sure are your worst enemy!" Sula spattered from across the room with a condescending look, as if he had everything figured out. It was not the first time he said this to me, as he blurted the same last week to which I paid little attention. Typically, I would have responded with some sarcasm, reminding him to stop psychoanalysing me and focus on his issues. I was not in a mood to pick a fight, so I let it passed.

"What do you mean?" Reshani was curious to unpack the comment. We were gathered in her house for our usual Thursday night dinner catch up. Keeping true to our weekly ritual, we have selected our personal drama as the after-meal entertainment. Today, there was nothing more interesting than my reluctance to accept Niranga's proposal.

"There is a girl, a boy and a villain in all love stories." Sula phased across the small room as if he were in a stage drama, lifting his shoulders and head and commanding attention like a narrator.

"Prince Saliya and Asokamala, the Gypsy woman, had Queen Vihara Maha Devi as their villain. King Kashyapa and Mahamatta, a lady from the Yakka clan, had Queen Wesamuni, Kashyapa's queen-wife, as their villain. Niranga and Saku do not have a villain in their story, so she had become her villain." He stopped phasing to stare at me, forcing me to glance away in unease. I saw Reshani and Ravidu nodding absently. That critical person in my head smirked, knowing neither of them would have a clue about the historical figures Sula mentioned, although they seemed to agree.

"What do you mean, I am my villain?"

"Are you that dumb?" Sula stared me down, making me feel insecure.

"You are finding reasons not to be with Niranga instead of identifying reasons to be with him." Sula's voice was laced with displeasure. "I can't figure out what your struggle is all about, Saku? You have been pinning for him since day one. He wants to marry you and start a family with you. What the fuck is wrong with you not wanting to accept it!" Sula sounded frustrated and annoyed. *'Why is he disheartened?'* I wanted to know.

"How come you are on his side?" I inquired with irritation.

"Because I feel sorry for the man. He had been obsessed with you, jumping through all the hoops you had for him! When he is doing the right thing, you are messing with his emotions. You are being a *praying mantis* !" I couldn't stop wondering if Sula was talking about Niranga and me, or Nilush and him.

"I think you are so happy for the first time in your life that it scares you to shit. So, you are trying to purposely sabotage your own bliss." I stared at Sula, bewailed. *'How did he figure it out?'*

I had never been this happy before Niranga came into my world. There were so many moments I had to pinch myself to confirm if I was not trapped in a dream. When I was with him, everything else became immaterial. He made me complete.

The emotions I felt scared me. Those utopian sensations were keeping me up at night. Sometimes I would wake up to watch Niranga, who was in a deep sleep, listening to the soft fall of his breath, wondering how I got this lucky to be lying next to such a gorgeous man.

I cherish how he possessively put his arm around me and pulled me to him in his sleep. I love the way his eyes light up when he catches me smile and the way he grins like a child when he is after a favour. Still, I haven't learned to accept the way my heart crumbles with the fear of losing him.

Those emotions were choking me. The happiness and fear I felt around Niranga were two sides of the same coin. The hedonistic lifestyle I gained when Niranga stormed into my life made me grapple with a visceral fear of losing them. I have become a slave, heedless, consumed by the desire to be with Niranga. I couldn't breathe anymore without obscene thoughts of him occupying my consciousness. I hated myself for being obsessed and vulnerable, and Niranga for how his poignant power made me annihilate my *'vanilla'* self. For the first time in my adult life, I have become dependent on someone for my happiness, and I despised it.

I loathed how quickly I forgot about our fights and disagreements that made me feel belittled. My willingness to let all misgivings get washed away by the overpowering sexual desire repented me.

While I couldn't imagine a life without Niranga, I cursed the day he walked into mine. I wanted to be that independent woman again. He brought so much that I did not realise I was missing or needed. He shattered my equilibrium in a way I was not equipped to glue it back.

I was lost, not knowing how to recant my life before Niranga. He brought a rainbow of colours to the black and white world I merely existed. I float across the golden glow that wrapped around me after our passionate lovemaking, the warm fuzzy redness that enfolds me with his warm hugs, and the calming blue that floated around with his sexy Australian Sri Lankan mixed husky voice. I had fallen for the rainbow, not making any plans on how to live when it vanishes.

"It is all too soon… we haven't even been together for six months." When I muttered, the three of them stared at me.

"What is holding you back, Saku? You love this guy. Your families get along, and most of all, he loves you and wants to marry you?" Reshani confronted me.

"I am not ready for marriage. There is so much to do before."

"Such as?" I picked up the sarcasm in Reshani's tone.

"I need to figure out how to support Malli in Sydney."

"What does it have to do with your marriage?" So, I told them how would both our parents espouse us to each other and how Thaththa would happily spend the last bit of the money he had on a wedding I didn't wish to have. None of them thought it was a good enough reason to turn down Niranga.

"What is the real issue Saku?" When Sula turned to me with dissent, I wished I could tell him *'You.'* I wanted to be there to support Sula when things eventually got worse. It is no longer a question of *'if'* Nilush would betray and leave Sula, but *'when'*. That inevitable dissolution will tear Sula's heart, and I wanted to be there to lend him my shoulder to cry. Still, I was not ready to share my prediction with others.

"I don't believe he proposed for the right reasons." Three of them were waiting for me to go on and enlighten them. I was so used to their condescending stares, so I continued.

"It is not me he wants; he just needs *'a woman'* to get married and have a child with because he is crazy about kids." Even before I finished my sentence, all three of them laughed.

"Are you insane?" Reshani asked, disdained. Her eyes were shooting daggers.

"Don't be naïve, Saku; it doesn't suit you. Let's try again. What is the real reason?" Sula's voice was oozing with sarcasm, ridiculing me.

"I am not sure I can trust him. He had never had a long-term relationship."

"Is it him you can't trust, or is it you who you can't trust?" It felt like a physical blow when Ravidu challenged me. All three of them waited for my response, and I didn't have the answer.

***

"Niranga, I am not ready to get married."

Niranga straightened, his head bobbing, reminding me of a cobra responding to the sound of a pungi played by a snake charmer. I watch his eyes filling with dismay, studying my face, searching for clues. I couldn't bear the silence, so I repeated myself.

"Ran, I am not ready to get married. I need time." I spoke with determination.

"I can't understand. How come?" He asked.

"Niranga, you are moving too fast! I don't have the same assurance you have. You said you knew what you wanted: marriage, kids… Um… I am not ready for any of that."

"You mean you don't love me enough to be with me?" Niranga challenged, confronting my emotions.

"I wish I have a simple answer for you. But I don't want to lie to you. My mind is jumbled like a ball of thread. All I can tell you for sure is at this point, I don't want to get married." I said it without telling him there was so much I wanted to achieve before I got married and let him override my life plan.

"How much time do you need?" Niranga was calmer than I expected him to be.

"I am not sure. I want to figure things out on my own time without a time limit."

"What do you mean?"

"I want us to stop seeing each other."

"That is going to happen, anyway. I wouldn't be able to come back for the next six to nine months with my current plans." He sounded calm and enduring, as if he was explaining basic math equations to a kid.

"It could take me more than that, and I mean a real separation."

"What?" Niranga's shoulders stiffen, and his eyes widen.

"No contact at all. I want us to stop seeing each other. If we feel the same when we meet again, we can be together." I explained. It was the only way I could confront my demons.

"I didn't realise you don't trust me!" Niranga's slumped in his chair, his eyes filled with disbelief. He was staring at me, expecting an explanation.

"It is not you I don't trust!" If I confused Niranga before, I have perplexed him now. I wanted to tell him he wasn't the only one I have shocked. I witnessed the same expressions on my friends' faces a few days ago.

"If it isn't me, then what?" Niranga's voice cut through my flashback, dragging me back to the living room.

"It is not what; it is who. And it is me I don't trust."

"What do you mean?"

"I want to marry you for me. I am scared if I say yes to you now, I will say yes because that is what you want… or because marrying you will help me walk away from my problems… I am worried I would say yes for the wrong reasons. If I get married now, I will lose myself."

Niranga was confused, not being able to follow me. I could resonate with him, as I found it difficult to follow my logic. I no longer could point out what or who I was fighting against.

"Because you have never been one for a long term relationship, I assumed ours would be merely a holiday romance. If I am honest, that is why I started flirting with you and slept with you. I expected you to leave me the way you have left others." I watched Niranga's face darkening with frustration, tired of explaining the same things to me repeatedly.

"Every week when you dropped me off, I was expecting you to tell me it was our last time together, and this it is not working. Not only have you proved me wrong, but you also made me crave more. Your presence is overwhelming."

"Why is that wrong?" Niranga didn't take it as a point to be concerned about. Instead, he started kissing me, pulling me to him. I didn't resist. I kissed him back, making him shiver with anticipation. I wanted to enjoy the power I had over him, forcing him to stretch and moan, yearning for me the way I crave his touch.

"So, you will give all this up?"

"No, it is my way of making sure I say yes for the right reasons," I said.

"What could be the wrong reasons?"

"This!"

"You mean sex?"

"Yes, isn't it the biggest pull between us? We haven't been able to keep our hands to ourselves when we are together."

"That is because we have over ten years of catching up to do." When I didn't laugh at his joke, Niranga let go of me and got up from the sofa. He walked to the windows and stayed staring outside for a while. There were deep lines on his forehead when he came back, and his eyes were heavy with concern.

"Do you seriously believe sex is the only thing between us?"

"I am not sure, Ran. I don't know you any more than I know myself." That was the absolute truth. I thought I had known him ten years ago, yet I couldn't recognise he was in love with me. It was the same for Niranga. He believed he knew me. Still, he couldn't pick up how heartbroken I was, assuming he had chosen Akka over me. Even now, we haven't grasped the other's dream! I didn't expect him to propose, and he never expected me to turn him down. So, what are the odds of us having clarity of the situation when things are more complicated than when we were kids? If we had a pinch of understanding each other's dreams, we wouldn't have this conversation.

"I don't think anyone ever gets to grasp everything about the other, babe. I will not say I understand you because most of the time, I don't. You always will be an enigma to me." Niranga sat beside me. He combed his hair, using his fingers to deflect the worry.

"All I can tell you is, I am happy when I am with you. Not that I was miserable earlier. You somehow make me feel content. It is not just sex! I felt at ease and peaceful for the first time in a long time on the day we drove to Kandy. There was no sexual tension between us. We were only sharing a journey. That night I didn't want to leave your place. After that, I was dealing with an emptiness that took me days to shake off." Niranga said, stroking my fingers as somehow his touch could transfer the confidence he had in his heart to mine.

"When I am with you, I don't have to fill in the silent gaps constantly. You are strong and independent; you care about people, not only your family and close friends. I love that about you. Maybe I am selfish. I need you. Not because I will be good for you, because you make me whole." Something made me not wanting to interrupt Niranga as he was baring his soul.

"I want to build a life with you, have a family, visit places, grow old together. I haven't felt this with any other woman I have been with." When he bared his soul to me, I was unsure if this was what I wanted to hear.

"Thank you for your honesty." I wished I could show him how much I appreciate his honesty. "That is what is missing in my life. You are at a stage in life that you can plan your life to have that vision. I am not there yet. I have a few more steps to get through before I reach that point." I checked if Niranga could follow my thoughts, and he nodded.

"I don't want to sign up for your dream, not knowing what mine are." My voice flutter with anxiety. The truth I was devolving gave me tremors. "I understand if you don't want to wait around for me until I decide because things can change in the future."

"Are you saying you want to break up with me?" Niranga uncoiled his back, looking deep into my eyes. His eyes got wider as if he just saw the earth open up in front of him.

"I guess I am. At least until I have some clarity on my needs. I don't want you to wait for me. I want you to be free to be with anyone you wish to be with. Search for your missing piece. You haven't kept true to your gap year. Go and enjoy it, don't tie yourself up to me. If I remain the thing that makes you stop searching, you will also have the confidence."

"I don't need to search anymore. I already know the answer. It is you!" I have annoyed Niranga. His voice elevated, and he puffed.

"I am not." I blinked to keep my eyes dry and tighten my hold on his hands. "I want to take the chance to understand what I want in life. If we connect in the same way next time we see each other, then we can plan our future." I was determined not to give in to his demands, no matter how romantic and intense they were.

"Are you sure one of my friends didn't put you up to this?" Niranga asked, eyeing me suspiciously.

"Are you crazy? Why would I talk to them about my emotions?"

"Because what you said sounded like what I would say."

"Then you must understand what I mean." I gave him a sly smile, pleading my case.

"That is the problem. I know what you mean, and that scares me. I don't want to lose you, Saku."

"I wish I could tell you; you wouldn't. I do not know which one of us would change. I think we both owe it to ourselves to try this out."

Niranga didn't speak for a while. The heaviness of my heart was getting worse with each passing second. I was not sure why I was doing this to myself; however, I knew if we were to have any chance of surviving; I needed to do this.

"Is that what you want?" Finally, when Niranga spoke, he sounded defeated and drained. I nodded, no longer able to hold the tears that filled my eyes.

For a long time, neither one of us spoke. Niranga left me to cry, lost in his thoughts. As if he could bear my sniffles, he got up from the sofa and walked to the window. Outside the window, dusk was settling in, and street lamps were lighting up. I could hear the squeaky calls of crows return to rest for the night.

"Okay." I blinked in amazement when Niranga returned and sat next to me. I expected him to be angry, yet he wasn't. I wailed, as I could no longer hold on to the heaviness I felt in my heart. He pulled me into his arms, stroking my back as he did the other week.

"Are you really okay with it?" I asked him once my sobbing faded away.

"No, I am not." He shook his head with sadness. "I have to figure out how I am going to live without you. Seeing you again made me realise what is possible. After being with you, I don't know how I could settle for someone else. I know love can't be forced. And I also know you don't know how much you love me!" He cupped my face in his hand, attempted to smile and failed.

"If there is any future for us, I have to give this space you need." He kissed me gently as if he didn't want to leave a mark.

"I want the same confidence you have."

"You will." For the first time since we began talking, Niranga smiled.

"You sure?"

"Very." He stroked my cheek as if he wanted to pass some of his knowledge across to me.

"How?"

"Once you learn to trust yourself, you will accept that we belong together."

When Niranga silently took me in his arms, his eyes were filled with tears. I sensed the heaviness of his breath and disappointment in his heart. I hope one day I will find it in my heart to forgive myself for today. Sula was right. I was my own enemy.

I have walked away from the greatest love I may not come across again in my life, all because I wanted to discover myself.

***

I don't think I have ever cried this much before. The front of Niranga's shirt was wet with my snot and tears. He was holding me tight to his chest with his chin resting on top of my head, stroking my back, trying to ease my pain.

I wish Niranga was angry. It would have made our parting easier if he just stormed out or accused me of playing with his emotions. But he didn't do any of that. Instead, he was calm and understanding, holding me so close to him, as if he was trying to imprint everything about this moment into his memory.

"Babe, you are going to end up with a headache." Niranga stroked my short hair and mumbled.

"I already have one." I muffled between sobs. My head was pounding like one of those drums beating in the evening service at Maligawa.

"Babe, look at me." Niranga pushed me away from his chest and lifted my chin, struggling to smile.

"You are such a cry baby. Look at you, snot and tears all over." He ruffled my hair the way he used to do when we were kids and wiped my face with his handkerchief. I was so drained and felt no shame about the mess I had made on his shirt. After cleaning my face, he kissed my forehead.

His eyes were wet with sadness.

"Just hold me." Again, I buried my face back, this time in the crock of his neck, inhaling his smell that I would miss so much.

We both were up last night, lying there holding on to each other, grieving the loss of the warmth and comfort we were so used to. We had decided Niranga was going to drop me at the annexe and wouldn't come in. When that moment came, neither one of us could honour that decision.

I burst out crying the moment Niranga walked inside and closed the door. The tears I kept in tack in the morning came pouring down as the floodgates were open.

"I am sorry," I murmured.

"I know." Niranga sounded sad and empathetic. I wish he had accused me of creating this, but he didn't.

'*What the fuck is wrong with you, woman? You have to go and create this mess?*' I ignored my inner voice that had been screaming since last night.

Niranga's demeanour changed. He became the older, wiser guy I grew up with, not the sexy, demanding, impatient man I had been spending weekends with. He was more concerned about my well being and my comfort than his. He reminded me of a parent waiting patiently for his child to have his own experiences.

"Babe, do you want me to stay?" After a long silence, Niranga asked me gently. It was late, and he had to leave to avoid the dangerous drive back to Nuwara Eliya. As much as I wanted to wrap my arms around him, basking in the warmth I would miss, I had to let him go.

"No, you have to leave. Can you do that when I go for a shower? I don't want to watch you leave." I uttered miserably. Instead of responding, Niranga kissed me hungrily, knowing this could be our last embrace. When we finally pulled apart, he slowly walked me into the bathroom and pushed me inside.

I avoided glancing at Niranga when he closed the bathroom door. I listened to his fading footsteps and slumped to the floor, sobbing. When there was no more water left in my body to shed, and I ran out of energy to cry, I turned on the shower, hoping the cold water would wash away my pain.

29 BLISS

I was on a mission, climbing up to the pinewood, coming to the flowing stream. The stream didn't care that my heart was heavy, or I was longing for the man I turned away. It didn't laugh at me for creating my misery the way my best friends have been. The water flow just continued with its journey, not bothering anyone.

I paused to catch my breath, leaning back on a young pine tree. I stood there staring at the clear water that was trickling down the rocks as if nothing had happened. This stream had witnessed my young love turning into an ardent desire that burned with each breath. Yet, it was oblivious to the fear I was carrying with me here and now.

It was getting colder as the sun had slowly begun its descent. Soon it will get dark. The surrounding reminded me of Baba Yaga, the flying witch from the Russian fairy tales that scared me. When I was a kid, I was obsessed with reading those stories repeatedly. And when I visited the stream, my heart would pound heavily, expecting her to appear any moment in her giant mortar and pestle, sweeping the road with the silver birch broom she carried around everywhere. I wondered what Baba Yaga would say if she saw me now yearning for Niranga.

Since our separation two years ago, I came to an understanding my longing was no longer a *'want.'* It was a *'need.'* I felt empty without Niranga in my life. He filled a void that I didn't recognise in myself. Sula was right when he said I was my own enemy.

When Niranga started filling my life with a rainbow full of colours, I got overwhelmed. After a quarter-century of living in a world full of black, white and grey, I didn't have the experience of riding that rainbow to the other side. Each time I saw a slight bleed in the colours, I wanted to run away. When I was in Niranga's arms, the happiness I felt didn't equip me to weather the anger I felt when things didn't go the way I wanted, so I ran away in search of *'me.'*

I have been living in a nightmare, constantly searching for that missing piece, the one that would make me whole again. Now I understand what Niranga meant when he declared, I completed him. Niranga was my missing piece.

I have tried to bury him and reclaim my life. Still, I missed him more as the days went by. I didn't learn to live without him, just to live with that massive 'need' I carried with me ever since then.

I tried dating, trying to fill the emptiness in me. Despite how much effort I invested, I couldn't go beyond the initial flirtation. There are so many gorgeous men where I live now, in many colours, shapes, and sizes. Still, no one could hold my attention beyond a couple of minutes. I didn't sense the excitement I felt when I had Niranga standing next to me. I searched for him in every man I came across and realised I would never find that wholeness again. The life I was building would not be complete without him and never will be.

Would Baba Yaga understand me? Would she get how I needed to know my dreams, not become a vase for someone else's dream. Would she be able to accept that this was why I turned Niranga away? Questions were churning in my mind, with no answers.

Maybe if Baba Yaga was around, she would reward me by showing me a way back to Niranga, leaving my vanity aside, the way she helped Vassilis by giving her light to face her fears and follow her intuition. I hoped the flying witch would understand why it was vital for me to walk away from Niranga's dream to discover mine. I didn't want to be trapped in a maze, continually searching for *'myself'*, trying to live up to others' expectations. So, I tried to stand tall and discover **the labyrinth of my life.**

My journey had been arduous, stretching myself, challenging, and transforming. I learned to observe deeply, listen to my intuition, not getting distracted by my inner negative voice, let alone others. Though it had been painful, it has been a rewarding journey.

If I had accepted Niranga's proposal, Malli wouldn't be in Sydney following his dream today. I knew both our families would have welcomed our union in the same way drought-stricken farmers embrace the rain in the country's dry zone. Our parents have been dreaming of the day for us to join our two families.

When we were young, our parents actively advocated Niranga and me to become our life partners. They always laughed when we played house and when I boldly declared I would not marry him when I grew up or when Niranga innocently promised he would build me a home. I would always admire our parents for allowing us to be who we were when we were teenagers, stepping back, and letting the forces take their course.

None of our parents got involved when the teenage Niranga started having an array of girlfriends. Nuwara Eliya was a small town, and he was a popular boy. They always knew what was going on. They never meddled and not once tried to alter the trust that allowed us to go in and out of each other's bedrooms whenever we wanted. When Niranga and I drifted apart, our parents were devastated. Still, they didn't pry. They continued to observe, hoping we would overcome our differences.

When we met the last time, they watched us the way a nosy neighbour would: standing behind a window curtain, waiting for us to fall for each other. They all did their part trying to orchestrate a union with subtle manuring. Amma finding little excuses to send Niranga into the kitchen. Aunty Nelum forcing Niranga to drive me to Kandy when he shouldn't have been behind the wheel. Uncle Sarath getting him to return my shawl after the anniversary dinner, Thaththa making me go to Kandy early in the morning. All these acts were soaked with our parents' dreams of seeing us as a couple.

If I had made their dream come true, Malli's vision would have got pushed out to the edges with the distraction of our union. We would have spent the little money we had on a wedding and a dowry that I didn't want.

I am slowly learning to live without Niranga. However, I would not have lived with myself being responsible for sabotaging Malli's dream. It was not an easy battle to win.

Saman Aiya had woven a grand plot to keep Malli in Sri Lanka; even Machiavelli, the economist, would have been proud. He had shrewdly used Amma's motherly love and her ironclad attachment to glue his scheme. He didn't want Malli to go overseas for his studies; he wanted Malli to stay behind to help with his business. Behind this was Saman Aiya's attempt not to return the money he had secretly borrowed from Thaththa.

"If Manoj leaves, who is going to be around to help when Uncles gets sick?" One day, Saman Aiya challenged me, realising I was on a mission to persuade Thaththa and Amma to support Malli's dream.

"Why, that's why we have you. You are technically our oldest brother now. So, we have you to support us." From the corner of my eyes, I saw both Amma and Akka eyeballing me in disbelief. It was not a secret in our family that I despised Saman Aiya from the early days. I always felt a cold vibe around him, the way one feels when walking to a haunted house.

Though he picked up my sarcasm, Saman Aiya was smart enough not to draw attention to it in front of Amma and Akka. He has been great at portraying himself as a devoted husband and son-in-law to those two naïve believers for a few years now. I was silently provoking Saman Aiya to come out and show his natural, selfish characteristics.

"Of course I will when I am in Sri Lanka. I am talking about when I travel for work overseas." When he spoke with concern, both Amma and Akka nodded their heads in agreement.

"On those days, Akka and I can manage. If needed, I can also ask Sula to help. I am sure you will take the next flight home in such a situation. Besides, why sabotage Malli's future, assuming Thaththa is going to be ill? Thaththa has been doing great since he started working again." I watched Saman Aiya deflating like a balloon out of air. His face darkened, realising he had lost the battle.

"Saman Aiya, can you return the money you borrowed from Thaththa? We need that money for Malli's bank statement." Later, I asked him in private. I didn't want to confront him in front of Amma and Akka, who believed in his charade.

I watch horror flashing through his eyes. He didn't like me being aware of his extensive borrowing from Thaththa.

***

I remember the look of despair on Thaththa's face when he found out how much money it would cost Malli a degree at the University of Sydney.

"Can't we borrow against the land, Thaththa?"

When we moved to Nuwara Eliya, Thaththa had a big plot of land. Over time, it shrank in its size. He sold a part of the property to pay for Akka's wedding. Thaththa divided the rest into four, allocating a piece of land to Akka, Malli and me, and keeping one for their retirement. Akka's one was given to her as her dowry when she got married. Mine was there for me to take when I wanted. Malli had the one with the house as the youngest -he was the rightful owner of the land that belonged to Thaththa.

Akka and I deserved nothing. Thaththa had given us enough. He raised us as his children, provided us with a lifestyle above our means. But mostly, he had given us a free pass to his heart when we needed him, despite how many times we have trampled it, disregarding his emotions.

Thaththa didn't speak for a while. I watched his eyes getting hazy. I turned away, uncomfortable, as I hadn't seen Thaththa weak and helpless before.

"I have already borrowed some money against the land and house, kiddo."

"For what?"

"Saman needed some money to expand his export business."

I should have known that was how Saman Aiya operated. He couldn't forge his path in the business world without the backing of an investor. The land was not his to be used as collateral, yet he had got around Thaththa to do his bidding.

"Can't you ask Saman Aiya to return the money now that he had the start he needed?

"I don't think so. Saman wants to borrow a bit more for his next product launch." Thaththa sounded helpless, torn between wanting to help Malli and not knowing how to.

"Then we have to sell my land and get Malli to Sydney."

"That is out of the question!" Thaththa straightened in his chair, giving me a warning stare. Usually, it would have worked, and I would have backed away. Still, it was Malli's destiny we were talking about, and there was no way I would allow misguided respect to stop me in my tracks.

"If we can't get Saman Aiya to return the money he borrowed, we don't have any other choice. We will sell my piece of the land to support Malli." Thaththa sensed my anger when he turned to me with hurt and disappointment written all over his face. I watched the stubborn look on his face that screamed, *'I don't care what you say. My decision is final!'*

"So, you will sacrifice Malli's happiness for a damn piece of land?" I was discontented. Still, I was not surprised by his response. Thaththa always went above and beyond for Akka and me. For some convoluted reasoning I couldn't understand, he thought we had to come before Malli.

"There is nothing wrong with universities in Sri Lanka, and Manoj does not have to go overseas to study. You and Amali both went to Sri Lankan universities. It is all nonsense." Thaththa brushed it off, showing that it was the last time he would discuss the topic.

"You understand what Malli wants to study is not available in Sri Lankan universities, don't you? And besides, becoming a Game Designer has become his dream." I leaned across and peered into his glazed eyes, tried reasoning.

"I don't believe Manoj has thought this through. Why study something when there aren't any job opportunities in Sri Lanka? Manoj had spent too much time with Niranga and his friends. That boy always wants to live a high life, above his means!. He can work for Saman and learn a thing or two on how the real-world works." I knew those were not Thaththa's thoughts. They reeked of Saman Aiya all over.

Thaththa wouldn't have a clue what a software game was, let alone talk about its industry. I knew it was Saman Aiya who had fed that information to Thaththa.

I could not understand why neither one of our parents could not recognise Saman Aiya's selfish behaviour. I wanted to scream and seriously hurt someone, and that someone was Saman Aiya. I wish I could cut him into tiny pieces to let him bleed. The viciousness roaming in my head scared me as I realised how long I had been harbouring such anger against him.

"Well, it is technically my land, and I can do what the hell I want with it." I pushed back the chair with force and stood up. "I am going to sell it and give the money Malli needs for the first semester. After that, he will have to find himself a job and manage on his own. Niranga promised to help him once he got there." I loomed over Thaththa and raised my voice at him for the first time in my life.

It disappointed me that circumstance brought me to a point where I challenged the man I idolised growing up. Seeing the disheartening in my eyes must have hurt Thaththa much more than the tone of my voice or the words I used.

"You need to accept what you have done for Akka, and me are more than enough! It is time to take care of Malli. Thaththa, I need you to do this. We are going to send him to Sydney. You are the only one who can talk to Amma. Make her understand. This is what Malli wants, and we all owe it to him." I lowered my voice, staring at Thaththa pleadingly. Tears were filling his eyes, which made me uncomfortable.

I strode across and stood behind him, putting my arms around his hunched shoulders, and hugged him. He grabbed my hands and squeezed them silently.

When I felt the coldness of one of his tears gracing my fingers, I pretended I didn't notice it and kissed the top of his head.

Thaththa had been my hero; despite that fragile moment, he will forever remain the beacon that brightened our gloomy existence after Appachchi passed away. That day, I finally graduated from being Thaththa's little girl to an adult in his eyes. After that, our relationship moved to a different place. Thaththa began treating me as an equal and started sharing more.

He reluctantly agreed to sell the land to fund what Malli needed. I didn't have any qualm about the land. For me, it was time to get the best out of my inheritance. I was so thrilled to give something back to the man who paved our way with immense sacrifices.

When the money we got from the land sale didn't cover what was required, Thaththa reluctantly sold the house. It was an agonising decision for all of us. We all had so many memories trapped inside those walls. I felt sad, realising I could no longer catch sight of my parents sitting on the veranda waiting for my return home. More than anything, I grieved anticipation of the loss of lingering recollections of Niranga's presence in my room. While I was supporting the decision to sell, internally, I struggled with the strange attachments I never thought I had on those walls and windows, my favourite bench under the lonely pear tree, the stone steps I loved taking to gather flowers for the vases.

When we sold the house, the new owners agreed to rent out the place for a couple of years. We all had tears in our eyes when we graciously accepted their offer and sent Malli off to follow his dream.

***

It was challenging to go on with my life without Niranga's presence. Even after two years, I am still not used to it, and I don't believe I will ever be. My heart yearned to meet him again.

I am home for Christmas break. Since returning a week ago, knowing that Niranga was also home on holiday, I have been patiently waiting for him to seek me out. I had caught up with Uncle and Aunty several times, but Niranga was never there. They have been fabricating excuses for his absence, covering their discomfort with the politeness that I had witnessed many times on Amma's face when she had to conceal the lack of my presence. We all knew he was avoiding me, as I avoided him.

After several days of waiting, I took things into my own hands. I went to Senege's house to find Niranga. Aunty Nelum said he had gone to the stream. So, I climbed the hill in search of him.

I was hoping to find him at the next corner, where the stream widens a bit before it descends from the hill. I expected him to be sitting at his favourite spot where we sat and chatted the last time we were here together. I needed to tell him a thousand unspoken words. There was no point in having the insight into what I want in life if he wasn't there to share it with me. I want to hold his hand and breathe his musk until the day I die.

"What brings you here?" When I heard Niranga's voice, the reality of seeing him there didn't stack up with my imagination. I stopped in my tracks, absorbing the hit of a thousand volts of electricity on me. Seeing him and hearing his husky voice startled me.

He had changed little. He was striking in his burgundy Polo sweater and dark blue Levis. His hair was way shorter than last time, making him appear younger. I searched for a reaction in his face, but I couldn't find any. There was no light in his eyes or a smile on his lips. He stood there, hands in his back pockets, staring at me indifferently. I froze with uncertainty.

They say one gets to relive a lifetime's worth of memories on their deathbed in a split second. That was how I felt at that moment. All my favourite moments had with Niranga stretched across my mind like a movie. The cherished recollections from the first time I met him to the day I let him go clenched my heart with an overwhelming desire to pull him to me and hug him, holding him closer to my chest.

"Hmm... Thought I'd come around to visit the stream," I uttered. Being so used to playing *'hard to get.'* I didn't expect a subtle contempt to flash across Niranga's eyes. I paused, assuming I was misreading him, leaving space for him to respond.

"I will leave you to it." He said with a dismissive stare and walked past me.

"Please, don't go." I panicked, grabbing his hand to stop him from leaving. The moment our hands made contact, I felt sparks flying, reflections of hundred sensual moments we shared in the past crowding my mind. Niranga didn't make a sound. He silently stared at the hold I had on his hand. Something told me he would have preferred me not to touch him.

It was Déjà Vu. My mind snapped to a similar incident two years ago, in the same place where our roles were reversed. I quickly let go of my grip, trying to contain the sudden urge to weep as I felt so helpless and desperate. I blinked rapidly to hold the tears building in my eyes.

"Please don't go! I came here to see you." Mustering all the courage I had in me, I glanced at Niranga. I shifted my feet uneasily, not knowing how to break through the invisible wall that stood between us. He didn't ask me why. Yet, I could read the question on his face.

"I was hoping to catch up with you…." Still, there was no response from Niranga, looking as if he was a million miles away, not bothered about the torment I was going through.

"I thought you would come around…… It has been a week…." I stammered reluctantly. Niranga didn't show any emotions or speak. He was aloof, cold, and nonchalant. I cleared my throat in unease.

"When the mountain doesn't come to Muhammad, Muhammad must go to the mountain!" Seeing that Niranga was not keen to join the conversation, I joked, trying to wipe my sweaty palms to hide my nervousness.

"What if the mountain doesn't want to see Mohammad?" When Niranga asked, my heart plummeted. I remembered Aunty Nelum saying Niranga had asked her to set up an extra plate at their Christmas dinner table. She was excited that finally, he was going to bring his girlfriend home to meet them.

Two years ago, when I asked him to give me space to grow, I told him not to wait for me. I told him it was ok for him to go out with others. I was naïve and arrogant, believing that he would wait for me. The reality of losing the love of my life shocked me, disorienting me. I swayed with dizziness, losing my footing, and would have fallen into the stream if Niranga didn't grab my hand, breaking my fall.

"What is it with you, woman? Can't you pay any attention to where you are going? You could have hurt yourself." Niranga pulled me to safety with a wave of anger. I noticed how he didn't call me *'Cookie'* or *'Saku'* in his usual way. There was a subtle coldness in his voice that cut through my heart, making me wish if he would have at least called me 'Sakunthala.'

I felt the warmth of his fingers spreading through my body like wildfire. I was giddy with apprehension and gazed into his eyes, looking for absolution and an invitation. Not seeing either for a moment, I was not sure what I was going to do. Desperation made me give in to the hope building in me, waiting for Niranga to hold on to my hand for a few extra seconds. There were times in the past he seized every opportunity to hold on to me a bit longer.

When he dropped my hand like a burning piece of charcoal, my heart sank. He was not interested in me anymore. Niranga had moved on with that *'extra plate'* Aunty was going to layout for dinner, and it was not me.

I had two choices. I could hold on to my pride and let Niranga go, or I could fight for my missing piece.

"Ran, can we talk?" Back in the day, Niranga said he had never experienced such warmth and sensuality hearing me calling him 'Ran.' He adored the desirable way I shortened his name to convey how precious he was to me. I was purposely trying to evoke the deep emotional and physical connection we shared in the past. I wanted my voice to warm his heart like an electric blanket in the winter, spreading the heat to his bones. As the name *'Ran'* implied, I just had to remind him he was my precious metal, *'gold'* .

"What about?"

Niranga didn't seem to be swayed. He leaned back on the tall pine tree next to him, crossing his arms across his chest. I wasn't sure if it was to protect himself or he was defensive.

"About us." I hated how desperate I sounded, as if I was begging for a handout. I shifted my feet with discomfort. However, underneath that egoistic feelings, I was not ready to give up.

"Make it quick. I need to get back." It felt as Niranga was punishing me away.

"Ran, I made a mistake. I want you!" I no longer could hold the tears; they were streaming down my cheeks. I watched Niranga pushing himself to stand and saw a light flicker in his eyes. I grabbed on to that subtle change and took a step towards him.

'Now or never.' I heard myself encouraging.

I knew I had to fight for him the way he fought for me. I nervously took another step closer to Niranga. Keeping my eyes on his face, I stood on my toes, putting my arms around his neck, pulling his head for a kiss with all the bravery I could find. This was my last resort. I didn't want to imagine the bottomless pit that would house me through my life if Niranga rejected me.

Niranga didn't resist, neither did he find it surprising. I felt his arms going around me slowly, drawing me closer to his body, away from the edge of the stream. When he lifted his head to gaze into my eyes, I choked, unable to hide my anguish anymore.

"I was wrong. I don't want you; I need you!" I whispered. Niranga breathed heavily and pulled me closer to his chest. We stood there holding on to each other before he gently guided both of us away from the stream where we could comfortably sit. Although the ground was full of pine needles, I didn't mind. At least Niranga will sit next to me and not run away.

"Say that again." Niranga cupped my chin in his hands and laid his forehead on mine; his voice was trembling.

"I need you!" I leaned across, gently capturing his bottom lip, closing my eyes to savour the moment, taking in all the sensations. I was so glad that we were already sitting on the floor when Niranga's lips caught mine, as my legs would have collapsed with nervous excitement.

The force between us didn't leave room for anything other than breathing. I could taste the saltiness of the tears that were streaming down my cheeks. The ache to be with each other was uncontrollable, and the universe stopped, leaving us with our raw desires, making us one. In that ecstatic moment, I thought I saw Baba Yaga in her flying motor and pestle, staring down with a satisfactory grin.

"What was that smile about?" Niranga was curious when he saw me peering over his shoulder.

"You remember Baba Yaga?"

"That flying witch you pretended to fear when you were a teen just so you could hold my hand?" He raised his eyebrows with a grin on his lips.

"You knew and said nothing?" I was horrified.

"Why would I? I loved holding your hand." He chuckled, his eyes laughing with him.

"So, what about her?" He was curious.

"I think I saw her, looking down with a smile." I lay my head on his chest and muttered. It felt good to lie there and hear his heartbeat. He stroked my arm and chuckled.

"You are delusional."

I giggled. I was happy. Whatever our future held after this moment, I was delighted laying here, having needle-shaped pines prickling me. I lifted my face and inhaled deeply, filling my lungs with Niranga's pinewood and mint scent.

"Oh, how much I missed how you smell."

"Why did you run out of my aftershave?" Niranga gave me a wicked grin. I pretended I didn't know what he was talking about. Just before we packed our bags that last Monday morning two years ago at Niranga's cousin's house, I slipped Niranga's cologne into my bag. It had little left; still, there was enough to keep my memory of his smell alive. I used to dab a bit of his cologne on my wrists and cry myself to sleep, remembering the warm comfort I felt been held in his arms. Wallowing in misery, as Reshani took the liberty to remind at every opportunity.

"Don't give me that innocent look, you little thief." Niranga pulled my chin up and kissed my lips roughly.

"Who are you calling a thief? I stole nothing." I would not tell him how miserable I have been. I didn't want him to laugh at me the same way Reshani, Sula, and Ravidu have been mocking me for creating my desolation.

I didn't tell Reshani I bought a bottle of the same cologne later to keep the memories alive. I wanted to hold on to my recollections of Niranga so desperately when the strength of the smell started wearing off in my mind. One day Niranga will find it waiting for him on my bathroom cabinet, expecting him to wear it. Today wasn't the day to tell him that.

"Did you think I wouldn't notice that you kept my aftershave, did you?"

I pulled his head down and kissed his lips. He inhaled slowly and buried his face in the hollow of my neck with a smile in his eyes. We lay there silently, feeling content.

"I love you, babe," I whispered in his ear.

"I waited over twelve years to hear that, Saku." There were tears in his eyes when he glanced into mine. I stroked his cheeks, feeling the tiny pricks of a day-old stubble. I stare into his brown eyes, trying to apologise for making him wait that long.

"You will forgive me, won't you?"

"You do deserve punishment for putting me through hell."

"You can punish me in any way you want." I watch his eyes spark with anticipation.

"I have to come up with something fitting." Niranga ran his fingers across my arm and stopped. He blinked and grabbed my forearm.

"Are those biceps? Have you been strength training?" He got up, pulling me along to a sitting position to run his fingers through both my arms, feeling my muscles. I watched his face changing from wonder to admiration. I no longer have skinny arms that resemble slender pods from a moringa tree. I have been exercising and building my upper body strength.

I took up exercise to channel the frustration, anger, and disappointment in life. Soon after Niranga left, our tour company collapsed. Nilush left the country with the married teacher he was having an affair with.

Sula hit rock bottom. He had lost his career, money, and the love of his life. There was nothing more that could go wrong with him. We all rallied around him, helping him to pick up the pieces. We took turns to watch over him and keep him away from plummeting into a big hole of depression. I remember Ravidu laughing at my attempt to help Sula saying, *'This is like the blind leading the blind. You are struggling with your own demons.'*

I never expected Sula to leave the country for a new life. He said it was too much for him to live around with memories. He didn't want to be with us, as we all reminded him of a time when he failed. It devastated me. I was angry and disappointed because I had sacrificed a part of myself for the business and Sula. It turned out he didn't need me or a shoulder to cry on. So not only I had lost Niranga, but Sula too.

Ravidu was the one who suggested I should go to a gym because I struggled with an overwhelming need to punch someone and desperately needed a boxing bag. I tamed my anger through exercise. Strangely, each time I went to the gym, it felt as if I was closer to Niranga.

I smiled and nodded, remembering how I used to hate exercising when Niranga tried his best to make me join him in the mornings.

I slowly removed the hairband behind my neck and let my hair fall, framing my face. I have not had a haircut for over a year now, and it had grown way past my shoulders. I looked a bit older with my hair down. I waited for Niranga to notice the difference. When he saw my loose hair, he reached out and playfully pulled me towards him.

"You are growing your hair?" Niranga asked in awe, kissing the back of my ear and base of my neck, making me see stars I hadn't seen for a long time.

"I am", I grinned.

"I miss your short hair. What made you grow it?"

"I want to dress up in proper Kandyan for our wedding." One day I will tell him about those dreams that got me scared and lost searching for myself in a hideous white wedding dress. I realized until now, I never acknowledged why I was growing my hair. When those used to see me in my short hair asked, I always said I needed a change. I chuckled silently, amazed at how my subconsciousness had worked.

"We are getting married?" Niranga uncoiled his torso and inquired in surprise.

"You asked me to marry you before you left." I reminded him.

"That was two years ago. What makes you think I haven't changed my mind?" I felt the rise of my heartbeat and nervous tick on the side of my temple. *'Is he joking, or has he changed?'* I glanced away, not wanting Niranga to witness the tears forming in my eyes or my desperation.

"You just showed me how much you love me!" I turned to look where we lay a few minutes ago with longing, missing that intimacy already.

"There was never a question about my love, Saku. My love wasn't enough for you." He sounded angry. I watched him, trying to gauge if he was truly annoyed with me. I couldn't read his face. He was looking at me with keen eyes, seeking to understand me in the same way I was.

"Niranga Praveen Senege, will you marry me and make me yours?" I knelt in front of Niranga and clutched his hand. His facial expressions still didn't change despite the surprise. I am pretty sure he didn't expect me to propose. How could he, when I didn't imagine such a thing, until a second ago.

"Have you thought this through? You are studying in Greece, and I am in Sydney. Unless I have missed something, they haven't introduced a super jet as a commercial flight."

Niranga paraphrased a conversation we had two years ago. I had been lucky enough to be awarded a scholarship from the university and have been living in Greece for the last nine months reading my PhD. As Niranga did last time when he proposed, I haven't worked out the logistics yet; how we would consummate our union living in two different countries and time zones. If I have learned anything in the last two years, you never get to have a perfect plan.

"Are you seriously turning down my proposal?" Niranga nodded his head, saying nothing. *'Gosh, this man is so good at poker.'*

"Let's go." I got up swiftly, brushing the dry needles from my clothes.

"Where?" Niranga was startled but got up and helped me with my jumper.

"We are going home to tell our parents about us, and I am going to tell your parents that I proposed to you, and you didn't accept it." I stood in my Wonder Woman pose and glared at Niranga. *'Let's see how you will deal with that,'*

"You wouldn't do that!" I saw the laughter he was trying to hide slowly creeping into his eyes.

"Watch me." I shrugged my shoulders and walked past him.

"I didn't go to your parents when you rejected me three times." Niranga stopped me in my track, pulling my hand. He was adorable, like a hurt little boy complaining about a fight he had with a friend.

"Whose fault was that?" I turned to him and smirked.

"Who are you? What have you done to my girl?" Niranga gathered me in his arms and gave me a passionate look. His face was bright with happiness and laughter.

"Get used to the new me, my darling. I will take what I want when I want it." I pulled his head and claimed his lips.

"Why do you want a marriage Saku? You don't believe in any of that." I saw the inquisitiveness in the depth of his eyes that were looking at mine.

"Oh, I am just after the Australian passport." When Niranga didn't laugh at my joke, I uttered. "True, marriage, kids and a house to call ours isn't my dream. But you are! We can work out what and when to compromise later. I don't care as long as we are with each other."

Hand in hand, we began our descent from the stream. While we were lost in each other's embrace, dusk had settled in. It was dark, and we could see the neon lights that were burning in both our homes. The mist was creeping in like a thick blanket, and I pushed myself closer to Niranga to shelter myself in his warmth. He gave me a sideways glance and put his arm around me, drawing me tighter to him. He knew I was cold, and he started rubbing his hand on my forearm to warm me up.

"Do you think it's normal?"

"What?" Niranga stopped walking, turning to face me.

"This infatuation that I have to be with you?" I asked. Niranga seemed pleased. A victorious smile spread across his lips, reaching his eyes. He hugged me and looked deep into my eyes before responding.

"I hope it will remain till death do us part." I could recognise the love in his eyes. I tightened my grip on his waist and laid my head on his chest.

"You didn't answer my question."

"We have a lot of catching up to do, babe." How much I missed hearing him calling me that. I love it when he calls me *'babe.'* Since the night we got together, it just rolls off his tongue, warming my heart and making me feel like I am floating on air.

"Hmm... Yes, two years," I said.

"Actually, it is much more than that. I have been lusting after you ever since I was a teenager. My longing was so strong that I had to purposely distract myself." Niranga explained. "I never felt complete with anyone other than you. It took me a while to understand you were the missing piece I was searching for. In the beginning, I couldn't figure out the emptiness I felt when I had it all. Initially, I didn't notice that emptiness was no longer there when I was with you. So, if it lasted all these years through all the challenges we had, I believe we will last for a long, long time."

"Why, does it worry you?" When Niranga inquired with concern, I didn't rush back to answer. I was processing what he said earlier.

"Yes... I am scared... You are a giant magnet pulling me... I don't have any control when you are around... I am not used to that... It scares me when this desire becomes overwhelming."

"Why?"

"Because the reality is, things change. Nothing is permanent in this life... I am scared I would not be able to pick up the pieces if that happens." He said nothing; he just cradled me up in a tight hug. We were glued to each other for a while before he spoke again.

"I have the same fear. Fear that I will lose you again. I can't think of living on my own anymore. You are not alone. Fear is real to both of us."

"So, what are we going to do about it?" I asked with desperation.

"Let us live this evening and figure out the rest together." I stared at the burning lights through the fog, creating a mystical pathway towards our houses. It was like the journey we had in front of us. I clutched Niranga's hand and nodded in agreement. Yes, I was not alone.

"Ran. Why didn't you come to see me all this time? I have waited almost a week." I watch Niranga's eyes brightening up with a satisfactory smile, learning how much I have missed him.

"I didn't know how to be normal around you," Niranga said.

"I didn't think I could handle being in the same room and not touch you, kiss you, and have you in my arms. I didn't want to influence you with my desire. I was waiting for you to realise how much you love me." He waited for those words to sink in.

"I already knew you loved me." I didn't have to raise the question as Niranga picked it up in my eyes.

"You wouldn't have done any of the things you did if your love wasn't strong. You even kept that old rag, my sweater, for years because you couldn't forget me despite the superficial anger you harboured against me." Niranga chuckled, pulling me closer to his body.

"You fought like hell to avoid me because your desire was burning you. Sleeping with me was out of character for you. You can dress it up any way you want. Still, you are not the type to have flings. Though you were projecting this modern liberated woman, you are a traditional woman in your heart." Niranga said, pinching my chin with a smile.

"You didn't know who you were. Two years ago, you were still searching for yourself." He said, reminding me of my dream, how desperately I was searching for myself.

"You didn't get tired of waiting?"

"I went through all the emotions Saku, shock and denial, pain, anger, depression … I hook up with other women hoping to forget you. But in the end, I knew if I needed any solace in life, I had to be your Gorky and give you space to grow."

"While you became a *praying mantis* to me, I turned into a *penguin*, one who mates for life. Of course, I had to be patient and wait for you to realise it yourself." I had an internal chuckle hearing Niranga's reference to animal behaviour. He reminded me of Reshani's obsession with watching 'Animal Planet.'

"You knew I would?"

"Yes, when Manoj told me you were coming home for Christmas, I knew."

"In the last two years, you have been avoiding me in every possible way. You were fully aware when I came home. I made sure Manoj passed on those details to you. In case you were ready for us. You didn't have to come home this Christmas. Manoj told me you were planning a ski trip with some of your friends. So, when I heard your plans had changed, and you were returning home, I was relieved and hopeful. I had to be patient and wait for you to make a move."

He was right. I changed my plans from going on a ski holiday with my newfound friends in Greece to visit home. I also passed on my travel plans to Malli, hoping he would share the details with Niranga. I have been manifesting a dream to accidentally bump into Niranga and fall into his arms. I can't recall how many versions of that beautiful moment of the reunion I replayed in my mind.

"Is that why you told Aunty to have an extra plate for Christmas dinner?" He nodded his head in response.

"So why did you imply I could be two years too late when I saw you earlier?" I was still mulling over his disinclination.

"You had me going through all the hoops two years ago, babe. I was not going to make it easy for you." Niranga gave me a quick kiss and grinned.

"Promise me one thing?" I turned to him in desperation.

"What?"

"Don't let me become my own enemy." Niranga turned to me, confused. "Just remind me to tell you all about it later." I laid my head in the crook of his neck and whispered.

One day, I will tell Niranga how I have changed my life's maze into a labyrinth. As the Greeks say, I have taken the journey to my soul, and I have come out to the world knowing who I want to be, and I am becoming 'her.' Though the path I travelled was complex and lengthy, I can look in the mirror with reassurance that I am where I need to be.

As we continued to walk away from the stream following the yellow lights beckoning us to our families, I heard the echo of Kanmali, the Gypsy fortune teller's premonition at Sigiriya.

"Mark my word, my precious; your stubbornness is going to harm your love. Don't doubt his love. Your prince will love you more than his life."

I glanced at Niranga and smiled; I have found both my Gorky and Prince Charming in him.

ACKNOWLEDGEMENT

One clarification before I appreciate everyone who had contributed to my author journey. As this story takes place in Sri Lanka, any deviations from the facts are solely my responsibility. Those familiar with the country will notice how I have not referenced some critical aspects related to the timeline of this story. There was no disrespect or disregard to any in creating a safe environment for my characters to exist.

As a first-time novelist, much gratitude goes to various YouTubers, authors, editors who freely share their lessons, experience, and tips on writing, editing, and publishing on their sites. Having access to free information made my author journey a little less daunting. Closer to home, I am indebted to following people who have assisted me in many ways; without their support, this story would have stayed in my imagination. Also, my heartful appreciation to beta readers for their valuable feedback.

I am thankful to my editor, Malapia (Mala) Singleton, my personal Gypsy palm reader. Your vision, belief, dedication, and encouragement were just what I needed to come out of my self-imposed closet. But, most of all, I am gratified to you for making me look like I have a good handle on English (*my second language*) than I do.

I am ever in debt to Pushpika Mullakanda for introducing me to Mala and connecting me with Sumith Imbulana at Piyapath Graphics. Thank you for always being willing to help, no matter how busy you are with life.

I am grateful to my friends, Gimhani Jayasunera, Dilrukshi (Rushi) Munasinghe, Thushari Wijewardena, Shirley Mower, Tracy Baulman for reading various drafts. Your candid insights, suggestions, criticisms and most of all, your love gave me courage. You ladies rock!

A very special thanks to Nayomi Munasinghe and Dr Darshini Goonathelika who constantly checked on me (writer) with nourishment for the body and soul. I am blessed to have such wonderful friends.

A thousand-fold thanks go to my family scattered around the world, especially to Akka, Kumari Pearcey, for putting up with my stubbornness and foul moods, loving me no matter what.

And finally, to my exceptional husband, Asanga Perera. I can't begin to tell you how much everything you do means to me! Your humour and practical sense always calm me down and gives me strength and encouragement, especially when I want to give up. Thank you for being who you are and making room for me to grow. I will carry this love for you to my next life (yes, you will not get rid of me that easily). I love you.

CPSIA information can be obtained
at www.ICGtesting.com
Printed in the USA
BVHW082354161121
621782BV00005B/528